PERSPECTIVES ON MODERNIZATION
Essays in Memory of Ian Weinberg

EDITED BY EDWARD B. HARVEY

Perspectives on Modernization is published in memory of Ian Weinberg, a sociologist of brilliant promise who died at the age of thirty. It consists of essays by his colleagues, students, and teachers which reflect upon and carry further Ian Weinberg's major scholarly concerns – the processes of industrialization and modernization of societies.

The book begins with an essay by Ian Weinberg which was presented at the annual meeting of the American Sociological Association, 1968. It is followed by a paper of wide scope and interest, Wilbert E. Moore's 'Normative Conflict in Stages of Cultural Change.' Noting that the study of rapid social change can no longer be confined to the so-called modernizing countries, Moore argues that comparable normative conflicts occur at comparable stages of cultural change. Rainer C. Baum and Charles Tilly are concerned with the serious gaps in the theory of modernization and politics. Baum is specifically concerned with developing a political analogue to the theory of economic development; Tilly concentrates on a longitudinal study of the relationship between modernization and collective political conflict. S.D. Clark writes of patterns of urban growth, looking at two exceptions to the well-studied outward movement of immigrants in Canadian cities. Edward Shorter studies the modernization of sexual attitudes by analysing illegitimacy. The last three papers approach modernization through economic changes and development: H. Nishio analyses the relationships between political control and economic development in Japan over two centuries; Stanley R. Barrett studies the transition of the economy in a Nigerian Utopian community from communalism to partial private enterprise; and L.R. Marsden, E.B. Harvey, and J. Bulcock explore the relationship of literacy and economic development in thirty-nine African countries. The volume includes an introduction by the editor and an outline of Ian Weinberg's short but brilliant career.

These essays are, like the work of the man they seek to honour, wide ranging and intellectually provocative in their approach to a complex question. The volume is a fitting tribute to both the man and the spirit of intellectual vitality to which he was committed.

EDWARD B. HARVEY is associate professor of sociology at the Ontario Institute for Studies in Education and the University of Toronto.

EDITED BY EDWARD B. HARVEY

Perspectives on Modernization: essays in memory of Ian Weinberg

UNIVERSITY OF TORONTO PRESS

© University of Toronto Press 1972
Toronto and Buffalo
Reprinted in paperback 2017
ISBN 978-0-8020-1798-7 (cloth)
ISBN 978-1-4875-9149-6 (paper)
Microfiche ISBN 0-8020-0114-9
LC 79-185716

Contents

Contributors

STANLEY R. BARRETT
Department of Sociology and Anthropology, University of Guelph

RAINER C. BAUM
Department of Sociology, University of Pittsburgh

J. BULCOCK
Department of Sociology, Memorial University

S.D. CLARK
Department of Sociology, University of Toronto

E.B. HARVEY
Department of Sociology, Ontario Institute for Studies
in Education and University of Toronto

L.R. MARSDEN
Department of Sociology, Princeton University

WILBERT E. MOORE
Department of Sociology, University of Toronto

H. NISHIO
Department of Sociology, University of Toronto

EDWARD SHORTER
Department of History, University of Toronto

CHARLES TILLY
Department of Sociology, University of Michigan

Preface

This book is a collection of essays by the colleagues, students, and former teachers of Ian Weinberg. Ian was a sociologist who showed brilliant promise. Tragically, the realization of this promise was cut short by his death at the age of 30. The essays in this volume attempt, in a variety of ways, to reflect upon and carry further one of Ian Weinberg's major scholarly concerns – his concern with the processes of industrialization and modernization in societies. The introduction of this book and the essays directly engage and carry forward this debate. This preface is concerned with something else. It is concerned to try to say something about the man for whom this book serves as a memorial. I think there is no better way to say something about Ian Weinberg, the man and sociologist, than to quote the words of Professor Wilbert E. Moore who taught Ian and knew him well.

E.B.H.

Ian Weinberg (1938–69)

Ian Weinberg was born in London, England, and obtained his secondary education in King's College, Taunton, and Hele's School, in Exeter. He went to Oxford on scholarship and took his BA in 1960, with First Class Honours in History.

Weinberg came to Princeton to do doctoral work in sociology with virtually no previous formal work in the discipline. He had discovered sociology at Oxford pretty much on his own, and, indeed, was the founder and first president of the Cole Society, Oxford's sociology club.

He was neither a quiescent nor an angry student. He was accustomed to arguing with tutors, and defending himself. His manner, though characterized by great civility, was not a little jarring to some of his peers and instructors. When the emperor was wearing no clothes, he had the commendable habit of saying so. It did not ease his relations with his fellow professionals-in-training that he stood for the Graduate General Examination at Princeton rather sooner than the norm, that he performed brilliantly on that examination, and went on to complete his PH D in short order on the basis of an observational study in England relating to public (that is, private) schools. Now he might have been forgiven if he had done a kind of get-the-licence work, even though he did it promptly and without endlessly changing his subject and his evidential materials. However, he had the bad manners to do a thesis which was published shortly in a moderately revised version.

Ian had a great many other defects: he knew things; he was professionally committed; he was remarkably intelligent; he liked to teach and did so superbly; he liked to write, and he wrote in a way that could lead most of us to wonder if we had not cheated on the sixth-grade or College Board literacy test.

His colleagues at the University of Toronto, aided by some of us at Princeton, have assembled an approximately accurate set of his publications, a few of which I shall mention in this memorial note. Ian was a dear friend of mine, and he dedicated his first book to my wife, Jeanne, and me. I have dedicated my half of a two-essay book to him, and

Reprinted, with permission, from *The American Sociologist,* 1969, vol. 4, no. 4, p. 341.

knowing his precarious (and soon terminal) physical state, I told him about the dedication before the book's appearance. The graduate students at Princeton, aided but not prompted by the faculty, are establishing a memorial shelf for Ian in their library reading room. A volume of essays in his honour is being put together by an editorial committee under the chairmanship of Professor Edward B. Harvey of the University of Toronto, Weinberg's colleague, and also a doctoral product of Princeton.

I should mention here only a small part of Weinberg's precocious publication record, but I want, by titles, to indicate that he was already both a specialist and a generalist. His revised doctoral thesis, *The English Public Schools: The Sociology of Elite Education*, was published in 1967. At the time of his death in March 1969, he had a second book in press, *English Society: A Reader for Comparative Sociology*. Among his seven or eight technical articles was one which showed his earlier training in history: 'Social Problems Which Are No More,' for the *Handbook of Social Problems*, edited by Erwin O. Smigel; and one that attends to the very lively topic of convergence theory: 'The Problems of Convergence of Industrial Societies: A Critical Look at the State of a Theory,' published in the January 1969 issue of *Comparative Studies in Society and History*. He was also an excellent and conscientious critic. Professor Raymond W. Mack, the editor of the *Sociologist,* testifies that Weinberg was one of his most valued associate editors on this journal.

Man's mortality we have come to expect, or we have found various ways of explaining away. To attempt such rationalization for a good and brilliant man dead just beyond the age of 30 would strike me as the ultimate indecency. Ian Weinberg is gone, and we survive, and I grieve, and I think that chance can be cruel. Those of us who had the privilege of knowing him will try to deserve his confidence, his competence, and his sense of professional calling. If I knew how to do more, I should do it.

WILBERT E. MOORE

Introduction

Accounting for the large-scale long-term changes taking place throughout the world has attracted scholars from many disciplines to a study of a process termed 'modernization.' The exact meaning of 'modernization' has not been agreed upon, as psychologists, sociologists, demographers, economists, and historians grapple with theoretical formulations of the problem in the light of new methods of data gathering and analysis. Where is the general theory of modernization? Not here and now and, probably, not just around the corner.

In an attempt to define and test some parameters of the problem, writers have often limited themselves to a discussion of industrialization, that is, the application of technology to the production of goods and attendant social change.[1] But, despite the work of many people exploring and documenting economic development,[2] its causes[3] and consequences,[4] many have felt that a more comprehensive term is required. The arguments about the term continue. Tilly, in his essay on page 50, while noting that the term modernization is 'deft and slippery,' also notes the need for such a term to describe '*what else* happens before, and while industrialization ... occurs.' Weinberg thought that

1 Ian Weinberg, for example, uses this description in his article 'Modernization, Elites and Class in England,' an unpublished article written for his *Reader on British Society.*
2 While no attempt is made to be exhaustive, examples are W.W. Rustow, *The Stages of Economic Growth: A Non-communist Manifesto* (Cambridge University Press, 1960); G.M. Meier and R.E. Baldwin, *Economic Development: Theory, History, Policy* (New York: Wiley, 1957); Wilbert E. Moore, *The Impact of Industry* (Englewood Cliffs, NJ: Prentice-Hall, 1965); and Cyril S. Belshaw, *Traditional Exchange and Modern Markets* (Englewood Cliffs, NJ: Prentice-Hall, 1965).
3 Besides economic etiology included in references above, psychological causes can be found in the discussion of David C. McClelland, for example, *The Achieving Society* (Princeton: D. Van Nostrand Co., 1961) and Everett E. Hagen, *On the Theory of Social Change: How Economic Growth Begins* (Homewood, Ill.: Darcey Press, 1962). The area of value change has been extensively discussed. See, for example, Neil J. Smelser 'Mechanisms of Change and Adjustment to Change' in Bert J. Haselitz and Wilbert E. Moore (eds.), *Industrialization and Society* (Paris: UNESCO, 1963), chap. 2 and other articles in the volume.
4 Moore has summarized the findings and literature in his volumes, *Social Change* (Englewood Cliffs, NJ: Prentice-Hall, 1963), and *Impact of Industry.*

the need for the term modernization rested on somewhat different bases. 'Industrialization was always a somewhat ethnocentric term,' he says, 'because it implied that the
application of technology to the production of goods, and the social changes which followed, was purely a Western phenomenon. Since the end of World War II, scholars have
come to use the term 'modernization' which can be applied to industrialization in both
Western and non-Western societies.'[5] Levy, in describing his use of the terms 'relatively
modernized' and 'relatively non-modernized,' argues that 'for many, the term "industrial" literally means factory-ized,' that industrialization may be present without factories in segments of a society, and that modernization is a broader term.[6] Again, Black
tells us that industrialization refers only to economic process and does not 'convey the
complexity and all-pervading character of the process.'[7]

These writers, among many others, sense the necessity for this broader term but do
not agree on a general definition of it. For example, Tilly includes in his use of modernization the development of an industrial labour force, an educated population,
urbanization, and political participation with the concomitant changes and inevitable
interrelation between them.[8] Weinberg, in his essay on the historical evolution of the
study of modernization and the changing use of the term, attempts a synthetic definition 'rooted in the career of social theory and in the present challenges before social
scientists.'[9] Weinberg argues that 'modernization is a process of social change which
describes the career of new nations since their independence.' He then goes on to give
a series of assertions about modernization of new nations: nations are small, ruled by
elites, have intellectual leadership from an emerging middle class, are committed to the
idea of progress, and so on. This type of modernization, Weinberg argues, is different
from Western development. Changes since the late eighteenth century in Western nations he terms remodernization. Different again are the processes of change in countries
which achieved their independence during Western industrialization (or during its early
stages). These countries, for example those in Latin America, must rid themselves of
part of their cultural past to develop economically – a process which Weinberg terms
demodernization.[10] Weinberg's embryological typology begins with substantive assertions of differences in processes and attempts to build theory inductively. While Weinberg seeks the common processes in each of the three types of change he describes, he
concludes that modernization theory 'must be a theory of the common properties in
different processes rather than a theory of one process or model alone.'[11]

Levy takes a rather different approach. He attempts a definition which is a 'parsimo-
nious tool for the identification of the class of phenomena referred to'[12] rather than a

5 Weinberg, 'Modernization, Elites and Class in England,' 1.
6 Marion J. Levy, Jr., *Modernization and the Structure of Societies* (Princeton: Princeton University Press, 1966), p. 9.
7 C.E. Black, *The Dynamics of Modernization* (New York: Harper and Row, 1966), p. 6.
8 C. Tilly, contribution to this volume, 'The Modernization of Political Conflict in France,' see p. 50 below.
9 Ian Weinberg, 'The Concept of Modernization: An Unfinished Chapter in Sociological Theory,' un-published paper read at ASA meetings, 1968, 6.
10 *Ibid.*, 8.
11 *Ibid.*
12 Levy, *Modernization*, p. 10.

realistic description of the thing referred to. His definition is: 'A society will be considered more or less modernized to the extent that its members use inanimate sources of power and/or use tools to multiply the effects of their efforts.'[13] This avoids dependence on the presence of factories, which Levy found a problem with the term industrialization (see above), but is still closely tied to the economy.

Black thinks of modernization as 'the process by which historically evolved institutions are adapted to the rapidly changing functions that reflect the unprecedented increase in man's knowledge, permitting control over his environment, that accompanied the scientific revolution.'[14]

If these writers, and many others not mentioned here for reasons of space, have looked for a broader, more comprehensive approach to this aspect of social change, they have certainly found a multi-faceted one. Psychological change, economic change, political change, educational change, family change, all these areas and many more have been studied, pondered, and debated in recent literature,[15] even if no common conceptualization of the term has been agreed upon.

This volume adds to this multi-faceted body of literature. It reflects the broad range of concerns of the man in whose honour these papers have been written.

Conversing with Ian Weinberg was not an experience in received wisdom or complacency. Seldom did one leave a discussion with him without pondering a new question or a new perspective on an old question. We have tried to show the fruits of the intellectual churning which we experienced in our relations with Weinberg in this collection of papers brought together in tribute to him. This is not to say that each of these papers grew directly out of Weinberg's own work or out of our conversations. Yet the link between Weinberg's continuous debate in the area of modernization, evident both in his published work and in his lectures and colleagual debate, is to be found in these contributions.

The contributors to this volume include a wide range of Ian Weinberg's friends, from his graduate school professor, W.E. Moore, to his own students, Stanley Barrett and Lorna Marsden. The majority of the papers, however, come from his colleagues at the University of Toronto whose decision it was to honour his memory with this collection.

The book begins with a paper of wide scope and interest, Moore's 'Normative Conflict in Stages of Cultural Change.' Noting that the study of rapid social change can no longer be confined to the so-called modernizing countries as it once was, the thrust of Moore's argument is that, at comparable stages of cultural change, comparable normative conflicts occur. The distinction – and the lack of its possibility – between norms (the means) and values (the ends) of action is neatly made. 'To distinguish normative conflicts and "cultural conflicts" may be impossible in the concrete case.'[16] With modernization

13 *Ibid.*, p. 11.
14 Black, *Dynamics of Modernization*, p. 7.
15 See, for example, the references above and the following: Alex Inkeles, 'Making Men Modern: On the Causes and Consequences of Individual Change in Six Developing Countries,' *AJS*, vol. 75(2) (September 1969); Eugene Staley, *The Future of Underdeveloped Countries* (New York: Praeger, 1961); Joshua A. Fishman, Charles A. Ferguson, and Jyotirinda Das Gupta, *Language Problems of Developing Nations* (New York: John Wiley and Sons, 1968); UNESCO, *Changes in the Family*, reported from the *International Social Science Journal*, vol. XIV(3) (1962).
16 Wilbert E. Moore, contribution to this volume, 'Normative Conflict in Stages of Cultural Change,' p. 15.

come new normative conflicts or new versions of conflicts found in traditional societies, as well as new means of solving problems of increasing cultural diversity. From the generational and individual conflicts of the village in the grip of economic change to the conflict between managers and managed in the post-industrial economy, we can predict, Moore argues, the sorts of conflicts that will emerge.

Baum and Tilly both address themselves to the problem of filling serious theoretical gaps in the area of modernization and politics. Baum is specifically concerned with developing a political analogue to the theory of economic development. He analyses the problem of the generation of societal power, using – and developing – the theory of stratification and its role in modernization and the generation of societal power. In doing so, Baum is concerned to move away from the current emphasis on political structure to considerations of political process. He presents three ideal-typical stratification orders and develops the relation of each to the generation of societal power. He argues that of the two extreme types of stratification orders (complete stratification of inequalities and no stratification of inequalities) the second does not give rise to societal power, the first gives rise to limited societal power, but partial stratification is the most satisfactory agar for its development. In opening up in this area of political modernization, Baum gives us a lead into a wealth of future considerations in the field.

Tilly concentrates on a longitudinal study of one aspect of political modernization, that is, the relationship between the familiar dimensions of modernization (industrialization, urbanization, demographic shifts, etc.) and the incidence of collective political conflict. To use his own words, Tilly seeks the 'order to disorder' in an analysis of collective political conflict in the last few hundred years in France. The conclusions to which he steers his way through the painstaking presentation of the available evidence[17] clarify some important points in the debate over the connection between the process of modernization and mass political action. After reviewing those dimensions of modernization which do not appear to have a direct link to political violence, Tilly states, 'it is justice – and conflicting conceptions of justice, at that – which is at the heart of violent conflict. That means violent conflict remains close to politics in origin as well as in impact.'[18]

Clark has written a new chapter on a familiar topic – that of urban growth patterns. Instead of approaching the topic from studying the movements of foreign immigrants to the centre city and then out to the suburbs, Clark takes a different tack. He looks at two exceptions to the well-studied 'out-ward movement' of immigrants in Canadian cities. Clark looks at the settlement patterns of the immigrant who is partially assimilated culturally before moving to the city, illustrating his case with the communities of immigrants from the United Kingdom to Toronto from pre-War years, and he looks at the settlement patterns of rural migrants both to the urban centres and to the new Northern industrial communities. Those newcomers, whose immigration has not been so culturally decisive, have a different relationship to the urban centre than others. For example, in contrast to the poor European immigrant, the Canadian Indian who uses the city for some purposes need not develop a community within the city, for a meaningful one still exists on his reservation.

17 Tilly, pp. 50–74.
18 *Ibid.*, p. 94.

In 'Sexual Change and Illegitimacy: The European Experience,' Shorter, in his study of illegitimacy in Bavaria, has used a clever empirical approach to a difficult topic in social change. Shorter's thesis is that a modernization of sexual attitudes can be studied through examining data on one manifestation of sexual behaviour – illegitimacy. Illegitimacy, in this analysis, stands for premarital intercourse, attitudes towards which Shorter regards as indicative of modernization (secularization) of sexual attitudes generally. Concentrating on dramatic changes in the Kingdom of Bavaria between 1750 and 1850, Shorter makes persuasive use of his data. As he points out, this is part of a larger study of changing sexual patterns which hitherto has not been within the boundaries of social science concerns.

The last three papers all approach the modernization issue via a concern with economic changes and development.

Nishio, like Tilly and Shorter, takes an historical situation and analyses the changes in sociological terms. He considers the period of Tokugawa Japan and the relationships between political control and economic (commercial) development which occurred in that period of over two centuries.

In an interesting analysis of the political strategy of centralism adapted by the founder of the Tokugawa regime, Nishio shows that the economic system resulting from the political strategy itself weakened the political equilibrium. The implications of the political, social, and economic events of the period have had long-lasting effects on the modernization of the Japanese economy.

Barrett, one of Weinberg's students, has studied the transition of the economy in a Nigerian utopian community, from communalism to partial private enterprise. Although Barrett limits his exploration of the theoretical significance of this smooth, though radical, structural change, in favour of a detailed description of the changes within the community, the reader will immediately see the contribution which this case study makes to the theoretical analysis of change within a social system. The characteristics of Aiyetoro which isolated it from the surrounding communities indicate that the economy changed in relative isolation from the external environment. While Barrett offers some interpretation of his findings, his case study offers tantalizing possibilities to the student of modernization.

In another study of economic development, this time in the area of literacy and economic development, Marsden, Harvey, and Bulcock explore some of the variables intervening between literacy and economic development in 39 African countries. In particular, they are interested in the question of homogeneity of language, and the use of the vernacular in the elementary school system. These variables are found to relate differently to economic development at different levels of literacy.

The papers in this volume are, like the work of the man they seek to honour, wide ranging and intellectually provocative in their approach to a complex question. Ian Weinberg is gone, but the vitality of his approach to his work continues to influence us. Perhaps this volume in some measure does justice to the goal of honouring both the man and the spirit of intellectual vitality to which he was indeed truly committed.

EDWARD B. HARVEY

PERSPECTIVES ON MODERNIZATION
Essays in Memory of Ian Weinberg

IAN WEINBERG

The concept of modernization: an unfinished chapter in sociological theory

PROLOGUE

In reviewing Smelser and Lipset's *Social Structure and Mobility in Economic Development*, Nathan Keyfitz remarked that the volume signalled that 'good minds are once again focussing on modernization, the central problem of social science in its best days.'[1] What he presumably meant is that the former occasion when good minds focused on the problem was during the eighteenth and nineteenth centuries when there was an extraordinary explosion of social scientific genius, co-terminous with the political revolutions in France, the United States, and elsewhere, the 'vital' revolution in population, the increased productivity of agriculture, and the beginnings of urbanization and industrialization. A transformation of western society had begun as these dimensions of change began to mesh together in a new, interdependent social system.[2] A striking fact about this new social system was that it did not immediately and automatically diffuse throughout the globe. It bypassed Spain, Latin America, Asia, and Africa; it greatly affected the vast area between France and Russia; and with few historical obstacles triumphed in North America. Eastern Europe and Russia were much slower in receiving it.[3]

We usually refer to this complex of changes as 'modernization.' We do so because the changes were cumulative, and because novel integrative mechanisms were fashioned which institutionalized and possessed the capacities to absorb the effects of differen-

---

This paper was read at the Annual Meetings of the American Sociological Association, Boston, August 1968.

1 *American Sociological Review,* 32, no. 3 (June 1967), 508.
2 I am using 'system' as most recently defined by Ackerman and Parsons as 'an ordered aggregate embedded in, and in interaction with, a fluctuating environment.' See Charles Ackerman and Talcott Parsons, 'The Concept of "Social System" as a Theoretical Device,' in Gordon J. Di Renzo (ed.), *Concepts, Theory and Explanation in the Behavioral Sciences* (New York: Random House, 1967), p. 28.
3 The main authority on the diffusion of industrialization in Europe is, of course, Alexander Gerschenkron. See his *Economic Backwardness in Historical Perspective* (Cambridge, Mass.: Harvard University Press, 1962).

tiation.[4] The question of whether this is exactly the term we can fruitfully use is broached later in the paper.

The initial reactions to these changes were philosophic, as men tried to understand the transformation within their traditional categories of thought. For some this meant a retreat into secular philosophies of religion, as in France, or into Romanticism, as in Germany. But the pressing need for understanding the societal and trans-societal changes led to specialization, to a division of labour, and to precise empirical and theoretical formulations. As natural science, and its subdivisions, became differentiated both intellectually and in terms of role and organizational structure from philosophy in the seventeenth century, so the social sciences began to differentiate from speculative, inchoate, social theory. But specialization was merely the device for interdependence. The grand design was to produce universal laws, or at least principles, after the fashion of the natural sciences. These laws would be laws of social development, explaining the transition from a primitive to a more advanced society.

Thus the beginnings of understanding were initiated. That men were universally self-seeking was an arresting philosophical concept derived from Hobbes, and refined by the Utilitarians, but the economists constructed from it the model of a market which enabled descriptive and predictive statements to be made. As Marx once said, 'Hobbes is the father of us all.' It was obvious that agricultural and economic growth was intensifying the extensity of the market and drawing families, villages, provinces, and countries into it.[5] *Cognoscenti* in the seventeenth century were fascinated by the accounts travellers brought back to Europe of alien tribes and cultures,[6] and these influenced the debate among contract theorists concerning the origins of the state and early Romantic notions on the nobility of the primitive. But it was the task of scientific anthropology, beginning in the nineteenth century to codify these accounts, to re-examine them with the latest empirical techniques, and to construct workable theories. Nietzsche and Carlyle were enthralled by the hero, the *übermensch*, but it was left to the sociological skill of Weber to develop the operational notion of the *charismatic* leader. The chroniclers and the antiquarians gave way to the comparative history of Von Ranke and his disciples. History became scientific with the role of the historian becoming increasingly professionalized. Sociology came into its own because its practitioners tried to understand the transformation which was taking place *in toto*, presenting grand theories, and by investigating dimensions of the process, such as

4 This is the sense in which Eisenstadt uses modernization. See his 'Modernization, Growth and Diversity,' *India Quarterly*, 20 (January–March 1964), 17-24, and 'Social Change, Differentiation and Evolution,' *American Sociological Review*, 29, no. 3 (June 1964), 375-86; 'Education and Political Development,' in Don C. Piper and Taylor Cole (eds.), *Post-Primary Education and Political and Economic Development* (Durham, NC: Duke University Press, 1964), chap. 2, pp. 27-47; *Essays on Sociological Aspects of Political and Economic Development* (The Hague: Mouton, 1961); *Modernization, Protest and Change* (Englewood Cliffs, NJ: Prentice-Hall, 1966).

5 For the extension of both the agricultural and industrial market in this early period, see M.M. Postan, 'Agricultural Problems of Under-developed Countries in the Light of European Agrarian History,' in *Second International Conference of Economic History*, 2 (Aix-en-Provence, 1962), 13.

6 Margaret T. Hogden, *Early Anthropology in the Sixteenth and Seventeenth Centuries* (Philadelphia: University of Pennsylvania Press, 1964).

urbanization. As Gellner has written, 'the emergence of industrial society is the prime concern of sociology.'[7]

The major field of social science which suffered in this process was political theory. Indeed, it seems that the more industrialization engulfed the West, the less likely were major political theorists to emerge. There has been no lack of eager obituaries on the demise.[8] In pre-industrial Europe and America, the problem that plagued intellectuals – I use the term reservedly as it only gained wide currency during the Dreyfus *affaire* – was how nations were to be built, who was to rule them, and what were the limits of obedience. Despite the centuries separating them, John of Salisbury's decision that a bad king could and should be removed was still of prime concern to Hobbes, who stated that men had a duty to rebel against a weak sovereign who, by definition, could not protect them. It did not matter that John represented an aggressive, reformist, and anti-monarchical Church, and Hobbes the new scientism of the seventeenth century. Increasingly the new specialized theorists of modernization simply drew on the existing stock of political theory or else contemptuously dismissed its new directions. Marx has often been criticized for being an unreconstructed utopian because his final picture of the classless society simply repeated the progressivist ideas of his eighteenth-century predecessors, and contained no theory defining the relations between man and the State. Durkheim, in a famous passage, could dismiss socialism as a 'cry of pain,' whereas Locke, in the first of his treatises, felt duty bound to counter Filmer's arguments step by step, instead of dismissing them as a 'cry of paternalism.' The basic reason why political theory was of declining significance was that industrialization and modernization were becoming of pre-eminent concern, and not nation-building. Existing political theory was adequate to the activists who worked to change the composition of legislatures, the increasing role of the State, and the existing franchise. The unsettled questions in political theory were not those concerning the relation of the individual to the State, but of the relationship between states.

Thus, turning away from philosophy because of the pressures towards specialization, and evading the unsettled questions in political theory because modernization and not nation-building was all important, the social scientists of the eighteenth and nineteenth centuries tried to understand, to analyse, and to quantify the process of which they themselves were the products. Yet specialization did not rule out interdependence, because a shared concern was the discovery of universal laws of development. Of course, tactical suggestions for political action, moral pronouncements, and normative prescriptions riddled the works of these scientists, generating the great controversies over the possibilities of a value-free social science. It could be argued that this occurred because of the lack of differentiation of the role of the scientist at this point in time from that of the philosopher, and because the new roles of economist, sociologist, and historian had not yet been fully institutionalized within the traditional organization of the university – which forced the development of new organizations for social research outside the walls of the academy. The natural sciences, after all, had experienced the

7 Ernest Gellner, *Thought and Change* (Chicago: University of Chicago Press, 1965), p. 35.
8 *Ibid.* See also Thomas D. Weldon, *The Vocabulary of Politics* (London: Penguin, 1953).

same process of inadequate role differentiation, lack of institutionalization within the university, and extramural groups and societies bearing the weight of research. Yet even when specialization and institutionalization had reached high levels within the social sciences, the same controversies continued.

The reason for controversies over the possibility of a value-free social science and the rivalry rather than interdependence which seemed to accompany specialization was simply that social scientists had failed to produce universally applicable laws or propositions concerning social development or modernization. Some disciplines, such as history, simply forsook the search for laws, which were left to marginal theorists such as Spengler and Toynbee, taken seriously only by historians of ideas but not by the body of the profession. Social scientists generally turned away from macroscopic to microscopic concerns, and tried to improve their middle-range theories and technical expertise to justify their intrinsic failure to explain modernization. Despite the similarity of approach of, for example, the historian concerned with the intensive study of one year of the Civil War, and the sociologist juggling with two variables within the confines of one community or nation, interdisciplinary rivalries increased.[9] Even economics, considered the most successful of the social sciences in terms of its development of theory and its utility, shared in the failure. As Spiegel has said:

there exist in economic science a number of propositions which may be characterized as more or less rudimentary theories of economic development of varying levels of generality. Thus far, however, economic science has failed to produce a single, general theory of economic development to become part and parcel of the main stream of economic tradition in the sense in which this is true of the theory of price or of the theory of income determination.[10]

In some areas of social science a false argument even began over equilibrium analysis as against change – false because the disputants were often arguing past each other or else trying to discover hidden ideological assumptions.[11]

9 The fact that history and the other social sciences were most *en rapport* in the nineteenth century is noted by Richard D. Challener and Maurice Lee, Jr., 'History and the Social Sciences: The Problem of Communications,' *American Historical Review*, 61, no. 2 (January 1966), 333; on the divergence between anthropology and economics, see Melville J. Herkovits, 'Anthropology and Economics,' in *Economic Anthropology* (New York: Norton, 1965), chap. III, pp. 42-64. This book is a revision of Herkovits's *The Economic Life of Primitive Peoples*, originally published in 1940.
10 Henry William Spiegel, 'Theories of Economic Development,' *Journal of the History of Ideas*, 16, no. 4 (October 1955), 523.
11 The general impossibility of 'static analysis' is explained by John C. Harsanyi, 'Explanation and Comparative Dynamics in Social Science,' *Behavioral Scientist*, 5 (1960), 136-45. In sociology, of course, the *soi-disant* structural-functionalists were attacked as theorists of *statis* despite Davis's work on urbanization, Moore's work on industrialization and general theories of social change, Levy's broad attack on the problems of modernization, and Smelser's theory of structural differentiation. See, for example, Kingsley Davis and Hilda Hertz Golden, 'Urbanization and the Development of Pre-Industrial Areas,' *Economic Development and Cultural Change*, 3 (1954-5), 6-27; Kingsley Davis, 'The Role of Class Mobility in Economic Development,' *Population Review*, 6, no. 2 (July 1962), 67-73; Wilbert E. Moore and Arnold Feldman, *Labor Commitment and Social Change in Developing Areas* (New York: Social Science Research Council, 1960); Wilbert E. Moore,

THE RETURN TO GENERALITY

The lack of interest in general theories of social change may have persisted, given inter-disciplinary hostility, intellectual conservatism, and the microscopic–parochial interests of many, except for two important events. The first was that social scientists, particu-larly economists, became concerned with the slow growth rate of Western economies after World War II; the second was the retreat from imperialism of the European coun-tries and the sudden appearance of 'new nations.'

It was with the second event that the term 'modernization' came to be associated. Yet it must be emphasized that the birth of the term occurred under inauspicious cir-cumstances. During the war governments had found that social scientists were useful in various ways, and the exigencies of the situation had reinforced the timid steps to-ward interdisciplinary activity noticeable before the war.[12] It was natural for govern-ments to turn to social scientists to explain to them how and why the new nations were developing. This presumably did not occur in the Soviet Union where sociolo-gists, at least, were merely regarded as ideologists.[13] The situation was urgent for West-ern governments because of the fear of the appeal of communism to the peoples of underdeveloped areas.[14] Moreover, foreign aid now became a factor in the international flow of capital. Foreign aid involved a government-to-government relationship. Western governments were accountable to their constituents for the correct use of aid, so that successful economic development in emerging nations became an internal political fac-tor in the donor nations. The modernization of the United States, and of other areas peopled by Europeans, had been financed mainly through the money markets of Lon-don, Paris, and elsewhere, and had been private and speculative. The crucial latent function of European credit had been to make available risk capital for innovation in North America and elsewhere, while European, particularly English, plants suffered from senility and lack of renovation. This is not to deny that the State did not play an important role in Western development, particularly in guaranteeing credit and actively supporting certain types of industrial enterprise. Furthermore, the emerging nations were given ready-made political institutions, whereas in North America, South Africa, and Australasia, the indigenous political institutions were brought by the settlers.[15] As the ex-colonial powers exported these political structures, they became, as in the in-

Industrialization and Labor (Ithaca, NY: Cornell University Press, 1951); 'The Social Framework of Economic Development,' in Ralph Biarbanti and Joseph J. Spengler (eds.), *Tradition, Values and Socio-Economic Development* (Durham, NC: Duke University Press, 1961), chap. 2, pp. 57-82; 'Industrialization and Social Change,' in Bert F. Haselitz and Wilbert E. Moore (eds.), *Industrializa-tion and Society* (The Hague: Mouton, 1966), chap. 15, pp. 299-359; Marion J. Levy, Jr., *Moderni-zation and the Structure of Societies* (Princeton, NJ: Princeton University Press, 1966); Neil J. Smelser, 'Toward a Theory of Modernization,' in Amitai and Eva Etzioni (eds.), *Social Change* (New York: Basic Books, 1964), chap. 30, pp. 258-75.

12 Julian H. Steward, *Area Research, Theory and Practice* (New York: Social Science Research Coun-cil, 1950), p. xii.

13 See Lewis S. Feuer, 'Problems and Unproblems in Soviet Social Theory,' *Slavic Review,* 23, no. 1 (March 1964), 117-24.

14 Morris Watnick, 'The Appeal of Communism to the People of Undeveloped Areas,' *Economic Development and Cultural Change,* 1 (1952-3), 22-36.

15 The problem of the transfer of structures is considered in William B. Hamilton (ed.), *The Transfer of Institutions* (Durham, NC: Duke University Press, 1964).

stance of economic development, committed to successful political development, and, again, accountable to their constituents.

As we have seen, social science in general and in each of its specialized fields, did not have at hand any universal laws of development. Ponsioen's analysis showed how bad the situation was, though his avoidance of some of the latest theorists of social change is curious.[16] If social scientists had been unable to agree on Western social, economic, and political development, what could be expected of their advice on processes of change in countries that were, to most of them, exotic and afar? It did not help much that economic, let alone social, indicators were hard to come by – and 'national social accounting' was a new phenomenon in the West.[17] Only the anthropologists, perhaps, took delight in the discomfiture of their colleagues in economics, political science, and sociology, whose generalizations were based on so small a part of the world. Kushner and his colleagues, in developing a propositional inventory of sociocultural change, virtually ignored the other social sciences.[18]

Yet in the late forties and early fifties, there was considerable optimism among social scientists and others that the emerging nations would become independent in foreign policy, economically developed, and democratic in the sense of having a tolerated opposition.[19] At this time, the phrase 'modernization' hardly appeared, except as 'economic modernization.' One reason for optimism, apart from the not inconsiderable fact that the emerging nations had hardly been in existence long enough for them to be evaluated, was that the importance of interdisciplinary co-operation to generate some universal laws or propositions of development, again became salient. The economists, such as Hagen and Hoselitz, perhaps took the first steps.[20] An important group of political scientists undertook to revamp their traditional vocabulary, and to borrow heavily from sociology, to understand the politics of the developing areas.[21] It did not seem entirely improbable that not only would more industrial societies appear in the world, but that there would be some convergence of structure among them.[22]

THE END OF OPTIMISM

This optimism did not last for very long. The debt levels of the new nations began rising so fast that the interest alone ate up new foreign aid. Some of the most important donor

16 J.A. Ponsioen, *The Analysis of Social Change Reconsidered* (The Hague: Mouton, 1965).

17 Bertram M. Gross, 'The State of the Nation: Social Systems Accounting,' in Raymond A. Bauer (ed.), *Social Indicators* (Cambridge, Mass.: MIT Press, 1966), chap. 3, pp. 155-271.

18 Gilbert Kushner *et al., What Accounts for Sociocultural Change? A Propositional Inventory* (Chapel Hill, NC: Institute for Research in Social Science, University of North Carolina, 1962).

19 See, for example, Bert F. Hoselitz (ed.), *The Progress of Underdeveloped Areas* (Chicago: University of Chicago Press, 1951).

20 Everett E. Hagen, 'The Allocation of Investment in Underdeveloped Countries: Observations Based on the Experience of Burma,' Center for International Studies, MIT (New York: Asian Publishing House, 1961), pp. 56-94; *On the Theory of Social Change* (Homewood, Ill.: Dorsey, 1962); Bert F. Hoselitz, *Sociological Aspects of Economic Growth* (Glencoe, Ill.: Free Press, 1960).

21 Gabriel A. Almond, 'Introduction: A Functional Approach to Comparative Politics,' in Gabriel A. Almond and James S. Coleman (eds.), *The Politics of the Developing Areas* (Princeton, NJ: Princeton University Press, 1960), pp. 3-64.

22 See Ian Weinberg, 'The Problem of the Convergence of Industrial Societies, a Critical Look at the State of a Theory,' *Comparative Studies in Society and History* (unpublished).

nations began to have balance-of-payments problems that involved cuts in aid. The flow of private capital to these nations began to fall.[23] Economic development was rarely a success, and political instability often seemed to be the norm.[24] It was at this crucial point that the word 'modernization' began to appear in the literature.

That 'modernization' became part of the language of social science in the early sixties signified, therefore, a disappointment with the social, political, and economic development of the new nations, although it was acknowledged that they were not old enough even yet to be evaluated as successes or failures. It was as if the theorists of social change were observing that the new nations were moving in the direction of social, political and economic development, but that when, or if, or how they would get there was unknown. In this sense, 'modernization' acts as a 'raincheck term' by which observations can still be made but judgment suspended. It also signified the extent of interdisciplinary co-operation, and an unwillingness, in the present state of knowledge, either to assign priority to one or other factor, whether it be, for example, economic or political, or to estimate the relative weight of these factors in a situation where prediction was demanded.[25] For this reason 'industrialization,' emphasizing the economic factor, or 'development,' which usually assigned the first priority to an admixture of the economic and political, were dropped.[26] 'Modernization' signified a process which was open-ended, and gave both the observer and the observed maximum autonomy. As a 'raincheck term' it serves the admirable function of allowing theorists the time to digest the phenomena they are interpreting, instead of being caught in the position of constantly having to alter their concepts and vocabulary to fit observed changes. This is really the dilemma that Almond and his fellow political scientists find themselves in, a vicious spiral known technically to philosophers as the 'parallelism theory of meaning.' The implications of the constant alteration of concepts and language are outlined by Gellner: 'If we invent rapidly changing concepts to deal with changing societies, or contradictory concepts to cope with societies in conflict, we may find ourselves with an unmanageable language, but we shall still not be able to be sure that the concepts change or internally conflict in just the way the society is changing or conflicting.'[27] It was perhaps to be anticipated that once social scientists began to try to analyse esoteric phenomena, which were themselves part of a process of global

23 W.M. Clarke, *Private Enterprise in Developing Countries* (New York: Pergamon Press, 1966).
24 For a particularly revealing essay on the problem of the export of experts, see Dudley Seers, 'Why Visiting Economists Fail,' in David E. Novack and Robert Lekachman (eds.), *Development and Society, The Dynamics of Economic Change* (New York: St. Martin's Press, 1964), pp. 375-91.
25 The extent of interdisciplinary co-operation and the degree of tolerance to all points of view is illustrated by Clifford Geertz (ed.), *Old Societies and New States. The Quest for Modernity in Asia and Africa* (New York: Free Press, 1963); Myron Weiner (ed.), *Modernization, The Dynamics of Growth* (New York: Basic Books, Inc., 1966). See also Cyril E. Black, *The Dynamics of Modernization, A Study in Comparative History* (New York: Harper & Row, 1966).
26 See J.P. Nettl and Roland Robertson, 'Industrialization, Development or Modernization,' *British Journal of Sociology,* 17, no. 3 (September 1966), 274-91. It is ironic that just when social scientists were re-examining both the realities in the new nations and their own views, they should be attacked as culture-bound by Moskos and Bell. See Charles C. Moskos, Jr. and Wendell Bell, 'Emerging Nations and Ideologies of American Social Scientists,' *American Sociologist,* 2, no. 2 (May 1967), 67-72.
27 Ernest Gellner, 'Time and Theory in Social Anthropology,' *Mind,* new series 67 (1958), 192.

change, they might find themselves in this dilemma. Marx consciously took the same direction in the nineteenth century, because in his social and economic theory he knowingly forged a new language in reaction to the liberal philosophers who had gone before him, a language which was avowedly violent, polemical, and destabilizing.

MODERNIZATION: TOWARDS A DEFINITION

If we understand the background to the introduction and use of the term 'modernization,' a synthetic definition becomes possible. For its definition is rooted in the career of social theory and in the present challenges before social scientists. Modernization is a process of social change which describes the career of new nations since their independence. As it is used, the term is limited both by geography and by history – the geography and history of colonialism.[28] These new nations are, for the most part, small.[29] They are ruled by elites, generally with a Western education and an orientation to the metropolis.[30] The leadership is distinctively intellectual, under the ideological rubric of socialism, a European set of ideas constantly changing in its new environment.[31] The stability, the pace, and the timetable of development, hinges on the integration of these elites.[32] The elites are often inseparable from an emerging middle class which, because it is relatively small, 'contributes to the persistence and importance of kinship relations.'[33] The elites, whether through their education, or their contact with the West, or through the utopian elements in socialist theory, are committed to the idea of progress for their nations. Often they are in a situation in which their nation is hardly more than a boundary line marked out by the politics or plain bad cartography and ethnology of colonialism, so that they are forced to mobilize and build a nation from a heterogeneous mixture of tribal, peasant communities. A potent means of achieving this lies in the use of radio and other communications techniques – which often results in an accelerated, though differential, loosening of former norms.[34] Indeed, the very potency of such means has moved some scholars to view modernization primarily as a communications process.

28 I have in mind S.D. Clark's remark that 'the eyes of sociology are geography and chronology,' in 'Sociology, History and Social Change,' in *The Developing Canadian Community* (Toronto: University of Toronto Press, 1962), chap. 14, p. 224.
29 'In effect, the typical new nation is a small country ...' Morris Janowitz, *The Military in the Political Development of New Nations* (Chicago: University of Chicago Press, Phoenix Books, 1964), p. 17.
30 Edward Shils, 'The Intellectuals in the Political Development of the New State,' *World Politics,* 12 (April 1960), 329-68.
31 See Charles W. Anderson, Fred R. von der Mehden, and Crawford Young, 'Socialism as a Program for Development,' in *Issues of Political Development* (Englewood Cliffs, NJ: Prentice-Hall, 1967), chap. 10, pp. 175-219.
32 See Lester G. Seligman, 'Elite Recruitment and Political Development,' *Journal of Politics,* 26 (1964), 612-26.
33 Morris Janowitz, *The Military,* p. 73.
34 Through such media as radio Lerner says 'traditional societies are passing from the face of the earth because the people in them *no longer want to live by their rules,*' Daniel Lerner, 'The Transformation of Institutions,' in William B. Hamilton (ed.), *The Transfer of Institutions* (Durham, NC: Duke University Press, 1964), p. 14.

Education is another device for mobilization – yet the enormous growth of literacy in the world is seen by Lerner as perhaps dysfunctional to the modernization process.[35] However, for various reasons, the efficiency and span of control of the central government is limited.[36] It is, perhaps, external factors which most influence and limit the process of modernization. New nations have to choose among donor nations for risk capital, thus incurring obligations they may see as a threat to their fragile sovereignty. The elites are generally hostile to private capital from abroad, which they fear may result in the repatriation of profits or in an economic neo-colonialism which has as its consequence economic development stuck at the stage of raw material production. If they follow Western advice and opt for agricultural development as a prerequisite to industrialization, they may draw their peasant communities out of local exchange systems and into, not national markets creating an internal surplus, but international commodity markets. The demand and price of these commodities fluctuates wildly and may erode rather than strengthen development plans.[37] Some new nations may never industrialize because they lack the basic resources. If they do, the social organization of the industrial sector may turn out to be completely different from that of Western experience. In the advanced industrial countries water and then steam power meant that production had to be centralized, so that factories emerged, and a labour force was created, with well-known sociological consequences. There is no technical reason why light industries in new nations should not be decentralized, with the use of electricity, and heavy industries automated – this follows, after all, the logic of being latecomers to industrialization. Without factories and a labour force the normative structure and institutional arrangements of the new nations may not erode but traditional behaviour patterns could be preserved if not reinforced. However, the means employed to cope with over-population and over-urbanization, if intrinsic unemployment were standard, might lead to the appearance of novel structures specific to the new nations. The problems of agricultural and industrial development, fortified by international politics and finance, are resulting in federations of new nations for protection and mutual help. Thus we may be observing a process not only of nation-building, as the literature puts it, but of supranation-building. For if the new nations are heirs to the technological cornucopia of industrialism, they are also born to *atimic* status in relation to advanced industrial nations, which accelerates their movement into regional economic and political blocs.[38]

OTHER TYPES OF MODERNIZATION PROCESSES

This synthetic description of modernization is, as Charles Tilly has pointed out, only a series of assertions. It is not a model of development. It is based on the fundamental

35 *Ibid.,* p. 18.
36 Felicia J. Deyrup, 'Limits of Government Activity in Underdeveloped Countries,' *Social Research,* 24, no. 2 (Summer 1957), 191-201.
37 'Many underdeveloped countries are "open" economies, heavily dependent on the export of one or two products into a world market that is utterly beyond their control.' *Ibid.,* p. 197; see also Gustavo Lagos, *International Stratification and Underdeveloped Countries* (Chapel Hill: University of North Carolina Press, 1963).
38 The concept of *atimia* is found in Gustavo Lagos, *International Stratification.*

idea that modernization in the new nations is a quite different process from modernization elsewhere. Western development followed a different course. Capital flows were structurally different. The elites, whether political, or intellectual, or military, were marginal to the process. The factory, the city, the labour force developed because industrialization was centralized and labour-intensive. Industrial Man, with his well-known psyche, relations with kin, mobility orientations, and organizational loyalties, appeared. In fact, before the late eighteenth and early nineteenth centuries, there had been previous growth periods in the West, such as the twelfth and sixteenth centuries, but these had faltered. They left a pool of scientific principles and a machine orientation among crucial groups, which were of the utmost importance when industrialization occurred. Agricultural development preceded industrialization and created a national market, a surplus, and a labour supply. Extensive urbanization and population were both concomitants and consequences of the modernization process. Furthermore Western nations had passed from the stage of nation-building, and industrialization, whether autochthonous or derived, did not involve the creation of blocs. Thus, social changes before the late eighteenth century were crucial factors in industrialization. The changes which began to occur in the late eighteenth century may, therefore, be designated as a *process of remodernization*, of a quite different type from that of contemporary modernization in new nations. This leaves the third major world area – Latin America. These countries achieved their independence before Western industrialization, or when the process was in its infancy. In many ways their ideology and structures were modern for their times, and they had the benefit of such transplanted organizations as the university. But they did not develop economically at least, and the reason may be in their premature modernity. Thus their current attempts to develop may be seen as an attempt to rid themselves of their cultural heritage. Their social changes can be described as a *process of demodernization*, for their cultural heritage impeded modernization, whereas in the Western case, it aided it.

PROBLEMS OF THEORY CONSTRUCTION

This approach to modernization, which stresses historical factors, international relations, and different cultural areas, may not be the answer to some of the dilemmas inherent in modernization theory. It may be only a primitive and questionable typology which needs considerable revision. It also takes the extreme position of denying both the limited convergence of industrial societies, and the applicability of the Western model of development to other areas. It also faces a fundamental dilemma, to which Charles Tilly has pointed – that the process of mobilization and change, without the emphasis on industrialization, which is visible in the new nations and in Latin America may be quite similar to the growth period in the West from the thirteenth to the seventeenth centuries, which was a sufficient if not necessary condition to industrialization.

If the typology above makes any sense, the attempt to treat all modernization processes as similar may, then, be premature. One such approach is to theorize at so high a level of abstraction that the variations between time-periods and cultures are minimized. The problem with this is that there is often little agreement as to what constitutes the theoretical essence of modernization, and also whether it is the independent or dependent variable. Even lower levels of generalization fall into these dilemmas, as each analyst selects his own definition of the core of the meaning of the term. Our method is, theoretically, to begin with substantive assertions of differences in processes and to hope that theory will be forthcoming inductively and not deductively. This method avoids the danger of teleological explanation, and the other problems of neo-evolutionary functionalism.[39] This does not, however, imply a retreat from functionalism, especially in analysing the consequences of modernization.[40]

An alternative approach is in the Marxist tradition. This tends to deny the positive aspects of functionalism, or even that functionalist theories can explain change. It does stress the international aspects of modernization.[41] But it too is cognitively entrapped by suggesting that the new nations and Latin America must choose between models – that of the United States and that of the Soviet Union, and, naturally overemphasizes the similarities between modernizing states and the experience of the Soviet Union. The Soviet Union only gives aid, but the United States and her allies are neo-imperialist, in the tradition of Hilferding. There is a real problem involved in internationalizing the Marxist model of stratification and of viewing the rich Western countries as the bourgeoisie and the other nations as the proletariat, with the Soviet Union as their Leninist *avant-garde*. Basically the wrong assumption is made that there is a communality of interests among the rich nations and a lack of diversity and antagonisms among the poor ones. The notion that the modernization of non-Western nations will somehow lead to the disappearance of the Western nations, if the argument is carried to its logical conclusion, is insupportable. The polarization of the world into rich and poor is not as obvious as it seems merely from figures on GNP or *per capita* real income. The relations between them are too many and too complex for it to be assumed that they are mutually and irretrievably hostile. When analyses in the Marxist tradition are made concerning internal development, the problems in theory construction are strikingly akin to the dilemmas facing orthodox Marxists in explaining Russian communism. Indeed, the same solution is usually proposed – that in the absence of a middle class and a proletariat, the elites are the Leninist *avant-garde* who will spearhead the development movement. Thus the notion of the similarity between Russian and non-Western development implies convergence *ab initio*. In short, the problems facing analysts in the Marxist tradition is that Marx himself used the West to construct a model of development, the Russian experience necessitated a drastic Leninist–Stalinist revision to make the model applicable to the Soviet Union, and both of these contradictory strands have to be interwoven in the attempt to explain change processes in the new nations and in Latin America.

CONCLUSION

The use of the terms *modernization, remodernization,* and *demodernization* does, of course, imply that there may be similarities in each of the three processes and, at least,

39 Kenneth E. Bock, 'Evolution, Function and Change,' *American Sociological Review,* 28, no. 2 (April 1963), 229-37.

40 See Wilbert E. Moore, 'Social Change and Comparative Studies,' *International Social Science Journal*, 15, no. 4 (1963), 524.

41 For example, see Irving Louis Horowitz, *Three Worlds of Development* (New York: Oxford University Press, 1966).

that the search for them is what modernization theory is all about. What is striking so far is that theories drawn from the main body of sociological theory have been useful heuristic devices in trying to isolate these common properties. Indeed the emphasis on different culture areas is not a retreat into a modified historicism but can be seen as an ecological approach to the problem. Many of these heuristic devices have been drawn from structural-functional theory. Smelser's notion of structural differentiation, with its roots in Durkheimian thought, is one such example.[42] Another is reference group theory, which Bendix and Lagos have used in trying to understand the relations between developing nations and the West.[43] At this point in time it might be worthwhile for theorists of modernization to search the abundance of sociological and other propositions in order to find tools for analysis. Hopefully the result will be a meaningful theory of modernization basically sociological but generously interdisciplinary. But it must be a theory of the common properties in different processes rather than a theory of one process or model alone.

42 For the utilization of structural differentiation with reference to Western development, see Ian Weinberg, 'Social Problems Which Are No More,' in Erwin O. Smigel (ed.), *Handbook of Social Problems* (Chicago: Rand McNally, 1967).
43 Reinhard Bendix, 'Tradition and Modernity Reconsidered' (mimeo.); Gustavo Lagos, *International Stratification*.

WILBERT E. MOORE

Typical normative conflicts in stages of cultural change

Perhaps as recently as five years ago this topic might have been viewed somewhat conventionally as applying particularly to new nations, newly modernizing areas of the world, in short, to the 'Third World.' In Asia, Africa, and Latin America, and indeed in eastern and southern Europe, one encounters a conflict between old standards, time-honoured ways of behaving, and new ones. And since the young are often more receptive to change, and indeed insistent on it, than are those who have grown old in accustomed ways and adjusted to situations that were tolerable if not ideal, it is not surprising that old and new patterns of conduct have a fairly high relationship with old and young members of the population. To this theme of old and new criteria of what is desirable and proper, and the fact that what is traditional is more likely to appeal to people who are old and mature, and what is new is more likely to appeal to people who are young and immature, we shall return. This theme is a central one in this discussion, though not the only one. It is of great importance, however, for it unites much of the contemporary world, rich and poor, that otherwise has little in common. Rich lands and poor lands share not only a significant set of common human aspirations and values; they also share internal disorders which arise from a deep questioning of the equity of existing distributions of power and worldly goods, and an insistent voice from the young that they should be heard, be recognized, be counted, and even be given, *now*, the authority and treasure accumulated by their elders.

Five years ago, as I said, one might have assumed that the typical normative conflicts in stages of cultural change referred to far-away places. Those places are not without continuing interest, but we have learned, I hope, some recent lessons. One important lesson is that rapid social change is universal. Becoming a modern, or post-industrial, society does not bring things to a quiet and conflict-free state. Even if one attended to 'class' or interest-group conflicts in highly developed economies, it was commonly thought that almost all segments of the population shared certain elementary goals, such as power, status, and wealth, and even shared a sense of conventional ways of achieving those goals. Those conventional ways might range from individual competition for preferential treatment, through various organized efforts of occupational groups and political parties, to attempted revolutionary activities. But at least we thought we understood all this, even if we had, here and there, some misgivings about both the ends sought and the means used for their achievement. Now we have less reason to be sure of ourselves, whether as scholars or as concerned citizens. If some African or Oriental religious community seemed to be rejecting the appeal of the 'basket of goodies' [translator: an equivalent, please?], we had a fair basis in demonstrated evidence that such exotic beliefs were commonly a counsel of despair, easily defeated by clear and present alternatives. We must now know beyond any doubt that comparative sociologists and anthropologists (among whom I count myself) exaggerated the differences among the world's cultures with regard to the values attached to life, health, food, and the material comforts of life. Yet we still do encounter significant differences and conflicts. They are subtler than we had supposed. For it turns out that the relatively affluent can be as unhappy as the poor, and sometimes more so. The sociological concept of 'relative deprivation' accounts for most of this, but not all. The otherworldly belief systems that the sociologists and anthropologists discovered and exaggerated a half century ago or less may still be relevant after suitable discounting. We may still have proper misgivings about the probability of sustained efforts for economic growth in predominantly Buddhist countries, and the record of Catholic countries or regions on these grounds is almost uniformly dismal. We cannot, therefore, dismiss too casually the notion that belief systems make a difference. We must simply note where the difference lies, and that is at a point well above chronic disease and widespread starvation. No one enjoys that, whatever the priests and philosophers say.

Questions of equity always arise when the world's worldly benefits are distributed unequally – between and within countries. And equally urgent questions of equity would arise if all benefits were distributed equally. But it would be silly to suppose that the issues can be neatly organized by conventional distinctions according to class or even by reference to interest groups in the ordinary sense of diverse and competitive claims on economic distribution.

Our topic here is that of normative conflicts, and a few elementary definitions and distinctions must be noted, without being too tedious about it all. Strictly speaking, normative conflicts involve only rules of conduct, disputes over the right way of doing things. Whether any such activity should occur, whether the purpose of the action is a worthy one, is therefore not in question. Norms refer to means, not to ends (or values, in our sociological lexicon). And unquestionably much of the current manifestations of conflict in all parts of the world do indeed refer primarily to the meaning of conventional procedures, the efficacy of rules for accomplishing shared goals, and, of course, the equity of determining who is to decide.

Yet it is difficult to make that distinction between norms and values, means and ends, concretely, for norms are always related to values, which provide their rationale. Thus normative conflicts may, in fact, turn out to be disputes over values themselves. Are the understandings about the purpose of a national state, a planned economy, or a university genuinely consensual? Or does not normative conflict indicate an underlying divisiveness in the conception of the purpose of life and its organized manifestations? Normative conflicts, seemingly mere disputes over proper rules of the game, may well reveal that there is no agreement that the game itself is the right one or worth playing.

To distinguish normative conflicts and 'cultural conflicts' may be impossible in the concrete case.

Cultural change can mean a dismaying variety of things, but will be taken here to mean at least changes in the basic ways a society operates: its technology, and therefore the ways of making a living and the distribution of opportunity between generations and within single careers; changes in economic structure, including such major shifts in resource allocation as substantial developments in manufacturing and services, while the productivity of agriculture increases; changes in the forms of political organization and international relations; and changes in 'values,' such as universal access to educational opportunities. We thus neglect in this discussion such cultural changes as fads and fashions in clothing and art forms, literary styles, and similar manifestations of diversity and volatility in tastes. Such changes may well produce conflicts, and often noisy ones, but those clashes are in these days chiefly verbal and not especially sequential for the principal structural features of a society. For the few protagonists and antagonists involved, these may be matters of high moment. But they do not engage or even come to the attention of most of the population.

Even today, the clearest and most persistent cases of 'normative conflicts in stages of cultural change' are to be found in modernizing economies. Almost no part of the world is now untouched by the earnest quest for a better material basis of human life, or at least a deep frustration in the perception that the quest now seems vain. Yet the rejection of time-tested bases of social relationships, of trusted relations in kinship groups unless in communities and tribes, is difficult at best. What the eminent German sociologist, Ferdinand Toënnies referred to as the community – *Gemeinschaft* – is superseded by a somewhat tenuous assembly of associations – the *Gesselschaft*. Market principles or the cash nexus displace relations of mutual trust and traditional obligations. Mobility by demonstrated, competitive merit challenges secure but rather fixed positions in the social order, and transitory encounters gain at the expense of enduring ones. The formerly reasonable expectations of mature or aging parents are unrequited by their children, who are pursuing their own careers.

The conflict between the old ways and the new extends beyond lack of symmetry in traditional expectations and obligations. The conflict is perhaps most poignant in the shattering or undermining of well-established patterns of deference, of loyalty, and of a broadly based, if strongly conventional, mutuality of affection. It is not true that affection has no place at all in a modernized society, but its bounds are more narrowly drawn and its proper occasions less frequent than in the traditional community. What we encounter, additionally, in modernizing societies are several forms of normative conflict, which partly represent old conflicts newly brought to the surface, partly broader manifestations of the old and the new, and partly the early stages of conflict within the modernized sectors of society.

The conflict between generations and among kinsmen who represent 'traditional' and 'modern' orientations represents normative conflict in the fine. Beyond the family, however, there is the village, the tribe, the ethnic or linguistic group. Most national states in the modern world are in fact multi-communal, including some old and stable ones – for example, the United Kingdom, Belgium, Switzerland; others are somewhat newer and seemingly stable combinations, such as the United States and the Soviet

Union. Nation-building has more or less succeeded, despite regional, ethnic and religious distinctions. These examples should caution us against the view that various new nations in post-colonial Africa are not 'viable' because of tribal loyalties and internal diversity. Yet it is true that new nations have *somewhat* greater problems than old ones in dealing with diversity, in finding a common national identity that will 'plaster over' real and fundamental divisions. Here the old is the traditional kinship structure or village community – the *Gemeinschaft,* again – and the new is the multi-communal national state – the *Gesellschaft* – which may make concessions to old forms of allegiance and loyalty, but will attempt to organize its activities and administrative agencies in emulation of other national states. In a very real sense, the old conflicts may very well be exacerbated by being caught up into a common national political structure, and hostilities long suppressed may be brought into the open by being made public in a context where commonality is the official doctrine and diversity the fact. Common hostility to the former colonial power may be played up for a while, but the political utility of that device is bound to have only a short-term utility in the face of real and present differences.

Still referring to old hostilities revealed is the situation, commonly found in Latin America, in which a radically unequal land distribution (and therefore distribution of benefits from agriculture) leads to demands for land reform, credit for the newly established private cultivator, or some such alternative as communist collectivization. Political modernity threatens traditional tribal and other differences. The faint hint of economic modernity, in a political context of change, threatens existing forms of land tenure. Here, by conventional wisdom and conventional liberal values, the normative conflict involves the right to *share* in the broader processes of joining the modern world, rather than the fear of having traditional divisions threatened by an overly insistent national polity. The anomaly is clear; its subtleties we cannot explore here. Yet one is always safe, and wise, in asking, which interests are served, and which put in jeopardy? Our net conclusions have to include an obvious one: major cultural changes will not affect all interests favourably, even if those changes appear to be consistent with common, and commonly announced, values. But there is a slightly more subtle one: *the various forms of modernization need not be consistent.* A more substantial economic equity may threaten tribal identity, and the old certainties may have some perceived advantages over new opportunities that carry with them uncertainties. Life is never simple, and in the modernizing world it is especially complex. For the individual participant in trying to attend to the old and the new, the old understandings and the new and dangerous opportunities, the situation may be very close to that identified by the eminent French sociologist, Emile Durkheim, as *anomie*: normlessness. In a situation of total confusion about rules, and even values, *there are no norms*. The conflict, if any, is within the confused individual. He may try to act out his uncertainty by destructive acts against all conventions, old or new, but more probably he simply 'drops out' and fails to cope with any of those demands on him. He is essentially lost to the on-going business of maintaining a social order; it is the business of students of social deviance to predict whether he becomes a criminal, a dope addict, or some other form of non-conformist. But he is a waste, and therefore a cost, and one can regret that result without condoning it.

Let us move a step farther along in the process of modernization. Now our contrast is not with the mature man who would not leave his village when some of his children did so, and who does not understand their orientation to life, and precisely those ambitious youngsters. Rather, it is between those who, for one or another reason (perhaps ideological, perhaps economically self-interested) decide to join the modern world on a very limited and temporary basis, and those who have espoused modernity as a life-style, perhaps seeing no reasonable alternative. Now we encounter another instructive anomaly. On the one hand, the 'committed' worker is likely to fare better than the nominally temporary one, to rise at least slightly in the scale of monetary rewards and administrative position. And he is precisely the worker who is likely to be an organizer and leader in labour movements, to present not a confrontation of the old and the new, but a challenge to the equity of power and rewards in the new order of productive organizations.

Karl Marx observed this phenomenon over a hundred years ago, and correctly understood the radical disparity between the owners and the workers – we should now say the managers and the managed. He was suitably, from his point of view, contemptuous of the Lumpenproletariat – we should now say the uncommitted worker. In place after place this perception of radical polarization within the *modernized* sector of the economy has been reconfirmed. But only at similar, early, stages of economic modernization. What has happened is that Marx gets reconfirmed through comparable stages in economic development, for reasons almost irrelevant to *his* idea of his theory. And as a social prognosticator, he has to be viewed as among the more usefully wrong scholars in the field, for he was *totally* wrong about the dynamics of industrializing societies. In place of economic polarization, or political polarization, or any other kind of polarization in what Marxists call capitalist societies, we have a greater and greater movement to the middle positions. Anybody who now believes that the original Marxist forecasts about capitalist societies are to be taken seriously has to be certifiably insane. Anybody who fails to note what Marx noted about the *early* stages of industrialization and its normative conflicts is at least certifiably incompetent as a social observer. For we now revert to our theme: at comparable stages of cultural change, comparable (and indeed virtually identical) normative conflicts do occur.

Before we leave the subject of modernizing societies we should note some additional problems. We have earlier noted the conflict between the conventional expectations prevailing within kinships and lineages, within tribes and other communities. In the nature of the case, the break between old and new standards of social organization will be partly sharp (some outstanding examples of those normative conflicts we have outlined) and partly subtle. Two standard examples must serve us here for reasons of generality and grave difficulty.

The first example is that of the failure of the administrative structure of the modernizing state to meet the normal criteria for selection and competence. The administrative agencies of new states are even more rife with incompetence than are their counterparts in longer established and somewhat more affluent states. Favouritism still reigns, graft is almost taken for granted, and selection to position scarcely meets the announced criteria of competence. The situation is simple, if not pretty. With only a tiny segment of the population having the opportunity to achieve higher education, and with educational criteria formally announced as necessary for various positions in public administration, the probability is high that the upper levels of public administration form a kind of social and ideological cadre, not simply a technical one. The normative conflict here is between the dedicated technicians (often trained abroad) and the secure time-servers who countenance new bureaucratic forms, since it gives them a sinecure, but who have slight interest in novel and suspect programs.

Another problem we shall note briefly. New nations, and those who have newly discovered nationalism as a useful tool for internal purposes, often spend otherwise ridiculous sums on a national military establishment. Again, paintings in black and white or other stark contrasts are essentially silly, and not to be taken seriously. Let us concede: the modern international world is precarious; even for minor states, a semblance of military preparedness might help to add to the costs of a potential aggressor; for new nations a military establishment may have no politically rational basis at all, but only be a sign, like embassies and consulates and flags and elaborate border restrictions, that sovereignty over a territory has been established. Were I not a citizen of the United States, which seems, off and on, to be nervous about everything, I could with greater confidence assert a common principle: the newer and less secure a national state – witness the paranoia of the Soviet Union, which even exceeds that of the United States, and that of all sorts of new nations – the more it will attend to its national sovereignty.

Our attention here, however, is properly narrower. In modernizing societies, at least, we should say a few words of gentle praise for military organizations. Whatever their rationalized excuse (which, for example in Latin America, may be totally fraudulent), military organizations in developing countries serve several other functions: for raw military recruits they act as a great civilizing influence by bringing rather innocent persons into the modern world of technology; military organizations are often internationally professionalized in a degree far beyond that of, say, physicians and lawyers; and in the power vacuum which is typical of multiply divided national polities without a consensus, the military may be the only recourse for internal order. In these situations there is a powerful temptation for the military to take over in internal government. They often do. The military take-over is commonly a last resort, and that last resort may have no sensible consequence, for there is no standard way for the military to give up power. We have to expect such a pattern, time after time, and expect internal disorders as the military establishment proves itself incapable of internal rule. It is not a joyful prediction, but I think it is a true one over the short term. Thus, in modernizing states the military plays an extremely ambiguous role: as a modernizing element, and as an enemy of modernity. Politically sophisticated elements in national states will make that, too, a subject for contention and try to find reasons for putting the technically sophisticated, but presumably politically neutral, military back in its place. No modern state has yet succeeded in solving that issue.

We turn finally and briefly to normative conflicts in modernized societies. The conflict between the old and new is not solved by modernization. Rather, it is accentuated, for modern economies devote considerable resources to deliberate change. Only part of that deliberate change is technological in the strict sense, for attention is also devoted to changes in political organization and management and to attempted solutions to various identified 'social problems.'

All modernized societies – and the United States is perhaps extreme in this respect – have various disadvantaged groups. The ideal of equality of opportunity may fall far short in practice. It is still a disadvantage to be born poor, and if one has linguistic or racial handicaps as well, one may be in effect a 'local colonial,' cut off from many opportunities while surrounded by the more privileged. Moreover, the status of women, who form a kind of 'submerged majority,' will be increasingly subject to question and probable political tension.

The revolt of the young, particularly in the universities, indicates a deep dissatisfaction with organizations that have been in the forefront of change in their research activities and notably backward in revising courses and teaching procedures. One can scarcely condone sheer anarchy or nihilism. For if the young did not ask to be born, it is also true that they have yet done little to deserve their existence. Yet the young face an especially uncertain future, and may well share with some of us who are much older the conviction that as we solve or ameliorate the old problems of sickness and starvation we create new ones of continuous adaptation to unprecedented change, and without clear normative guides to what is right and what is wrong. Despite prosperity, we live in difficult times.

RAINER C. BAUM

On political modernity: stratification and the generation of societal power

Once 'development' had become a catchword in the years following World War II, students of politics set out to search for the political analogue of the industrial revolution. It has yet to be found. Studies in political development grew rapidly into a specialty. The emphasis in this field has been primarily on the growth of specialized political structures, such as parties, pressure groups, legislatures, executive and judicial offices. Such office proliferation and specialization was seen as a necessary accompaniment of the numerical growth of the politically relevant. It has hardly ever been a matter of dispute that industrialization increases the proportionate number of people who must be taken into account in politics. The connecting link in this relation is social mobilization. Whether one considers increases in mass media exposure, geographic and social mobility, urban living, literacy, or personal wealth, all of these, separately and jointly, tend to expand the politically relevant strata in society (Lerner 1958; Deutsch 1961). An essentially similar observation had already been made by Durkheim (1900), who noted a concomitant growth of 'individuation' and centralized state power. What remains in question to this day is the range of variability that the institutionalized forms of political mass participation can take.

On this question there has been a certain measure of ethnocentric bias. Perhaps this was inevitable initially. At one time it seemed to Western observers as though the 'democratic revolution' might be the political analogue of the industrial revolution (Lipset 1960; Cutright 1963). Democratization here referred to the extension of the franchise to strata previously excluded from regularized 'official' participation in the political system (Rokkan 1961) and the notion of representative government. Common-sense observation of such cases as Germany, Japan, and Russia, of course, always rebelled at the claim of an intrinsic link between industrialization, social mobilization, and democracy. Also theoretical and historical work soon helped to dispel hopes for any such direct relationship (Parsons 1960, 1956; de Schweinitz 1964; Moore 1966). Just how much of a shift in perspective has taken place is indicated by the following recent forthright assertion: 'The existence of an elected assembly is, in itself, an indication of neither the modernity of a political system nor of its susceptibility to modernization. The same is true for elections' (Huntington 1968, 402). But, modernization apart, since it is of marginal interest here, what *is* political modernity?

POLITICAL MODERNITY:
AN UNDERDEVELOPED CONCEPT

The desirable and the familiar continuously interfere with our vision of the real or the possible. In the present case this interference amounts to a predilection for the study of readily observable structures, the organizational forms of activities rather than process, the activities themselves, *and* a decidedly one-sided conception of power, defined as A's ability to make B do what A wants, even against B's opposition (Weber 1946; Dahl 1957; Banfield 1961).

The study of party structure with respect to political modernity seems to conclude that 'modern is what we in the West already have.' One-half of Olsen's (1968) measures of political development are 'Western democratic.' Even Huntington (1968) prefers to partially contradict himself rather than concede that contemporary Anglo-Saxon party structure may not be modern. In his analysis of the relation between party structure, stability, and capacity to manage social change, he first identifies party strength as the crucial variable. Here the party's major role is seen in the mobilization of support which is treated as one form of 'power generation.' Party strength is measured in terms of voting turn-out. On that measure, single-party communist systems outflank all others (Huntington 1968, 403). Single-party systems also tend to be more stable and less prone to coups than others (Huntington 1968, 422–3). Yet for 'sustained modernization,' which equals modernity, competition between parties, not within a party, or between a party and other structures, the two-party or dominant-party systems are singled out as most adequate (Huntington 1968, 426). Thus while Huntington would exclude the multi-party system, like the Dutch and Norwegian, from the status 'modern,' in the end it is an obviously democratic party structure *already in existence for a long time* in the Anglo-Saxon countries which remains as the pinnacle of modernity.

There is something seriously wrong here. First, we do not know why we have what we have. A recent review of studies on the genesis of democracy concludes negatively. All efforts to find the social forces necessary for democracy have so far failed to produce any conclusive results (Lepsius 1968). Consequently, prediction in this area remains precarious. Worse yet, much of what seemed to be known about the structural conditions making for stability in democratic regimes has apparently turned out to be illusory. Until recently the following conditions were deemed favourable for stability: (a) cross-cutting rather than superimposed social cleavages (Dahrendorf 1959; Lipset 1960); (b) interest rather than value conflicts, or pragmatic-bargaining rather than *Weltanschauungs*-parties (Nettl 1967); (c) relative value homogeneity rather than heterogeneity, lest interest conflicts escalate into value conflicts (Smelser 1963); and (d) two-party and majoritarian electoral systems rather than multi-party systems with proportional representation electoral rules (Hermens 1941; Duverger 1954). On all these counts there should have been no stable democracy in the Netherlands, Belgium, and Switzerland. Yet these countries enjoyed precisely that for long periods (Lijphart 1969). Finally, worse yet again for Huntington's identification of multi-party systems as traditional in function, the Dutch system has proved remarkably resilient in absorbing vast quantities of rapid modernizing social change following World War II (Lijphart 1968). The same is true for Norway (Eckstein 1966). Both have a multi-party system.

Next, concerning the conception of power, there is still a predominant concern with its distribution, not with its quantity, or *how much there is* to be distributed. This too seems to be related to a preference for studying structure rather than process. The situation has been noted and criticized as a one-sided preoccupation with the zero-sum or constant-sum conception of power (Parsons 1963a). That power also varies in sheer quantity, and indeed must be produced, has been pointed out more than once (Parsons 1960, 170-98; Parsons 1963a; Huntington 1968, 397-433). But, according to my reading, there has been no systematic attempt to delineate the social conditions favourable to the generation of power which compares at all with the parallel efforts expended on the problem of economic development.

Common sense tells us that some countries seem to have more power than others. Israel looks more powerful today than all the Arab countries combined. Given the propensity of common sense to associate power and force, it is no accident that the first attempts to measure power as a quantitative nation-attribute appeared in the field of international relations (Jones 1954). But as the example of Israel shows, power seems to be a function of *organization* more than of sheer numbers, population size, or quantities of resources.

Historical study also shows that modern states possess vastly more superior powers than previous polities. Limited control of the ruler and chronic disobedience, due in part to ownership of office by officials, was a feature characteristic of much of the *ancien régime* in France (Moore 1966). Effective control from the centre was severely limited in historical empires due in part to the limitations of transport technology (Eisenstadt 1963). Limited and non-expansive resources characterized most absolutist regimes, where universal conscription and universal taxation had not yet been invented (Beloff 1962). Strict barter-exchange politics characterized much of the relation between ruler and estates (Carsten 1959).

Theory also suggests that modern states have more power than earlier forms. The actions of modern states have far more penetrating consequences, their power goes far beyond 'this or that particular policy decision' (Deutsch 1963, 118). Not only do modern states command more power, they have more obligations. As Weinberg (1967) pointed out, segmental society had relatively fewer social problems in a technical sense than can be found in differentiated society. Cities apart, crop failure and hunger, plague or natural disaster resulted in the elimination of a few segments in agraria. There was a meaning problem of crushing dimensions, but the elimination of segments caused comparatively little direct social-organizational disturbance. For segments are self-sufficient; comparatively, they are little worlds unto themselves. With increasing differentiation and the resulting interdependencies in society, most disturbances become social problems. Regardless of the cause, the failure of any given unit has a much greater probability for disturbing the functioning of others than in a segmented social structure. Therefore, the more modern the society, the greater its susceptibility to social problems. As captured in the term 'welfare state,' social problems in most modern societies have become the business of government. Consequently, modern states not only command more power, they also need it to fulfil their function. Yet common sense, historical perspective, and theoretical suggestions notwithstanding, the theory of *the production of power* in society is still in its infancy (Mitchell 1967).

The preceding three paragraphs have utilized the language of common sense on purpose, almost with a vengeance. There are references to powers of countries, societies, states, governments, and polities. One point of this is that one should distinguish between the power of a governmental system, state, or polity *over* non-governmental and non-political units *in* society from the power *of* society, country or nation to achieve the kinds of ends commonly called public or national interest.*

Another point is that the study of political modernity which takes political structure as its major focus can say a great deal about governmental power but apparently little about societal power. In one of the most interesting essays of the more recent political science literature, Huntington (1968, 93-139) has characterized the structure of contemporary American government as outright traditional and backward. He claims its best parallel is to be found in the Tudor monarchy. It is discovered that in terms of the actual differentiation of legislative, executive, and representation functions the Soviet Union by far outranks the U.S. in modernity. The power of Soviet government is also superior to that of the United States. But by itself, this obviously does *not* mean that the power of Soviet society to achieve its goals is therefore higher than that of American society.

However, if we are interested in treating economic and political development as parallel phenomena in our conception of the modern society, it is precisely the power of society that is at issue. Societal power has been defined as 'the generalized capacity to get things done in the interest of collective goals' (Parsons 1960, 181). In terms of a first-step operationalization on the national level this simply refers to the attainment of national objectives. Goals authoritatively set, such as targets of economic plans, placing a man on the moon, school integration quotas, and the like may serve as examples.

Societal power in the above sense has been viewed as the *product* or *output* of the polity in a fashion parallel to wealth which *results from* economic action. When we speak of economic modernity as involving sustained economic growth, we have in mind the result, viz. wealth. We do not have in mind that economic activity as such increasingly pervades all social relations. In fact, in the wealthiest countries, aggregate labour force participation of the population has declined, even though individuals spend as much if not more years in the labour force as before. The latter appears to be a function of increased life expectancy. There has been an increasingly delayed entry into the labour force at the beginning of the life cycle, a longer time in retirement towards its end, and increased leisure or vacations from direct economic-occupational activities during the middle. With these developments, it would be difficult to argue that economic modernity involves economization of all social life.

A parallel logic in the area of politics would therefore specify sustained growth in societal power as the central criterion of political modernity. It would also specifically exclude politicization of social life as an accompaniment. With such criteria, our atten-

---

* Governmental and societal power in this sense are, of course, related phenomena. But the relationship between the two seems fairly complex, to say the least.

tion is directed to the interaction between political and overtly non-political structures, and its outcome, viz. power. Whether this approach will be more fruitful remains to be seen. But at least it will preclude continuation of a too exclusive preoccupation with the development of political structure. That approach, it would seem, has reached a certain impasse. For where the proliferation of political organizations constitutes the major measure of political development, the logic of differentiation, used in an over-simplified manner and left to itself, points to totalitarian regimes as the most modern. In terms of organizational richness and manifest claims to specialization, including specialization of the mass media, that type of political system beats all others (Orlow 1968; Schoenbaum 1967; Höhne 1967; Meyer 1965; Brzezinski and Huntington 1964).

But overt proliferation of organizations as indexed by sheer number does not measure differentiation. In addition, differentiation calls for actual functional specialization and increased efficiency in services performed (Smelser 1968). And so the logic of the model is not left to itself. Facts and common-sense impressions combine to save the situation by *ad hoc* arguments. In totalitarian regimes all of social life tends to be politicized. Since this signals relative fusion of polity and society, the case is not modern. Khrushchev's ambitions 'to bury the capitalist world under an avalanche of the good things in life' as the best strategy of peaceful co-existence have so far remained an empty threat. Consequently, the discrepancy between planning and knowledge (Berliner 1957), a utopian ideology and parallel structures that fail to work (Meyer 1965), and imperfect institutionalization of political conflict resolution (Huntington 1968) are the factors used to explain the glaring inefficiencies. A too liberal use of the concept differentiation and lack of measurements can hardly explain such a dismal ending of analysis alone. More likely it is also the result of the failure to distinguish systematically between governmental and societal power.

THE SUM AND SUBSTANCE OF THE PROBLEM
Possibly prematurely, and with a corresponding sense of precariousness, I should like to draw the following conclusions from the above remarks.

First, a conception of economic modernity that focuses on the idea of continuous sustained growth in wealth as a result of interaction between primarily economic and primarily non-economic organizations (Parsons and Smelser 1956) calls for a parallel conception of political modernity. Consequently, sustained growth in societal power as a result of interaction between governmental or political and primarily non-political organizations would fill the bill.

Secondly, a historical or contemporary-comparative approach that focuses primarily on political structures and ends up by identifying *any given* structure as 'all there is and can be' to modernity amounts to a failure by misplaced attention. All self-conscious efforts at avoiding precisely this dilemma notwithstanding, Huntington (1968, 114, 397-461) still failed to eliminate it. On the one hand, we learn that the Soviet Union is more modern by virtue of a greater differentiation of the political output structures. On the other, we learn that the West is more modern by virtue of a greater differentiation of the political input structures, the two- or dominant-party systems and legal institutionalization of lobbies. Other analysts agree with him on the last point (Parsons 1964; Pye 1966; Almond and Verba 1965). Yet many writers, Huntington included, identify continuous institutionalized change as the central characteristic of modernity. From that perspective some given stable developed political structural arrangement may indeed be conducive to the management of such change. But it is the latter, the phenomenon of change, which is of primary interest, and not the former, the stable structure, regardless of how it is constituted. Without identifying *on a requisite level of generality* just what is changing, one cannot even test impressionistically whether the developed structure is adequate to the task.

Thirdly, to the extent that 'sustained growth in wealth' has proven its utility in the conception of economic modernity, sustained growth in societal power constitutes the phenomenon of change at the requisite level of generality of the conception of political modernity. Consequently, attempts to develop a theory on the production of power in society seems at least as promising as anything else in advancing our search for an adequate conceptualization of political modernity.

Fourthly, contrary to Mitchell (1967, 134), who calls for the operationalization of Parsons's 'production function of power,' other and more simple tasks may also be usefully undertaken as a first step. According to Parsons the amount of power produced in a society is at least a function of the following: (a) values, including type of value-commitments, relative consensus on these, and their legitimation effectiveness (Parsons 1957, 1960); (b) six more direct components ranging from opportunity for effectiveness to legality of powers; six other components involving money, influence, and values which are interchanged with the six power-components listed under (b); and (c) all of the above embedded in an interchange system comprising a total of twenty-six interchanges (Parsons 1963a, 1963b, 1968a). If upon much needed clarification this scheme should turn out to be exhaustive, then operationalization would be the next logical step. In the meantime something equally fundamental yet much less complex in scope might also be examined.

Fifthly, this is the relation between the quantity of a society's power and its stratification system. The sociology of stratification has been characterized by a similar double view as the literature on power. But in contrast with the latter, where there has been much writing on the constant-sum conception and little on power as a quantitative societal attribute, in the field of stratification both horns of *its* dilemma have been given extensive attention. Here the Marxist tradition sees inequalities as inherently frustrating and therefore productive of conflict and change primarily (Bottomore 1965). But the other side, the functionalist interpretation has been equally well developed. According to this view, the major function of stratification is regulation of the allocative process and with that primarily integration in society (Davis and Moore 1945; Parsons 1953). The functionalist answer to the question 'why stratification?' has generated an unusually proliferating debate. This controversy helped much to shed considerable light on the complexity of the problem. So far, however, despite Lenski's (1966) effort at synthesis, it has failed to advance our knowledge about the primary function of stratification in any commensurate degree (Heller 1969, 479-87). Two components of the functionalist argument seem primarily responsible for the apparent intractability of the problem. These are the questions of value consensus and the relative objective importance of roles in societies. If one succeeds in identifying *some* of the *general conditions* under which the nature of stratification makes *primarily* for integration as contrasted with conflict-change, and does so *independently* of the questions of value consensus and objective functional importance of roles, a small advance would result. A small advance in the theory of stratification, however, *at the same time* might tell us something concerning the general societal conditions conducive to the generation of societal power. Both are the subject of the remainder of this essay. Both are also very complex matters. All that can be aimed at here is the opening of a discussion, hopefully to provide it with a focus, but certainly not to settle the issues.

STRATIFICATION AND SOCIETAL POWER:
LIMITATIONS OF SCOPE

The central role of stratification in the development of societal power in its evolutionary aspect has been clearly stated by Parsons (1964, 1966). Accordingly, it is the development of stratification which makes possible the increase in centralizing the taking of responsibility for society and with that for collective effectiveness. The emergence of stratification is seen as providing the means for increased collective effectiveness. For it is stratification that institutionalizes the concentration of power as well as of wealth. Therefore, it sets in motion a modernizing chain reaction. Such a process starts with the emancipation of resources from kin-ascriptions, creates a strain for legitimating such emancipation, involving a legitimation of both the policies and the position-advantages accruing to those who control power and wealth, and this in turn leads to the development of legal norms, universalism, bureaucracy, money, markets, and societal power. The last element, termed power as a generalized societal medium, is said to depend 'overwhelmingly on a consensual element, i.e. the ordered institutionalization and exercise of influence which links the power system with the higher-order societal consensus at the value level' (Parsons 1964, 355). My only advance beyond this position will be an attempt to show why and how some types of stratification systems are more conducive to the growth of societal power than others.*

According to this view then, stratification is an indispensable prerequisite for the generation of societal power. It is also a universal and inevitable aspect of more highly developed societies. Restricting the term 'class' to groups characterized by authority differentials has led Dahrendorf (1959, 219) to a similar conclusion, viz. 'a society is classless if it is "powerless".' Finding a convergence between Parsons and Dahrendorf, however, may not be enough. Since the inevitability issue of stratification and even of inequalities has raised considerable controversy (Tumin 1953, 1963; Huaco 1963), it has become inevitable to state one's own position on it. Therefore, concerning the universality of inequalities, agreement with Parsons (1953) and Wrong (1964) is registered. Complete equality in every respect would imply that men cease evaluating their action, an assumption I find neither useful nor plausible. Whether, how, and to what degree inequalities are or need to be stratified, however, is a different matter.

---

* Next to Parsons other writers have also noted the relation between stratification and collective effectiveness. Kimberley (1966) argues the case for economic organizations: the greater the stress on productivity, the greater internal stratification. Similarly, Lenski (1966) also predicted increasing inequalities with growing modernity at the societal level, a position from which he separated himself only by *ad hoc* argument after finding no empirical evidence for it. A positive correlation between stratification of a social system and 'its capacity to get things done' has also been observed in small groups, natural (Whyte 1961, 125-35) as well as experimental (Hare 1962).

Minimally, stratification refers to two variables, viz. (a) the degree to which people see others as arranged in discrete levels along some dimension of inequality rather than in a continuous hierarchy with no visible breaks, and (b) the extent of concordance of a ranked unit on all vertical dimensions or the degree of status congruence (Kahl 1959, 10-15). While both are empirical questions, the first turns out to be largely terminological. So far as we know, the number of levels recognized varies with position in the perceived hierarchy. Those placed fairly low and fairly high tend to see fewer levels than those in the middle (Bolte 1966). Those near the bottom tend to see least, viz. a dichotomy in society (Dahrendorf 1959, 282-4). Some, of course, have practically no image, i.e. see nothing distinct at all. The point is, however, that where there are images in terms of vertical dimensions, they vary in complexity, but all involve relatively distinct levels. Therefore, one may define stratification as the degree to which the vertical dimensions exhibit positive correlations.

Given this perspective, the more a society is stratified, the greater is status congruence among the ranked units. Status concordance and criss-cross, however, vary inversely and in constant-sum fashion (Galtung 1966). Criss-cross is defined as the sharing of one or more statuses of one unit each with two or more other units, which in turn share no status. Thus, the more a society is stratified, the lower is criss-cross. It also follows that criss-cross is at maximum when the correlations among the vertical dimensions are zero.

Two further considerations treated by Galtung largely as facts established by research, will be used here as assumptions. The first is that criss-cross cements society by uniting otherwise separate parts.* The second is a sociopsychological assumption, viz. that lack of status congruence makes for an active life and leads in the aggregate to a more dynamic society.†

Next, dealing with the relation between stratification and societal power largely independently of the value system means making no assumptions concerning any ranking of the vertical dimensions themselves. It also calls for assumptions concerning conversion attempts. Following Lenski (1966) and Kervin (1968), whatever is subject to ranking is here treated as a social resource. It is assumed that all units in society – whether individuals or collectivities – try to maximize all their resources. They attempt conversions to cumulate their resources until the net costs become prohibitive. Also, we have to assume sufficient transparency of the social structure so that the relative success and failure of conversion attempts become widely known. From this perspective, positive

---

* That cross-cutting cleavages imply cross-pressures and conflicting loyalties is, of course, well known. But instead of integrating status-separated groups, they may do nothing of the kind, leading to further fragmentation of the social fabric instead (Eckstein 1966). This is not only a theoretical possibility. There are known instances, as for example voting in Imperial Germany, where criss-cross had a fragmentation-effect (Lepsius 1966).

† Status incongruence is usually thought of as leading to attempts at equilibration in a direction of upward mobility. According to Kimberley (1966), however, the matter is more complex. Where function status is higher than ability status and aspirations and/or social pressures to get ahead are relatively weak, downward mobility constitutes the expected response to status incongruency. Pop sociology has registered the same phenomenon in the Peter Principle, where happiness is not being promoted beyond one's ability. For present purposes, however, it is only important to keep in mind that downward mobility also makes a position available that someone else can attain. Whether up or down, what counts here is that status incongruence leads to mobility attempts and with that to more activism in society than under perfect status equilibration.

correlations among the vertical dimensions constitute a constant invitation for conversion at relatively low risk, while negative correlations imply discouragement. Zero correlations, however, parallel the situation of the rat subjected to intermittent reinforcement schedules. Here conversion attempts are likely to be frenzied and generative of high tension. Other factors influencing vertical mobility cannot be taken into account; these must therefore be considered constant across the three types of stratification systems to be discussed.

Concerning the number of vertical dimensions employed, the practice among analysts has been quite varied, depending on the purposes of the study. Kahl (1959) and Barber (1968) used six, Weber (1946) three, and Galtung (1966) two. The purpose here being theoretical, four vertical dimensions will be used. This means saying less quantitatively than Galtung could with only two. It also means trying to say something more realistic in general, and with respect to societal power in particular. Furthermore, only one non-vertical dimension of stratification will be used, viz. class-barrier consciousness.

With respect to the vertical dimensions, Weber's (1946) famous triad of wealth, power, and social honour seems most useful. Only one alteration involving a separation of the last element into two seems advisable. Accordingly, social honour may be broken down into social prestige on the one hand, and what for lack of a better term may be called cultural honour or simply virtues, on the other. Parallel to usage in empirical research on occupational prestige (Inkeles and Rossi 1956), social prestige here refers to attribution of differential importance to positions in society. Such attribution in turn reflects the apperception of differential contributions to the smooth working of interdependencies in a differentiated social structure. Social prestige, then, is a reward rendered for contributions most directly relevant for maintaining the solidarity of society. It is also a facility used for managing solidarity. Prestige in this sense has always been an attribute primarily of interstitial roles and organizations in society that regulate competing claims. Therefore, a segmental society that hangs together chiefly by mechanical ties or cultural honour has less need for prestige, as well as for its unequal distribution. The major carriers of prestige are the professional experts.

Cultural honour or virtues as used here refers to attribution of differential moral worth to a unit. Virtues are somewhat parallel to what Cohn (1960) termed 'charismatic standards.' In his conception, however, these are opposed to 'worldly' standards, and this is the only respect in which cultural honour differs. No intrinsic opposition between differential moral worth and other evaluations is assumed. Thus virtues and prestige, for example, are not seen as intrinsically in opposition. For present purposes the postulate of such opposition would seem to hinge too much on the continued and essentially unaltered viability of the Judaeo-Christian heritage. Not only would this restrict the concept to Western society, but even here it seems out of place. Modern religious concerns seem to be differentiating (Parsons 1968b), or more modestly, perhaps just changing but still in a direction diminishing the fundamentalist ethic that subjected Western man to an unavoidable measure of conflict with instrumental rationalism (Schelsky 1965). The remaining two Weberian dimensions are used in unaltered form. Thus only one point needs emphasis In distinction to societal power, simple power from here on refers to the power-over conception. It will be restricted largely to mean governmental power over citizens.

There is a very simple reason for employing the four vertical dimensions just outlined. Wealth, power, prestige, and cultural honour jointly subsume most, possibly all, of the crucial cleavages in society. Wealth and power capture the dimensions most salient to Marx's industrial and political cleavages. Virtues capture the fact of ethnic ranking, the pervasive struggles over educational rights (i.e. the state-church issue), language use, as well as some aspects of regional cleavages. Prestige captures occupational ranking as well as standing in small groups.

Finally a cautionary note concerning the role of international relations and political structure in a society. In the international field, societal power is, of course, a vertical dimension. Obviously, too, societal power depends to some degree on a society's dependence on others and the regulation or lack thereof that can be established in this area. It is possible that international relations is a more important variable in the generation of societal power than a society's stratification system. However that may be, international relations must be excluded from the present account. It is therefore assumed to be a constant across the types discussed. A similar caveat is necessary concerning the nature of political structure. Since, in the view adopted here, societal power is an output of the interaction between polity and society, a fuller analysis must treat political structure as a variable. Nevertheless, it is contended that the nature of the stratification system has a partially independent effect on the quantity of societal power. To show how and why this is so constitutes the sole objective here.

STRATIFICATION, INTEGRATION,
AND SOCIETAL POWER GENERATION

A decade ago Dahrendorf (1959) placed the term post-capitalist society into circulation. He recognized that economic-industrial and political conflicts had become institutionally isolated from each other in the Western democracies. With that development, the central underpinning of Marx's conception of revolutionary change, the fusion of power and property, had changed. Instead of revolution and violence the institutional regulation of conflicts and built-in change in the social structure had become feasible. Dahrendorf also restated an insight already discovered by Marx, that stratification brings order to social conflict. One of the conditions for the organization of opposed interests is patterned rather than recruited by chance to quasi-groups (Dahrendorf 1959, 187). One cannot organize the *Lumpenproletariat* because its elements – dropouts from the strata above – are too diverse. Before the fight really gets under way, they fall apart under the weight of their own inner divisiveness. That this idea carries considerable plausibility is indicated by a contrasting case quite as famous as the 'down and outs' of the eighteenth century of Brumaire. A *Lumpen*-aristocracy can be organized. This happened in Japan, where the impoverished *samurai* succeeded in spearheading the Meiji Restoration (Nishio 1965; Moore 1966).

Yet concentrating on the conditions favourable for decreasing the intensity of conflicts and facilitating their institutionalization, Dahrendorf largely failed to exploit this idea. His conception of the social structure of the free society remained exclusively oriented to the maximization of cross-cutting cleavages where all conflicts become dissociated. He derived this conception of the institutionalization of freedom, treated as synonymous with modernity, in part from an incorrect empirical generalization of the monist totalitarian case where all conflicts and cleavages are allegedly superimposed (Dahrendorf 1959, 316-17). During subsequent years his simple identification of pluralism with dissociated cleavages and conflicts apparently did not change in any substantive way (Dahrendorf 1965). Thus, the notion that stratification – apart from rendering conflicts more intense and with that more difficult to control – also orders or patterns social conflicts, thereby rendering an indispensable prerequisite for their institutionalized control, had been lost again. Such a double effect of stratification was implicit already in Simmel (1908), who noted that, far from having only negative effects on the social fabric, various types of conflicts not only resulted from stratification they also maintained the class structure, authority differentials, and commitment to law. A general functional proposition may serve to make this double effect of stratification explicit. Where the system of stratification differentiates from the polity, just sufficient order is imposed on conflicts to predict them and just sufficient mixing or cross-cutting of lines of conflict group formation is preserved to control them. With these contradictory forces in balance, stratification integrates society better and the polity-society interaction produces more output, viz. societal power.

Since differentiation has been mentioned, a definition is called for. According to Smelser (1963, 1968), differentiation refers to a process whereby one role or organization splits into two or more with the result that the functions – previously under joint management as it were – are performed more effectively and with greater efficiency or less cost. Therefore, unless enhanced effectiveness and efficiency in performance results, one can speak of structural segregation perhaps, but not of differentiation.* The integration of differentiated units is therefore not simply another matter, as Smelser (1968, 129) claims, it is an integral aspect of differentiation itself. For it would be difficult to conceive how enhanced effectiveness could result without adequate integration.

Possibly the best analysed case concerning the differentiation of institutions is the one involving the family and the occupational system (Smelser 1959; Parsons 1955, 1961). There, as may be recalled, the double-role incumbency of father and worker by the same person has been seen as one of the principal integrating devices mediating between the family sphere and the world of work. In the parallel case of the institutional differentiation of stratification system and polity, we encounter two central integrating ties. On the one hand, there is the double-role incumbency of the citizen as subject to political authority and legitimating master over it (Parsons 1963a); and on the other there is the double-group membership of the status incongruent unit pressured by conflicting loyalties. Both mediate between the world of inequalities in society and society's capacity to get things done, or the societal power sphere.

Yet this conceptualization is only the beginning of analysis. For apart from recognizing that the need for integration varies directly with differentiation, our quantitative understanding of this matter seems still fairly primitive. Only one aspect appears to be

---

* Thus, to turn once more to Huntington (1968, 114), one cannot assert that Soviet political structure is more differentiated than that of the U.S. unless it can be demonstrated that the Soviet chief of state, the Soviet head of government, and the Soviet party chief, all separate offices there, perform their respective functions of representation, executive, and support mobilization more effectively than the office of the U.S. president which combines all three functions. Given the pervasive use of force in Soviet life this may at least be doubted with respect to representation.

clear: where there are only conflicting loyalties, social conflicts cannot be organized effectively and integration suffers. On different modes of integration we seem to know a little more. It has been observed that industrialized totalitarian society can exhibit quite stable features. These lie principally in the area of unidirectional changes in the standard modernization indicators, such as industrialization, communications, urbanization, etc. Furthermore, this stability in development seems possible without value-consensus and without widespread personal commitments to development. Given this perspective, Holzner (1967) proposed four modes of integration: through (i) operative interdependency, (ii) power on the basis of conflicting interest constellations (iii) values, and (iv) loyalty. Each mode can substitute to some degree for another. For present purposes the lesson to be drawn from this classification is a simple one: to the extent that a stratification system brings about integration, solidarity at the national-societal level need not be made a national goal. The resulting saving in societal power can be allocated to other objectives of the public interest.

For such a condition to obtain, the stratification system and polity must differentiate. Such differentiation seems to be primarily a function of the degree and manner in which the different vertical dimensions correlate. The analysis of this problem may be structured around the following hypotheses dealing with three ideal-type stratification orders:

1 Where there are positive near-perfect correlations between the vertical dimensions,
i/inequalities approach near-total stratification;
ii/stratification order and polity are relatively *fused*;
iii/criss-cross approaches zero and status congruence is maximum;
iv/activism in society is relatively low;
v/conflicts in society are patterned, therefore predictable but difficult to institutionalize;
vi/a hierarchical view of society capped by a ruling class obtains; and
vii/societal power depends almost wholly on consensus construction and therefore remains limited.

2 Where the correlations between the vertical dimensions approach zero,
i/inequalities approach structurelessness;
ii/the polity is *segregated* from other inequalities;
iii/criss-cross is maximum, status congruence minimum;
iv/activism in society is at fever pitch;
v/conflicts are not predictable and therefore impossible to institutionalize;
vi/the prevailing image of society is one of unordered complexity and anxiety-inducing confusion; and
vii/societal power, depending entirely on governmental power or force, is at minimum.

3 Where there are complex correlations between the vertical dimensions, constituting a mix of positive, negative, and zero correlations,
i/inequalities show partial stratification;
ii/the polity is *differentiated* from the stratification order;
iii/there is moderate criss-cross and moderate status congruency;
iv/activism in society is high;

v/conflicts in society are patterned, therefore predictable, and can be institutionalized; vi/the prevailing image of society is one of ordered complexity manifest in the perception of a strong centre, multiple functional élites, and multiple intermediary powers; and

vii/societal power, depending neither on force nor on consensus alone, is at maximum.

For the sake of greatest economy in analysing these propositions, a brief comment. Examination of the hypotheses will show that the first listed consequence, stratification of inequalities, follows by logic alone from the preceding specification of correlations among the vertical dimensions. Therefore, minimal comment, if any, is called for. The same applies to the relation between the third consequence, criss-cross and status congruence, and the fourth, the level of activism in society. Given our assumptions, here again one conditions the other. Therefore, the weight of the analysis should focus on the following topics: (a) the variable relations between polity and stratification system labelled fusion, segregation, and differentiation; and (b) the effects of this variable on: (i) integration-conflict in society; (ii) the prevailing image of society; and (iii) the variable quantities of societal power.

POLITY AND STRATIFICATION: FUSED SIMPLE ORDER

Turning to the first case, the fused polity-cum-stratification order, what does fusion mean? At this point the answer is charmingly simple. Those who 'run the show' in political affairs are also in command of economic life, the interstitial professional complex, and cultural affairs. The group that holds power over others also possesses a disproportionately larger share of wealth, prestige, and cultural honour. Put differently, high positive correlations among all vertical dimensions mean that a given attempt to convert one resource into another, for example prestige to participation in policy-making, has a much better than even chance of success. In aggregate terms, i.e. all conversion attempts, high positive correlations imply cumulation of resources whereby the acquisition of one does not cost a corresponding amount of the other, or a propensity towards monopoly in all. How far monopolization actually proceeds is primarily a function of the rate of social change, which in this case of low internal activism depends primarily on outside pressures.

So one is not surprised to find that empirical cases most clearly approximating this condition are mostly confined to the pre-industrial stage (Lenski 1966). Excepting virtues, an essentially similar interpretation has been rendered concerning contemporary American society (Mills 1956). Yet both theory and fact seem to argue against it (Riesman 1953; Parsons 1957). For purposes of illustration, Dahl's (1961, 15-16) concise portrayal of the eighteenth century New Haven patriciate remains one of the best. 'They (the patricians) were of one common stock and one religion, cohesive in their uniformly conservative outlook on all matters, substantially unchallenged in their authority, successful in pushing through their own policies, and in full control of such critical social institutions as the established religion, the educational system ... and even business enterprise.' Yet, as the famous case of the despised merchants of Tokugawa Japan shows, such a social order was not a universal characteristic of society immediately preceding industrialization (Bellah 1957; Nishio 1965). Apparently contradictions between the ideology and the reality of traditional stratification were frequent, and due in large measure to the rigidity of strata barriers (Goldthorpe 1969).

Next, given our minimal assumption concerning change, viz. its ubiquity, but leaving rate and amount unspecified, what can be said about conflict-integration in society? Any successful innovators who accumulate substantial amounts of a given resource encounter difficulty when they attempt conversion. According to Landecker (1963), status congruence – high in this case in the aggregate – relates positively to class barrier consciousness. The latter, furthermore, can be treated as an index of the visibility of social strata. Thus the few status incongruents gradually create conditions of superimposed cleavages into superimposed conflict groups. Therefore, when conflict occurs, it is likely to be intense, for there is little criss-cross. Here the double effect of stratification comes into view. The lines of conflict group formations are clear. The weaker in resources, usually the larger in number, square off against the richer and fewer. It is known where the conflict is likely to occur, i.e. what groups will be involved. Nevertheless, the opportunity to exploit this knowledge for institutionalization remains severely limited. For the more a society is stratified (the higher the positive correlations among all vertical dimensions), the lower is criss-cross and with that the supply of conflicting loyalties which facilitates subjugation of the conflict relation to common standards and subsequent regulation. With little criss-cross there is neither motivation nor a capacity to develop commitments to common standards. In short, in a highly stratified society there is order in conflict, but there are few restraining forces available to control it.

Concerning the prevailing image of society, high class barrier consciousness and cumulation of resources implies a hierarchical view of society topped by a ruling class. The principal variation here concerns the number of levels perceived and the level of antagonism. These two seem to vary inversely. Apart from the quantitative distribution of the population along the vertical axis, other important variables are the nature of work organization and communal organization. Middle groups see more gradations than marginal ones. They also have a stake in the system by virtue of the perception of lower orders beneath them (Bolte 1966). Therefore the larger the middle group, the lower the total amount of antagonism. Where work organization provides some direct contact between the 'higher-ups' and the employee rather than none, and communal organization is 'integrated' rather than strata-specifically 'isolated,' more levels are seen and status consciousness co-exists with class-conflict 'unconsciousness' (Lockwood 1968). To the extent that the indicated opposite alternatives hold, i.e. concentration of the population towards the bottom, no direct contact with higher authority at work, level-specific community organization, a dichotomized image of society develops. This is more productive of conflict.

In any event, wherever such an order is approximated, the fact that the goals of such a society are the goals of the ruling class (Lenski 1966, 41) is not likely to remain a secret to all members of the political strata for long. The lower members of this group in the past, the representatives of the estates, knew it (Carsten 1959). With modern communications – formal and informal – in dense urban settings, the chance to be aware of this is just as good if not better for the lower members of the political strata of the present, the citizens. It is this fact which tends to limit societal power in this case pretty much to the traditional tasks of internal order and external defence. For wherever men seek to mobilize resources for political ends, they must also seek legitimation in terms of common welfare. Simmel (1906) recognized this principle clearly in his formulation of the egoism inherent in altruistic concerns with poverty. Yet where political claims are advanced by or in the name of those who have more of all there is to have, the effectiveness of legitimation remains intrinsically limited. It is, therefore, no surprise that we find successful modernizing monarchs only among those who in one way or another succeeded in smashing the traditional stratification order (Huntington 1968, 140-91).

Concerning the generation of societal power then, there must be sufficient coalescence among those unequally blessed with resources to facilitate realistically workable policies (Parsons 1964), yet not so much coalescence as to impair unduly the legitimacy of the regime. Thus the social conditions making for the production of societal power are characterized by a similar dilemma of intrinsic contradictions as that found concerning the integrative effect of stratification. To describe this parallel the paradox of stratification may bear repeating. *Whatever forces make for stratification (increases in status congruence) also structure conflicts; but at the same time such forces also diminish criss-cross and with that the capacity to institutionalize structured conflicts.*

With respect to societal power the most important factor in the dilemma arises from the role of knowledge. This is, of course, glaringly obvious in modern societies where science and technical expertise have become an indispensable tool for effective policy-making. East or West, democratic or totalitarian, all policy makers who really care about the outcome have to share power with experts (Fischer 1966; Kolkowicz 1967; Fischer 1968). To give one example, the universalization of welfare-state policies such as family allowances, tax allowances for education, old-age security, health insurance, explicitly designed to increase equality of social rights and opportunities has had the opposite effect, at least in England and possibly elsewhere (Titmuss 1968). It does take specialized expertise to find that out, correct it, or prevent it in the first place. However, there is nothing specifically modern about the role of knowledge. The mistakes of past policy makers attest to the fact that knowledge was always indispensable to getting things done in the name of public interest. To give some more examples, Rome traded extensively with the Far East, a matter of considerable advantage. It was only discovered much later that this activity also related to political upheavals at the edges of the empire, a matter of grave disadvantage (Teggart 1939). During the fifth century Rome decided on a very modern type of bureaucratic recruitment, viz. the employment of achievement criteria as the only relevant ones. Capable barbarians and slaves moved into officialdom while the better-off Roman citizens preferred to languish on their latifundia. It was recognized only much later that this procedure undermined first the effectiveness, then the legitimacy, of the regime (Smelser 1968, 241).

Thus in order to achieve realistic policy-making, which forms the bedrock of societal power, *there must be differential access to governmental power.* Those with more knowledge must have a greater impact on decision-making than the ignorant. *Yet whatever favours differential access to governmental power also tends to impair the legitimacy of the regime by alienating excluded groups.* As the last example shows, it is only a question of secondary significance how the exclusion comes about. Furthermore, this dilemma may well affect different types of regimes to different degrees. That is a subject beyond the scope of this paper. What is not is the fact that it is a universal dilemma exerting some influence everywhere.

Having stated the principle, the discussion of our first case, the fused polity-cum-stratification order, can be brought to a speedy conclusion. Where a society is highly stratified the exclusion of some groups from policy-making, itself a prerequisite for the realization of societal power, becomes too obvious to permit its production in larger quantity. Deviations in political demands from those traditionally customary and therefore supported by consensus are met with immediate mistrust. In addition, past failures to perform traditional tasks come to haunt the regime's later efforts at political mobilization, even for traditional tasks. In this condition societal power remains intrinsically limited.

POLITY AND STRATIFICATION: SEGREGATED DISORDER

If near-complete overall stratification sets limits to both conflict regulation and societal power generation, the opposite, the absence of stratification, in no way signifies more favourable conditions. On the contrary, theoretical as well as empirical information suggests that, where there is no or hardly any stratification, conflicts are all pervasive and near chaotic, and societal power approaches a minimum.

Zero correlation among all vertical dimensions means that there is no stratification system or no order at all among inequalities. All these are segregated from each other instead. As in Dahrendorf's ideal-type pluralism, not a single social cleavage overlaps with any other. The wealthy have no more prestige than the poor, the prestigious no more wealth than the lowly esteemed. Neither of these nor the morally superior have any differential access to political power. Given maximum criss-cross and status disequilibration, conversion attempts are pervasive but with precisely random effects. Some try to use power to get rich and succeed, others attempting the same thing fail miserably, losing the power they had in the aborted bargain. Experiences of this type reinforce the aggregate motivation to try again on all fronts.

In this case the classical politicized cleavages of recent times, economic–industrial, church–state relations in the school question, regional, urban–rural, and ethnic–subcultural cannot coalesce. They all exist side by side. They cannot become effectively politicized either. Incapable of coalition they remain politically ineffectual. While the intensity of these conflicts should remain low, there is no status congruence to organize them.

This lack of order and developmental direction in society becomes manifest in the image created by its citizens. Without any stratification one does not know 'what's up and down,' 'what's right and left.' Where wealth outside conspicuous consumption, where knowledge outside some ivory tower, where moral excellence outside some church service, and where power outside the area of direct enforcement all mean virtually nothing in any ostensible fashion, there confusion reigns supreme. In this situation the only source of security is to be found with political authority; to stay out of the way of its wrath and assure oneself of its protection remains the only thing for sensible men to do. For, mutually isolated in dissociated groups and unable to overcome the dissociation, they have no place else to go. With no reliable and regular input of institutionalized expertise into policy-making, however, the generation of societal power approaches a minimum, appearances to the contrary notwithstanding. Appearances in this case are usually deceptive, for it displays some inherent tendency towards tyrannical rule. But there is only governmental power and to manage the divisiveness and maintain a resemblance of orderly development exhausts all available resources. Thus in comparison with the previous case, it is not lack of legitimation so much that limits the production of societal power, it is the lack of regulated differential access instead. This point deserves emphasis and may bear reformulation: where there is a maximum of diverse conflicts and practically no way to organize them, completely equal group access to governmental power amounts, in fact, to no access at all.

It may now be asked, has such a model any bearing on reality? The answer can be rendered in the clear affirmative. The social conditions preceding as well as those during totalitarianism approximate this case.

Concerning Germany voting, studies indicated the existence of dissociated conflict groups during the empire and extending well into the Weimar Republic. The labour movement was split into a Socialist and a Christian wing. The bourgeoisie was split into nationalist and progressive wings. The peasants were regionally divided, as were the Socialists. In fact Roth's (1963) 'negative integration thesis' respecting the Socialists has been generalized to cover four dissociated subcultures, a Catholic, a Conservative, a bourgeois-Protestant, and a Socialist (Lepsius 1966). Throughout the empire and into the Weimar Republic these four groups managed relatively peaceful coexistence in negative integration. None sought support for its aims among the followers of another. None achieved any measurable resolution of their conflicting aims, all experienced slowly mounting frustration. To be sure, before the end of the Weimar period, there was some line of basic cleavage, some status congruence that provided some small degree of organization of those conflicts, viz. the 'coalition of iron and corn' (Moore 1966). Subsequent developments suggest that this was not quite enough. This remaining bit of stratification was smashed by the Nazis.

Turning to totalitarian society, in the Soviet Union the evidence seems rather ambiguous at first sight. After the initial and apparently incomplete destruction of the stratification system through the revolution, there was some reconstruction under Stalin which later loosened up again under Khrushchev (Meissner 1966). At any rate, it seems doubtful that Soviet policies alone effected as systematic a destruction of stratification as occurred under the Nazis in Germany. But there were other factors to push developments to a largely identical result. Because of the fluctuating fortunes of three wars, the two Great Wars with their German invasions and the Civil War, and the waves of Stalinist terror, social inequalities assumed a pattern of wild and confusing fluctuation. The heroes of one day turned into the treasonous villains of the next. In addition, some always manage collaboration with any power, depriving the image of any remaining meaningfulness. These mobility patterns, therefore, assumed chaotic proportions adding their force to the destruction of stratification.

Despite Arendt's (1958) and Inkeles's (1954) warning against interpreting the actions of totalitarian elites in terms of a simple search for power, both the destruction and the reconstruction of stratification in the Soviet Union are still viewed as motivated by power aggrandizement (Goldthorpe 1969, 462). Yet, in the light of more recent research on the

Nazi case, Inkeles's contention seems clearly supported. Totalitarian elites, he argued, are like functional sociologists, with one difference: they are in a position to act on their assumptions. Like functionalists they believe that society can be analysed best as a system; unlike good functionalists they also believe that society *is* a system where everything is related to everything else and value consensus constitutes the *sine qua non* for the operation of the whole. Since their aim is to construct a new system, they start in logically consequent fashion with the destruction of any systematic relations they find and the imposition of a new ideology. Yet while they often succeed in the former, they seem to fail invariably in the latter. The general result is one they hardly desire, viz. the whittling down of societal power to a minimum. The last assertion, however, depends on granting some authenticity to their stated goals rather than seeing in these no more than propaganda fashioned to cloak personal power ambitions.

As to their failure in establishing a uniform ideological commitment, estimates for Germany indicate that the proportion of convinced Nazis ran under 10 per cent of the adult population. In the Soviet Union a 1961/62 USSR Academy of Sciences survey showed that, after decades of indoctrination, young adults still cherished traditional ideals concerning the nature of man, not the Communist conception of the good personality (Meissner 1966).

With respect to smashing stratification, Schoenbaum (1967) rendered an impressive portrait of this process in Germany. Here we find that the *virtuosi* of the new cultural honour, resplendent in brown uniform, had neither personal wealth, nor usually any influence on policy-making whatsoever. The correlation between official rank in any of the bureaucratic hierarchies of party, government, army, and economic institutions and access to power was practically nil. Himmler, next to Hitler the mightiest man in the Third Reich, remained an economic pauper capable neither of paying his medical bills nor of building himself the kind of home he desired (Kersten 1956). The only organized economic elite, if it can be called organized, the friendship circle of the chief of SS, had no influence on policy-making whether related to economic matters or not.

In all this, there was a twofold result. First, society was ranked with unorganized, all-pervasive, and highly intense social conflicts in the form of interorganizational rivalry. Second, society developed in a direction almost diametrically opposite to the goals officially proclaimed.

The SS was perhaps the purest organizational expression of Nazism. A study of this organization led the author to the conclusion that ideology and reality were as much at variance as they possibly could have been. Instead of a totalitarian system run from a centre of political will, a 'system of anarchical systemlessness was the practiced outcome (Höhne 1967). A study of factionalism in the Nazi party showed that under the cover of the *Führer*-principle a multiplicity of conflicting groups pursuing contradictory policies was the rule, and clarification or settling of policy issues an exception, indeed a last resort least desired by the top (Nyomarkay 1967). A detailed case study of a business firm reveals that whatever semblance of order existed was maintained by neo-feudal particularist ties cross-cutting the organizational realms of industry, party, army, SS, and government. Such ties were so tenuous, however, that it was only the war that gave the whole system its direction and its short-lived viability (Orlow 1968). For purposes of illustration this limited evidence seems sufficient. With the stratification system thoroughly destroyed, the outstanding characteristic of the Third Reich was continuously shifting short-life coalitions pursuing changing and contradictory goals, with an ever increasing severity of conflict constituting one of the few consistent threads. As Schoenbaum (1967, 275) put it, German society was 'united only in a negative community of fear, sacrifice, ruin.'

Finally concerning societal power, one may ask: do totalitarian societies achieve the things they stand for? Here the evidence seems equally clear and the result dismal. In the case of the Nazis the goals were a halt and, as soon as possible, a reversal of urbanization, preservation and strengthening of the rural community, continuous ties to the soil for all, conservation of the traditional female role and purification of the race. The results achieved were exactly the opposite of these objectives: continuation, and indeed acceleration, of urbanization, industrialization, flight from the farm, female participation in the labour force, and increased geographic mobility of ethnic and nationality groups (Schoenbaum 1967). During the Third Reich, modernization of society proceeded faster than ever before in Germany (Dahrendorf 1965). Political power over citizens was indeed high, but what the Nazis wanted remained a pipe dream. A similar examination of Soviet societal power hardly seems necessary. If one takes the unexpurgated version of their goal seriously, then 'from each according to his ability, to each according to his need' meant that the specification of needs and abilities was up to the autonomous individual. Today it appears doubtful whether any substantive progress towards this goal has been achieved. In fact, rapid social mobility, particularly downward mobility, suggests the opposite.

That those who insist on the ruthless pursuit of what are essentially non-modern utopias *with the use of modern means* should find themselves incapable of attaining their ends is hardly a novel idea. But that they may not even end up moving in the general direction of their intentions, let alone approach them, and instead move in a direction diametrically opposed to their goals might well be related to the destruction of stratification. For without stratification the direction of societal development rests on the shoulders of the political structure alone. Without any naturally coalescent alignments in society the forces of conflict, tremendous in their aggregate under conditions of intermittent reinforcement of conversion attempts, despite criss-cross, could only be organized by political authority. There is hardly any other force to tame these energies and channel them. If the German case is any indication, it seems difficult to imagine any political structure, no matter how constituted, that could withstand such a load. For in Nazi Germany there was neither a lack of enforcement means nor any great scruples concerning the use of violence. Nevertheless, with stratification effectively destroyed, the 'system of anarchical systemlessness' which resulted ground to its apparently inevitable ruinous end.

POLITY AND STRATIFICATION: DIFFERENTIATED ORDER

If neither full stratification nor the absence of it, provides optimal conditions for societal integration and power generation, the obvious hint is to look for something in between. Hence partial stratification suggests itself. With respect to integration-conflict, there must be sufficient stratification to pattern conflicts in society, yet also sufficient criss-cross to facilitate their institutionalization. Concerning societal power production

there must be sufficient and regulated differential access to policy-making so that politics as the art of the possible has a chance, but not so much as to undermine the legitimacy requirement of politics as the art of the desirable. A stratification system conducive to the maximization of societal integration and power generation may be said
to signal institutional differentiation of polity and social inequalities.

Before beginning the analysis of this most hypothetical of the three types of stratification orders, let us make a brief comment. First, a fully differentiated stratification
order does not seem clearly evident anywhere as yet. It has probably been absent from
societies in the past, but seems to be emerging here and there in the contemporary
world. Differential access to policy-making by outside and *independent* experts is a
growing practice. In some instances the practice has been incorporated into organizational form to a greater extent than in others. France appears to outrank many other
Western societies in this respect (Macridis 1963; Hackett and Hackett 1963). As that
case shows, however, formal organizational institutionalization by itself is unlikely to
guarantee the stability of differential access. Secondly, as this last case deals with present and future society, a value element has to be introduced. Egalitarianism and universalism have become increasingly prominent everywhere (Barber 1968). As used here,
these elements do not imply an ideology comparable in emotional strength to nineteenth century ideals. Instead, no more than the following is meant: on the general
societal level, and not in other specialized contexts such as the industrial workshop, it
is inequalities in wealth, including spending power and social rights, which have to be
justified. Equality in this area justifies itself. Universalism signifies that the evaluation
of means becomes nearly a sole concern with their effectiveness and efficiency. This
may be called pragmatic primacy where questions of style or principle become largely
irrelevant. Reprivatization of a previously nationalized business enterprise by the governing Swedish Socialists purely on grounds of economic rationality illustrates this
orientation.

The last point has been noted in the literature as the end of ideology. This may, in
fact, be specified as a first condition for the differentiation of stratification and polity.
Three reasons suggest this specification. First, instead of any intrinsic opposition between everyday social life and the experience of more ultimate meaning, there is some
evidence demonstrating an ever increasing indeterminacy between the two. For the
construction of meaning, modern man apparently has to rely more and more on himself as an individual. In the sociology of religion and art this has been recognized as
the individuation of meaning creations (Bellah 1964; Lieberman 1968). This does not
mean the end pure and simple of all mechanical ties but rather the use of generalized
meaning symbols in such a way as to permit individuals to pour variable content into
them. Secondly, this condition is changing the role of virtues. These can neither be
clearly ranked any more, nor are individuated conceptions of the moral as intersub-
jectively binding as old-fashioned morality was. Such developments find their manifestation in a growing moral tolerance which constitutes the only possible response
compatible with individual moral freedom and responsibility which results from the
indeterminacy between action and meaning. Third, these changes are altering that nature and consequences of man's collective-public flight from loneliness in meaning experience. Under the new conditions, attempts to re-ideologize the image of society may

still occur as a response to bearing the heavy burden of meaning creation by and for oneself alone. But protest movements now only retain the appearance of fundamentalist revolts; genotypically they differ. For in the classic fundamentalist uprising participants were mutually bound by a common interpretation of the symbols they shared and propagated. While governmental power suffered temporarily where such movements succeeded, the bindingness of moral commitments also facilitated some new majority thrust, gave society a new direction, and with that left societal power relatively intact. In modern disturbances, on the other hand, the symbols lend themselves to the projection of almost innumerable dissatisfactions and meanings. The New Order of the Nazis is a case in point. This slogan lent itself to practically unlimited conceptions. 'Bourgeoisie,' 'establishment' among our disturbed contemporaries are quite similar. Such freedom severely limits the chances for any consensus formation and conveyance of clear messages. Where disturbances can be interpreted as the projection of private neuroses onto the public arena as they are by some today (Scheuch 1968), societal power suffers through lack of a steering mechanism. It follows that charismatic political leadership has no place in a differentiated polity.

Specification of the end of ideology as a necessary condition for the differentiation of stratification and polity means dealing with a reduced stratification system. One vertical dimension, virtues, has been eliminated. Instead of four rank dimensions, there are only three; instead of six pairs of correlations there are also merely three. With this reduction, polity and stratification may be defined as differentiated when the following conditions hold:

1 The correlation between power and prestige is substantially positive.
2 The correlation between power and wealth is moderately negative.
3 The correlation between prestige and wealth approaches zero.

These conditions seem optimal for the integration of society. First, with two correlations, neither near perfect, and one zero correlation, there is sufficient criss-cross but also sufficient status congruence to pattern conflicts through viable coalitions and to institutionalize them. There is a basic cleavage between those in power and those high in prestige on the one hand and those out of power and the intermediate and low in prestige. But there is also a cross-pressured group, some high in prestige who are temporarily out of power, i.e. suffer in access to policy-making relative to their perceived rights and obligations. Secondly, the positive correlation between power and prestige helps to sustain a sense of distributive justice. For if there is any valid general interpretation of Inkeles's and Rossi's (1956) uniform findings concerning cross-national occupational prestige, it seems to be this: everywhere in industrialized society importance is associated with perceived technical-scientific expertise. The positive power-prestige correlation therefore fulfils a demand, viz. that those who are the important and competent should also have a differential say in societal decision-making. As contrasted with 'what' or 'what first' in politics, to be considered below, the 'how' seems relatively well assured. A positive correlation between power and prestige produces trust in policy makers. This too fulfils a demand because concern with and doubt about competence increases where society is seen as complex.

Thirdly, a moderately negative correlation between power and wealth facilitates translation of egalitarian demands into policy-making. There is more to this aspect than a mere dissociation of political and industrial conflict. With respect to wealth, including assets and the whole gamut of Marshall's (1965) social rights, egalitarianism signifies a growing demand for equalization of all of these. Thus a negative correlation between power and wealth indicates relative exclusion from policy-making of those 'who have all' as compared with the less well endowed. With that the wealthy have fewer opportunities to slow down the trend towards equalization of life chances. Their access to power runs via prestige. The zero correlation between wealth and prestige signals constant conversion attempts between these two resources with random success. For the few prestigious who succeed in reaching affluence, prestige is rewarded; being important to society does pay off. For the few wealthy who succeed, wealth becomes tempered through association with prestige. The influence John F. Kennedy commanded was possible despite the known fact that millions of private assets had to be spent to gain a very marginal victory. Yet he was not seen as a corrupt politician purchasing support. Apparently one important reason was that by surrounding himself with a brain trust he conveyed an aura of competence and responsibility that dignified his otherwise new wealth. A stratification system that guarantees access to power (participation in policy-making) to those who should have it, experts, and debars from access precisely those, the merely wealthy, who should not have it, is one that renders an appearance of justice. A stratification system that creates ordered conflict and provides for regulation of conflicts is one that produces order in change. A stratification system that does both is one that integrates society instead of tearing it apart.

In this type the image of society is just as complex as in the previous case. But there is some stratification. Therefore, this complexity can be reduced (Luhmann 1968), and given the nature of stratification; it can be reduced so that anxiety is minimized and trust maximized. First, this image includes the perception of a powerful national political centre (positive correlation between power and prestige). The executive is seen as constantly in touch with and advised by the major professionalized expert institutions in society, such as the scientific establishment, the defence establishment, the educational community, the national health and welfare complex, and the industrial-economic complex with its professionalized management. Secondly, however, some of the top leaders of some institutional complexes are always excluded from direct power (imperfect correlation between prestige and power). This creates an image of relatively independent functional elites (Keller 1969) who rotate in their access to power. Thirdly, there is a basic cleavage between those 'in' power and high in prestige and those 'out' of power and less prestigious. The latter makes for the perception of all manner of intermediary groups, special interests, regional and local governments, trying to garner wealth for conversion to prestige and subsequent access to power. Thus the image is one of relatively ordered complexity. There is a centre, independent functional elites, and intermediary powers who busily seek support from below in order to pressure the top.

Finally, what about the production of societal power in this case? There seem to be essentially two sets of forces which tend towards the maximization of societal power.

The first involves insuring the access of knowledge to policy design. The second comprises a balanced resource flow to the different needs of modern society.

It has already been suggested that the positive power–prestige correlation insures differential access of expertise to power and with that maximized politics as the art of the possible. But what about politics as the art of the desirable? A purely pragmatic officialdom may well get stuck in efficiency considerations of daily administration where overall policy results from drift out of the aggregate of detail decisions; there would be steering by accident, rather than by design. With ideology at an end, where does direction come from here? Two sources of direction appear to be given in this model. The first is an overall egalitarian trend in social rights. For this to work in direction-setting without re-ideologization, a general principle concerning the relation between action and legitimation must be emphasized. It is always easier to pursue a course of action which demands no special legitimation, a course of action that seemingly justifies itself, than one that calls for legitimation expenditure. The second is the exploitation of this principle by functional elites who compete for scarce societal resources.

In this model all of society's needs, economic–industrial, research–educational, health and recreational, etc. are organized in and represented by functionally specific expert institutions. These institutions are expected to compete for scarce resources. Seeing to it that society is well off in terms of increasing prosperity, better health, exploration, national security, and so on constitutes their responsibility. Societal power is being realized if all of these needs are being serviced in balanced fashion. Modern society is not characterized by one-sector dominance as captured in Marx's felicitous phrase 'production fetishism.' Serving society's different needs in a direction facilitating increasing equalization of life chances here constitutes goal attainment. Given an imperfect power-prestige correlation, not all functional elites are equally politically influential at any given moment in time. Some are relatively excluded from direct access. This means that their institutional interests, which are also their societal responsibilities, are very likely underserviced. The fact that the onus of proof lies on the defence of inequalities gives them their chance. They can claim that insufficient recognition of the needs in their sphere causes unnecessary continuation of inequities in life chances. Since the 'other side' has to disprove this charge, all the disaffected influentials need is to lend their expert opinion sufficient weight and they can gain a net advantage over the 'ins.'

In order to gain sufficient weight the intermediary groups must be involved. It has already been stated above that the prevailing image of society features the perception of a strong national political centre. This indeed seems to be a prerequisite for the functioning of intermediary groups. Therefore, in terms of perception, i.e. what people believe to be the case, it is not Riesman's (1953) dispersion of power but rather its opposite, viz. its perceived concentration, which counts for an effective marriage of politics as the art of the possible with politics as the art of the desirable. The reason is charmingly simple: where there is no perception of a powerful centre, intermediary groups malfunction in such a way that first they lose their effectiveness and subsequently their legitimacy. Examination of the forces underlying the failure of German intermediary groups to withstand the onslaught of Nazism has shown this quite clearly (Lepsius 1968). Where power is believed to reside nowhere in particular, intermediary groups turn against each other. Shifting pressure group alliances mutually locked in combat and mutually stalemated in outcome are the net result. Instead of mobilizing protective support against the centre and articulating interests for it (exerting demands from it), the intermediary powers dissipate their resources, achieve less and less, and finally lose their legitimacy.

But given the perception of a strong centre, coalitions have a focus for their organized struggle. Thus the influentials temporarily incapable of fully discharging their responsibilities are in search of interest alliances. They must seek power because the perception of a lack of effectiveness in the case of professionals automatically leads to fears concerning threats to their legitimacy and autonomy. The perception of a centre here provides the basis for a coalition between the disaffected functional elite, politicians out of power, and intermediary groups. The functional elite offers issues packaged in weighty scientific reports and numerous abstracts to the defunct politician and intermediary groups in search of constructive proposals. The ensuing triple alliance either partially succeeds the 'ins' or else effects a policy shift, thereby redressing the balance in society's resource flow. In order to maintain the power-prestige correlation, i.e. regulated differential expert access to power, such a triple alliance can only work in an atmosphere of de-ideologized politics. For if there is anything that uniformly characterizes all professions, it is a vehement insistence on professional autonomy. The interest position of professionalized expertise demands that one not turn to the people, for that intrinsically endangers autonomy. Instead, professionals generate technical information, a task to which they claim a monopoly in their respective areas of specialization. This information is then distributed to those who seek office or special legislation. As a result the centre becomes flooded with reports from three directions simultaneously, all predicting dire consequences unless something is done to correct imbalances. With the burden of proof that inequalities are not being maintained entirely on the shoulders of the 'ins,' the net forces in operation point towards a correction of imbalances, and given knowledge, to an enhancement of societal power. It must be noted, however, that only one partner in this triple alliance, the functional elite, has a direct stake in professionalized politics. But insofar as near complete professionalization of all services is a characteristic of modernity, the empirical chances for this model seem to be auspicious.

CONCLUSION

This has proved a rather lengthy way to open a discussion. For purposes of assessment concerning the most strategic directions of further analysis, a brief overview of the limited objectives pursued here may be helpful.

The search for a conception of political modernity that would parallel the case of economic modernity is called for by common sense as well as by historical and theoretical considerations. Last but not least such a conception seems necessary also to move us out of a noted impasse in current political sociology and political science research that derives from a too one-sided preoccupation with political structure. As a parallel to sustained economic growth, political modernity should involve sustained societal power growth. As the sociology of economic modernity involves consideration of social conditions primarily and of technical factors such as factory size, industry composition, labour markets, money institutions, etc. only secondarily, the sociology of political modernity might more profitably start with that social substratum that variably conditions the production of societal power rather than the more technical and detailed aspects of political structure. There seems to be little doubt that whatever success sociologists have had in specifying the conditions favourable for economic modernity have been intricately tied in with the analysis of the institutional differentiation of the family and the occupational complex. This suggests that a profitable strategy to advance our understanding of political modernity might be the analysis of the institutional differentiation of the polity and the complex of social inequalities.

Focused on this problem the present analysis covered three ideal-typical stratification orders. It seems fairly clear that the first two types, complete stratification of all inequalities and no or hardly any stratification of inequalities, do not render conditions favourable to the generation of societal power. Neither of these two types is capable of reconciling the contradictory forces productive of power growth. The first, complete stratification, succeeds neatly in ordering all conflicts and creating powerfully antagonistic groups but it also fails completely to provide for criss-cross and with that for the chance to institutionalize ordered conflicts. The strength and weakness of the second type, zero stratification, are precisely reversed. Here there is ample supply of criss-cross but no forces to order conflicts and create sufficiently stable conflict groups. In these two types the societal power dilemma remains equally unresolved. The highly stratified society ensures ample differential access to governmental power, but does so by sacrificing legitimacy of political power correspondingly. The unstratified or minimally stratified society ensures full legitimacy, but at the cost of sufficient differential access to political power.

The only thing that seems relatively clear concerning the last case of partial stratification is that there must be some mutual neutralization among the contradictory forces underlying societal power production if this is to develop into sustained growth. The forces that must be fashioned into some mutually off-setting blend are those that create order in conflicts on the one hand and those that make for criss-cross on the other, as well as those that ensure differential access to and yet allow sufficient legitimation of political power. One such arrangement has been suggested. This involved the disappearance of ranked virtues and a remaining correlational matrix of positive power–prestige association, negative power–wealth correlation, and a zero relation between wealth and prestige. Under the assumption that fundamentalist morality does in fact recede from public life in modern society, this patterning of inequalities may well be the optimal one for societal power growth.

Altering the assumptions, however, certainly opens vistas of other potentially favourable combinations. One of the possibilities worthy of exploration, and one empirically feasible, would be to study the impact of perceived equalization in social rights and wealth on power production. The Swedish case should prove illuminating in this respect. If it should turn out that a direct relation exists, such that the more equal the perceived life chances the greater societal power, a next step in theory might be to set wealth a constant and let virtues vary. As to a more complete analysis in this problem complex, political structure certainly would have to be included as a variable. Here one useful cross-national approach would involve examining the relative effects of stratification as contrasted with political structure on the societal power potential.

One might choose a setting where stratification varies and political structure is very similar or vice versa. In any event, this is still a new field where practically everything has yet to be done. But the distinction between governmental and societal power and the recognition of the role of stratification in the production of a society's power seems a prerequisite if we are to advance our continuing search for an adequate grasp of political modernity.

REFERENCES

G.A. Almond and S. Verba, *The Civic Culture* (Boston: Little Brown, 1965)

H. Arendt, *The Origins of Totalitarianism* (New York: Harcourt Brace & Co., 1958)

E.C. Banfield, *Political Influence* (Glencoe, Ill.: The Free Press, 1961)

B. Barber, 'Social Stratification Structure and Trends of Social Mobility in Western Society,' in T. Parsons (ed.), *American Sociology* (New York: Basic Books Inc, 1968), pp. 184-95

R. Bellah, *Tokugawa Religion* (Glencoe, Ill.: The Free Press, 1957)

– 'Religious Evolution,' *American Sociological Review*, 29 (June 1964), 358-74

M. Beloff, *The Age of Absolutism* (New York: Harper Torchbooks, 1962)

J.S. Berliner, *Factory and Manager in the U.S.S.R.* (Cambridge, Mass.: Harvard University Press, 1957)

K.M. Bolte, *Deutsche Gesellschaft im Wandel* (Opladen: C.W. Leske Verlag, 1966)

T.B. Bottomore, *Classes in Modern Society* (London: Allen & Unwin Ltd., 1965)

Z. Brzezinski and S.P. Huntington, *Political Power: USA/USSR* (New York: Viking Press, 1964)

F.L. Carsten, *Princes and Parliaments in Germany* (Oxford: Clarendon Press, 1959)

W. Cohn, 'Social Status and the Ambivalence Hypothesis,' *American Sociological Review*, 5 (August 1960), 508-13

P. Cutright, 'National Political Development,' *American Sociological Review*, vol. 28 (April 1963), 253-64

R. Dahl, 'The Concept of Power,' *Behavioral Scientist*, 2 (July 1957)

– *Who Governs?* (New Haven, Conn.: Yale University Press, 1961)

R. Dahrendorf, *Class and Class Conflict in Industrial Society* (Stanford: Stanford University Press, 1959)

– *Gesellschaft und Demokratie in Deutschland* (München: Piper & Co., 1965)

K. Davis and W.E. Moore, 'Some Principles of Stratification,' *American Sociological Review*, 10 (April 1945), 242-9

K. de Schweinitz, Jr., *Industrialization and Democracy* (New York: Free Press, 1964)

K.W. Deutsch, 'Social Mobilization and Political Development,' *American Political Science Review*, LV (September 1961), 493-514

– *The Nerves of Government* (New York: Free Press, 1963)

E. Durkheim, *Professional Ethics and Civic Morals* (London: Routledge & Kegan Paul, 1900, 1957)

M. Duverger, *Political Parties* (London: Methuen & Co., 1954)

H. Eckstein, *Division and Cohesion in Democracy* (Princeton: Princeton University Press, 1966)

S.N. Eisenstadt, *The Political Systems of Empires* (New York: Free Press, 1962)

C.W. Fischer, 'Scientists and Statesmen,' in S.A. Lakoff (ed.), *Knowledge and Power* (New York: Free Press, 1966), pp. 315-58

G. Fischer, *The Soviet System and Modern Society* (New York: Atherton Press, 1968)

J. Galtung, 'Rank and Social Integration,' in J. Berger, M. Zelditch, Jr., and Bo Anderson (eds.), *Sociological Theories in Progress* (Boston: Houghton Mifflin Co., 1966), pp. 145-98

J.H. Goldthorpe, 'Social Stratification in Industrial Society,' in C.S. Heller (ed.), *Structural Social Inequality* (New York: Macmillan, 1969), pp. 452-65

J. Hackett and A.M. Hackett, *Economic Planning in France* (Cambridge, Mass.: Harvard University Press, 1963)

P.A. Hare, *Handbook of Small Group Research* (New York: Free Press, 1962)

C.S. Heller, *Structured Social Inequality* (New York: Macmillan, 1969)

F.A. Hermens, *Democracy or Anarchy? A Study of Proportional Representation* (Notre Dame, Ind.: Notre Dame Press, 1941)

H. Höhne, *Der Orden unter dem Totenkopf* (Gütersloh: Sigbert Mohn Verlag, 1967)

B. Holzner, 'Integration in Sociological Theory,' *Sociological Quarterly*, 8, 1967, 51-62

G.A. Huaco, 'A Logical Analysis of the Davis-Moore Theory of Stratification,' *American Sociological Review*, 28 (October 1963), 801-3

S.P. Huntington, *Political Order in Changing Societies* (New Haven: Yale University Press, 1968)

A. Inkeles, 'The Totalitarian Mystique,' in C.J. Friedrich (ed.), *Totalitarianism* (Cambridge, Mass.: Harvard University Press, 1954), pp. 88-108

A. Inkeles and P. Rossi, 'National Comparisons of Occupational Prestige,' *American Journal of Sociology*, 61 (Jan. 1956), 329-39

S.B. Jones, 'The Power Inventory and National Strategy,' *World Politics*, vol. 6 (July 1954), 421-52

J.A. Kahl, *The American Class Structure* (New York: Rinehart & Co., 1959)

S. Keller, 'Beyond the Ruling Class – Strategic Elites,' in C.S. Heller (ed.), *Structured Social Inequality* (New York: Macmillan, 1969), pp. 520-4

F. Kersten, *The Kersten Memoirs* (London: Hutchinson, 1956)

J.B. Kervin, 'Formalizing Theories of Social Stratification,' Johns Hopkins University (mimeographed), 1968

J.C. Kimberley, 'Relations among Status, Power, and Economic Rewards in Simple and Complex Social Systems,' in J. Berger, M. Zelditch, and Bo Andersen (eds.), *Sociological Theories in Progress* (Boston: Houghton Mifflin Co., 1966), pp. 213-26

R. Kolkowicz, *The Soviet Military and the Communist Party* (Princeton: Princeton University Press, 1967)

W.S. Landecker, 'Class Crystallization and Class Consciousness,' *American Sociological Review*, 28 (April 1963), 219-29

G.E. Lenski, *Power and Privilege* (New York: McGraw Hill Book Co., 1966)

M.R. Lepsius, 'Parteiensystem und Sozialstruktur,' in W. Abel, K. Borchardt, H. Kellenbenz, and W. Zorn (eds.), *Wirtschaft, Geschichte und Wirtschaftsgeschichte* (Stuttgart: Fischer Verlag, 1966), pp. 371-93

– 'The Collapse of an Intermediary Power Structure,' *International Journal of Comparative Sociology*, 9, 1968, 289-301

D. Lerner, *The Passing of Traditional Society* (Glencoe, Ill.: Free Press, 1958)

A.B. Lieberman, 'The Well-Made Play and the Theatre of the Absurd,' *Sociological Inquiry*, 39 (Winter 1968), 85-91

A. Lijphart, *The Politics of Accommodation* (Berkeley: University of California Press, 1968)

– 'Consociational Democracy,' *World Politics*, XXI (January 1969), 207-25

S.M. Lipset, *Political Man* (Garden City, NY: Doubleday & Co., 1960)

D. Lockwood, 'Sources of Variation in Working Class Images of Society,' in J.A. Kahl (ed.), *Comparative Perspectives on Stratification* (Boston: Little, Brown, 1968), pp. 98-114

N. Luhmann, *Vertrauen* (Stuttgart: Ferdinand Enke Verlag, 1968)

R.C. Macridis, 'France,' in R.C. Macridis and R.E. Ward (eds.), *Modern Political Systems in Europe* (Englewood Cliffs, NJ: Prentice Hall, 1963), pp. 137-265

T.H. Marshall, *Class, Citizenship, and Social Development* (Garden City, NY: Doubleday Anchor Books, 1965)

B. Meissner (ed.), *Sowjetgesellschaft im Wandel* (Stuttgart: Kohlhammer Verlag, 1966)

A.G. Meyer, *The Soviet Political System* (New York: Random House, 1965)

C.W. Mills, *The Power Elite* (New York: Oxford University Press, 1956)

Wm. C. Mitchell, *Sociological Analysis and Politics* (Englewood Cliffs, NJ: Prentice Hall, 1967)

B. Moore, Jr., *Social Origins of Dictatorship and Democracy* (Boston: Beacon Press, 1966)

J.P. Nettl, *Political Mobilization* (London: Faber & Faber, 1967)

H. Nishio, 'Political Authority Structure and Development of Entrepreneurship in Japan.' Unpublished PhD dissertation, Berkeley, University of California, 1965

J. Nyomarkay, *Charisma and Factionalism in the Nazi Party* (Minneapolis: University of Minnesota Press, 1967)

M.E. Olsen, 'Multivariate Analysis of National Political Development,' *American Sociological Review*, 33 (October 1968), 699-712

D. Orlow, *The Nazis in the Balkans* (Pittsburgh: University of Pittsburgh Press, 1968)

T. Parsons, 'A Revised Analytical Approach to the Theory of Stratification,' in R. Bendix and S.M. Lipset (eds.), *Class, Status, and Power* (Glencoe, Ill.: Free Press, 1953), pp. 92-128

- 'The American Family,' in T. Parsons and F.R. Bales, *Family, Socialization, and Interaction Process* (Glencoe, Ill.: Free Press, 1955)

- 'The Distribution of Power in American Society,' *World Politics*, X (October 1957), 123-43

- 'Authority, Legitimation, and Political Action,' in T. Parsons, *Structure and Process in Modern Societies* (Glencoe, Ill.: Free Press, 1960), pp. 170-98

- 'Some Considerations on the Theory of Social Change,' *Rural Sociology*, 26 (September 1961), 219-39

- 'On the Concept of Power,' *Proceedings of the American Philosophical Association*, vol. 107 (June 1963), 232-62

- 'On the Concept of Influence,' *Public Opinion Quarterly*, 27 (Spring 1963), 37-62

- 'Evolutionary Universals in Society,' *American Sociological Review*, 29 (June 1964), 339-57

- *Societies* (Englewood Cliffs, NJ: Prentice Hall, 1966)

- 'On the Concept of Value-Commitments,' *Sociological Inquiry*, 38 (Spring 1968), 135-60

- 'Christianity,' in *International Encyclopedia of the Social Sciences*, 2 (Macmillan Co. and Free Press, 1968), pp. 425-47

T. Parsons and N.J. Smelser, *Economy and Society* (Glencoe, Ill.: Free Press, 1956)

L.W. Pye, *Aspects of Political Development* (Boston: Little, Brown, 1966)

D. Riesman, 'Who has the Power?' in R. Bendix and S.M. Lipset (eds.), *Class, Status and Power* (Glencoe, Ill.: Free Press, 1953)

S. Rokkan, 'Mass Suffrage, Secret Voting, and Political Participation,' *European Journal of Sociology*, 2, 1961, 132-52

C. Roth, *The Social Democrats in Imperial Germany* (Totowa, NJ: Bedminster Press, 1963)

H. Schelsky, 'Ist Dauerreflexion institutionalisierbar?' in H. Schelsky, *Auf der Suche nach Würklichkeit* (Düsseldorf-Köln: Eugen Diederichs Verlag, 1965), pp. 250-75

E.K. Scheuch, 'Das Gesellschaftsbild der Neuen Linken,' in E.K. Scheuch (ed.), *Die Wider-Täufer der Wohlstandsgesellschaft* (Köln: Markus Verlag, 1968), pp. 104-23

D. Schoenbaum, *Hitler's Social Revolution* (Garden City, NY: Doubleday Anchor Books, 1967)

G. Simmel, 'Soziologie der Armut,' *Archiv für Sozialwissenschaft und Sozialpolitik*, XXII, 1906, 1-30

N.J. Smelser, *Social Change in the Industrial Revolution* (Chicago: University of Chicago Press, 1959)

- 'Towards a Theory of Modernization,' in B.F. Hoselitz and W.E. Moore (eds.), *Industrialization and Society* (The Hague: UNESCO-Mouton, 1963), pp. 32-54

- *Essays in Sociological Explanation* (Englewood Cliffs, NJ: Prentice Hall, 1968)

F.J. Teggart, *Rome and China* (Berkeley: University of California Press, 1939)

R. Titmuss, 'Goals of Today's Welfare State,' in J.A. Kahl (ed.), *Comparative Perspectives on Stratification* (Boston: Little, Brown, 1968), pp. 89-98

M. Tumin, 'Some Principles of Stratification: A Critical Analysis,' *American Sociological Review*, vol. 18 (August 1953), 387-94

- 'On Social Inequality,' *American Sociological Review*, vol. 28 (February 1963), 19-26

M. Weber, *From Max Weber*, edited and translated by H.H. Gerth and C.W. Mills (New York: Oxford University Press, 1946)

I. Weinberg, 'Social Problems Which Are No More,' in E.O. Smigel (ed.), *Handbook of Social Problems* (Chicago: Rand McNally, 1967)

Wm. F. Whyte, *Men at Work* (Homewood, Ill.: Irwin-Dorsey Press, 1961)

D.H. Wrong, 'Social Inequality Without Social Stratification,' *Canadian Review of Sociology and Anthropology*, 1 (February 1964), 1-16

CHARLES TILLY

The modernization of political conflict in France

MODERNIZATION[1]

Modernization is like raising children; it takes longer, and costs more, than anyone imagines before he begins. The very emergence of the blurry word 'modernization' in discussions of contemporary nations which used to employ sharper terms like 'industrialization' and 'urbanization' suggests as much.[2] Industrialization turns out to be much chancier, and urbanization much more complicated, than the hopeful commentators of the 1940s used to say. To speak of 'modernization' is to point to a broader, longer, more complicated set of changes.

Not that as an analytical tool the concept of modernization serves more effectively than the concepts of industrialization and urbanization. The opposite is true. Modernization is too big and slippery for deft manipulation. Its virtue is as a warning: pay attention to *what else* happens before, and while, industrialization or urbanization occurs. Our adoption of the term modernization signals (1) that the development of an industrial labour force, an educated population, an urban way of life or widespread participation in national politics entails far wider changes than any of these terms suggests in itself, and (2) that these – and other – transformations depend on each other closely enough to justify imagining another grand process comprehending all of them. These signals (and thus the term modernization) became more important as students of con-

© Charles Tilly, 1972.

1 Substantial portions of this essay come from the unpublished draft of my chapter on France for a comparative study of modernization and collective violence in Germany, Italy, France, and elsewhere by Richard Tilly, Louise Tilly, and Charles Tilly, destined for publication by Basic Books under the title *The Rebellious Century.* Colloquia at the University of Wisconsin, the University of California (Berkeley), and the University of California (Riverside) heard and criticized portions of the argument. I am grateful to the Canada Council for generous financial support and to the Center for Advanced Study in the Behavioral Sciences for the leisure to do much writing.

2 See Ian Weinberg, 'The Concept of Modernization: An Unfinished Chapter in Sociological Theory,' unpublished paper presented to the annual meeting of the American Sociological Association, 1968; Reinhard Bendix, 'Tradition and Modernity Considered,' *Comparative Studies in Society and History,* 9 (April 1967), 292-346.

temporary nations began to realize that promoting economic growth was a risky and complicated business; that many other things might have to happen before stable and/or democratic government would even begin to emerge in new states; and that in the Western experience the appropriate analogies to current changes in non-Western countries might be the emergence of governments, national markets, bureaucracies and the like in the eighteenth century and earlier, rather than the swirling urban–industrial growth of the nineteenth and twentieth centuries. So the turn to the larger agenda signaled by the word 'modernization' included a turn towards reconsideration of the Western experience over a long sweep of time.

One portion of this reconsideration which has not gone far enough is the study of political conflict. In the contemporary world, poor countries appear to be much more turbulent than rich ones, despite all the recent wrangling and protesting in the richest countries.[3] That could be because wealth (or industrialization, or urbanization, or something else which goes along with wealth) pacifies men. It could be that political conflict changes form – becomes more subtle, shifts away from physical force – with advancing wealth. Or it could be an illusion based on bad information or faulty definitions. Whichever applies, it raises the question whether the historical experience of Western countries points to the same conclusions. Did modernization reliably transform political conflict? If it did, we could reasonably compare the historical evidence with the implications of the contemporary comparisons.

In Western countries, modernization clearly did not *eliminate* political conflict, even in its more violent forms. Within the most modern nations, men are fighting and protesting still. Just as clearly, modernization in those countries did bring changes in the issues, the styles, the personnel of political conflict. No one could mistake the Peasants' War for the Nazi Revolution, or the struggle of Tudor factions for the jockeying of twentieth-century MPs. The critical questions lie between those two extremes. Did political conflict in Western countries change in some regular way attributable to standard features of modernization? Did its intensity and disruptiveness diminish in consequence?

Let us take a serious look at those questions in a single country, France. We shall thereby run the risk of mistaking French idiosyncrasies for Western universals. In compensation, we get the opportunity to follow the well-documented, actual experience of a turbulent country continuously over a considerable span of time. One might think that the seventeenth-century Frenchmen who blamed the bickering and bloodshed of their time on an enduring moral weakness of their people were not only correct but prescient. The eighteenth century, after all, brought a revolution more far-reaching than the seventeenth-century Fronde; the nineteenth century was full of protest; and the twentieth century – well, here we are, and France is still crackling with conflict.

Yet the character of political conflict has changed. The contenders, the issues, the occasions for conflict in contemporary France have little resemblance to those of the seventeenth and eighteenth centuries. France is no longer her old self; why should her conflicts remain the same? Some parts of the change are, nevertheless, hard to understand, and worth trying to understand. The problem is to determine what essential

---

3 For a review of the literature on this point, see Samuel P. Huntington, *Political Order in Changing Societies* (New Haven: Yale University Press, 1968), pp. 39-59.

features of conflict changed, how they changed, and what connection those changes had with the modernization of France, which was proceeding simultaneously and, presumably, interdependently.

This essay takes up only a portion of that problem. Despairing (at least for the moment) of any hope of treating *all* forms of conflict comprehensively, I shall sketch some of the major alterations in French society over the last few centuries, review some of the major shifts in the character of the more violent, public and political forms of conflict, and offer some ideas and evidence concerning the relationships between the two.

That means taking up themes which mattered a good deal to my late friend, colleague, and critic Ian Weinberg. I am taking up the themes in his memory, although not in perfect agreement with the conclusions he had reached. Ian Weinberg argued that over the long run modernization had reduced (in Western countries) and would reduce (in others) the pervasiveness and violence of political conflict. As he put it:

The impact of modernization was not simply to 'break down' traditional authority systems as the literature so often puts it, because there was hardly any need to do this. What actually occurred in western political development was that the legitimacy of the political system itself was accepted as more of the population became participants. Institutional mechanisms were evolved which assured succession, opposition, and the greater effectiveness over time and in depth of governmental authority. The bureaucracy of government provided much of the stability because recruitment was more universalistic. France, for example was well-governed during the tempestuous Third Republic, even though the civil service was accused of harboring royalist elements. Intra-elite aggression became oral and bureaucratized, or formalized into the duelling system. Elite schools began to emphasize seminars and tutorials, education to styles of verbal aggression, rather than the lecture system. The greater mobilization of the lower socio-economic groups, with the expansion of the franchise meant that violence and riot as a political phenomenon began to decline ... The decline in violence intrinsic to the pre-modern political system is indicated by the romanticization of violence by intellectuals which begins in the nineteenth century. There were, and still are breakdowns in the process of modernization, which produce internal war and revolution. But persistent violence, as a common and pathological problem at every level of society, has disappeared.[4]

Much of this argument is correct and valuable. The standard portrayal of the emergence of modern politics as a 'breakdown' of traditional systems of authority does, indeed, obscure the way that emerging states accumulated authority where little had existed before. The bureaucratization of government did promote a continuity and predictability of administration which survived transfers of power. The style of elite conflict did become more subtle, more verbal. Larger and larger segments of the population did become directly involved in national politics.

4 Ian Weinberg, 'Social Problems Which Are No More,' to appear in Erwin O. Smigel (ed.), *Handbook of Social Problems* (Chicago: Rand McNally), pp. 25-6.

There the difficulties begin. Two questions deserve scrutiny. First, how smoothly did the participation of ordinary people in national systems of power expand? I shall suggest that the whole process went on with frequent fits, starts, and reversals, and that ordinary people often *resisted* incorporation into national politics (which meant the subordination of other political units to the national state) with rage and indignation.

Second, did the process of modernization somehow routinize and mollify political conflict? I shall suggest that any particular form of conflict did tend to routinize and become more predictable, if not more manageable, but that the structural processes we lump together under the name modernization, in transforming the identities and interests of the principal contenders for power, constantly threw up new forms of conflict to replace the old.

Whether the overall amount of conflict declined in Western countries over the long run of modernization is more doubtful. Final resolution of that question will take far more agreement on the facts, the definitions, and the measurements of conflict than is now in sight. I shall suggest that in France, at least, violent conflict was just as prevalent in the twentieth century as in the nineteenth, although its form changed fundamentally from one century to the next.

A QUICK VIEW OF THE HISTORY OF CONFLICT
In order to sense the magnitude and character of the change, let us go back to a time before the urbanization and industrialization of the nineteenth century. We stride through history in hundred-year boots. It is 1768, a year of dearth in France. Louis XV, no longer excessively *bien-aimé*, still reigns. When violence breaks out, it most often assumes the shape of a food riot. In the food riot's most developed form, mixed crowds of ordinary people gather angrily before the shop of a miller, a merchant, or a baker; they complain about prices, seize the food on hand, cart it off to the market square, sell it to all comers (so long as they belong to the community) at a price they declare to be just, turn the cash over to the owner of the grain or bread, and go home saying they have done justice, as the authorities themselves should have done justice. That year major disturbances following this pattern occur in Le Havre, Rouen, and Mantes; many more break out in the smaller market towns of Normandy.

A century earlier, the crowd would normally have smashed, manhandled, and looted. Sometimes they still do. But as merchants and royal ministers have painstakingly constructed a national market in grains (and thus assured the survival of monstrous Paris) ordinary people have shifted to more highly organized, more effective, and more nearly non-violent ways of bargaining through the threat of force. Through a decree of 1763, the royal government has made its greatest effort so far to knock down barriers to the shipment of grain from town to town and province to province; 'free trade' is the slogan, the prescription for France's economic ills.

Many provincial people see it differently. Confronted with a large and long-forecast food riot in April 1768, the Parlement of Rouen has reinstated many of the traditional controls – inventory of grains in private hands, requirement that all sales be made in the public market, strict control over the departure of grain from the community. It has declined to condemn the authorities of small Norman towns for actually setting the price of grain (no one questioned their setting the price of bread). And it has authorized the arrest of government commission agents sent out to buy wheat for Paris. The government's views of these 'hindrances to trade' appears emphatically in a letter from the controller general of finances, l'Averdy, to the duc d'Harcourt:

I see, Sir, by the report that M. Bertin made to the King a few days ago concerning the news he had from you on the present circumstances of the province of Normandy, that you were worried about the provisioning of the province and believe that it is completely stripped of grain. It gives me the greatest pain to see the state to which the province has been reduced by a very ill-considered decree of the Parlement of Rouen; for I cannot help thinking that it is the hindrance to the food trade brought about by that decree which produced the shortage about which people are complaining today. I do not know, Sir, if you have accurate information about the amount of grain which has arrived in Rouen since the tenth of this month and about the grain which is still expected. I am sure that when you have informed yourself on that score you will support the measures taken by order of the King, which I made as prompt and effective as possible, and you will agree that it was impossible to do more than was done in those unhappy circumstances. If the merchants had not been discouraged and if they had thought it possible to take part in the free competition guaranteed to them by government decree, they would have made greater efforts and the rise in grain prices would have been negligible in the province.[5]

But the provincials persist. In a letter of remonstrance of October 1768, the Parlement goes so far as to intimate that the king is in cahoots with hoarders and racketeers. The idea of a Pact of Famine is spreading.[6]

Behind this widespread belief in a conspiracy among merchants and royal officials to profit from the starvation of the provinces exists the usual refracted glimmer of truth. The king and his minions are bending every effort to pry resources from the grip of provincial particularism, in order to devote them to their own national ends: the feeding of Paris, the maintenance of the army, the payment of a growing bureaucracy, the creation of a national market, the promotion of agriculture. The struggle pits the centralizers not only against the holders of grain, but also against the hoarders of men, of land, of gold, and of loyalty.

The collective violence of the time expresses the titanic conflict. There is still a substratum of very old-fashioned violence aligning members of one more or less communal group against another: the brawl among rival groups of artisans, the free-for-all setting two adjacent villages against each other, and so on. In the mid-eighteenth century, however, the characteristic forms of collective violence involve angry resistance to demands from the centre. Food riots take first place, but revolts against conscription, tax rebellions, and forcible invasions of lands closed off from communal use by royal decree have essentially the same character. The century's largest series of disturb-

5 Letter of 27 May 1768: C. Hippeau, *Le Gouvernement de Normandie au XVIIe et au XVIIIe siècle* (Caen: Goussiaume de Laporte, 1864), part II, vol. I, p. 478.
6 Georges Afanassiev, *Le commerce des céréales en France au dix-huitième siècle* (Paris: Picard, 1894), pp. 163-4.

ances will be the garland of food riots draped around Paris in 1775, after Turgot's most vigorous efforts at freeing the grain trade. A very large part of the collective action of the Revolution itself will take the quintessential eighteenth-century forms.

We spring forward a century, to 1868. Napoleon III, no longer so lustrous as when he seized power sixteen years ago, governs France. By now, Frenchmen have virtually forgotten food riots and tax rebellions, although they were rife only twenty years ago. The gatherings which commonly turn violent nowadays are no longer casual congregations at markets or fairs; they are deliberate assemblies of men belonging to special-purpose associations. The International Workingmen's Association – later to be called the First International – is four years old, and actively organizing in France. In June of this year the Empire finally legalizes public meetings, although it still requires prior authorization for them. As settings for collective violence, demonstrations and strikes now prevail.

Now is the time of massive strikes, the first important wave of the Second Empire, strikes of a scale and sophistication never before seen in France. The workers of Lille and its vicinity have been striking, on and off, for two years. This year's *graffiti* on the walls and urinals of Lille go:

Vive la République!

Des balles ou du pain

Aux armes, citoyen

Ci nous ne voulons pas nous laissés mourir ou mangé par les Anglais

Je suis républicain parce que le bonheur est dans la République[7]

All of which are, naturally, defined as 'seditious slogans.'

In this year of 1868 major strikes break out in the Nord, in Marseille, and through much of the industrial region of Lyon, Saint-Etienne, and Roanne. Many of them pass more or less peacefully, if not amicably. Some few produce violence – typically strikers stoning the house of a mine's director, or scuffles between assembled strikers and the troops sent in to keep them in line. Although strikes have been more or less legal for four years, prefects are quick to aid the managers when workers show signs of turbulence and/or 'socialism.' However, the really bloody encounters of soldiers and workers – the so-called Massacres of la Ricamarie and Aubin in 1869, the struggles around the near-insurrectionary strikes of 1870, the Commune of 1871 – have yet to come.

The deliberately organized demonstration is rapidly becoming the usual setting for collective violence. Toulouse, for example, has seen no disturbances of any note since its republicans' futile resistance to Louis Napoleon's 1851 *coup d'état*. But now the government is beginning to organize the militia (the *garde mobile*) in preparation for a possible war with Prussia. On 9 March, there is a minor demonstration at the Prefecture: some singing, some stoning. On the evening of the 10th

7 Pierre Pierrard, *La Vie ouvrière à Lille sous le Second Empire* (Paris: Bloud & Gay, 1965), pp. 490-1.

56 Charles Tilly

... a crowd of 1,500 to 2,000 persons sings the Marseillaise, and breaks the gas lamps. Then groups of young men go to the Prefecture, where the police station is broken into and sacked. They then run through the streets to shout of Vive la République! Down with the Emperor!, break street lights and windows of public buildings, and besiege the mayor at his house, on which they fly a red flag. The next day ... many workers stay away from the job, and new disturbances break out; many women take part, thinking that the militia will be garrisoned far away ... youngsters take to the streets with a red flag (a towel drenched in an ox's blood at the slaughterhouse) and try to build a barricade of wagons. Another gang breaks gaslights around the Place des Carmes. A third goes to the School of Law, breaks in and smashes a bust of the Emperor. The authorities start preparing the military for action.[8]

Many of the disturbances of the time follow this script: a moderately disciplined demonstration shatters into rioting and vandalism. As the reporter of the incident tells us, 'It seems that the Republicans were behind the first demonstrations, but they were overwhelmed by the exuberance of the young people and the calculated intervention of a few troublemakers.' The well-organized mass demonstration, in which the usual violence takes the form of struggles between the demonstrators and the police sent to disperse or contain them, has not yet come into its own.

One more hundred-year bound brings us to 1968. General de Gaulle has survived ten years as president, but his popularity seems frayed. Strikes still shake France's industrial life frequently. But this year student rebellions steal the headlines. A series of student strikes blend agitation against the American war in Vietnam with demands for greater student participation in the running of universities. PROFESSORS, VOUS ETES VIEUX, goes one of the slogans.

In May, the main action in Paris shifts from the new campus in the industrial suburb of Nanterre to the ancient one at the Sorbonne. After some vandalism and some threats of rough-and-tumble between militants of the far Left and the far Right, the rector asks police to surround, and then, to disperse, a group of students meeting in the Sorbonne's courtyard to protest disciplinary action begun against some of the leaders at Nanterre. The clearing of the Sorbonne itself goes smoothly, but clashes between riot police and jeering students gathered just outside the old building began six extraordinary weeks of demonstrations, street fighting, strikes, sit-downs of a new style in schools and factories, speeches, elections, repression: the 'Events of May.' This year's *graffiti* have a more fantastic touch:

la culture est l'inversion de la vie

la lucidite est la blessure la plus proche du soleil

haut-parleur = ambiance programme = répression

quand le dernier des sociologues aura été pendu avec les tripes du dernier bureaucrate, aurons-nous encore des problèmes?

l'anarchie, c'est je

8 André Armengaud, *Les Populations de l'Est-Aquitaine au début de l'époque moderne* (Paris: Mouton, 1961), pp. 420-1.

And l'anarchie sometimes seems to be the point of it all. It turns out otherwise, at least in the short run. The elections at the end of June produce a Gaullist landslide. People are scared. Nevertheless, the Events involve far more than a handful of fanatics. In May and June, at least 20,000 Frenchmen take part in violent encounters with the police, perhaps 2,500 are wounded and 4,500 arrested during those encounters, and five men die as a more or less direct result of them. A far larger number of people join non-violent strikes, sit-ins, and demonstrations.

The violence itself does not distinguish the Events of May from a number of other disturbances since World War II: the insurrectionary strikes of 1947, for example, or the riots at General Eisenhower's installation as SHAEF commander in 1951, or the huge, bloody demonstrations during the Algerian war. For the great numbers involved, the destruction and casualties of May 1968 are slight. But the leadership of students, their reaching out to factory workers, the rejection of Communist patronage, the experiments with local control of schools and workplaces, the undercurrent of demands for communal autonomy within a complex society combine to give the Events a new and baffling character.

Veteran observer Raymond Aron finds the Events senseless and repellent, which is to say, baffling. Just after the fighting dies down, he rummages in his wordbag for the right label and chooses ... *psychodrama.*

The psychodrama brings into play the revolutionary propensity of the French people, the weakness of mediating institutions (accentuated by Gaullism, in which everything depends on General de Gaulle himself), the surge of irrational forces in a society which calls itself modern, probably the discontent of a number of Frenchmen in a phase of modernization lacking the morphine of inflation. There were enough frustrations, resentments and griefs among Frenchmen for a great outburst to occur, given the right circumstances. Is it the end of a civilization?[9]

No revolution, but mass hysteria, says Raymond Aron. No hysteria, but mass revolution, reply the students. Both agree that something deep in French society is coming to the surface. They disagree on whether it represents a change or a breakdown. A little later Alain Touraine will tell us that it represents both, with the change in French society being the more fundamental:

The movement of May is a new form of the class struggle. More than any other collective action of the last decades, this movement revealed and thus constituted the fundamental social conflict of our society. That way of putting it is farther than it might seem from the proclamations of the participants themselves, for it means that we are dealing with a new social conflict, whose nature and participants are no longer the same as in the previous society, in truly capitalist society ... The French students, like those of Berlin and Berkeley, began a struggle against the apparatus of integration, manipulation and aggression. It is these words and not the word exploitation which best define the nature of the conflict.[10]

9 Raymond Aron, *La Révolution introuvable* (Paris: Fayard, 1968), p. 44.
10 Alain Touraine, *Le Mouvement de mai ou le communisme utopique* (Paris: Le Seuil, 1968), p. 14.

And so – as in 1768 and 1868 – the analysis of the violent events quickly becomes an analysis of the society which produced them.

Our mythical journey is far from bootless. The two centuries we have paced off brought fundamental changes in the character of collective violence in France. That is the first and elementary lesson: collective violence has form – more than clumsy words like 'riot' or 'disturbance' convey. At any particular time and place, people have a limited and well-defined repertoire of violent forms. The repertoire changes systematically with time and place, as the basic forms of organization for *non*-violent action vary. That is the second (and more contestable) lesson: the predominant forms of violence depend on the basic structure of collective action. No tragic chasm separates violence from non-violence, in 1968 or 1768.

The third lesson follows directly from the first two, although it may be even harder to accept; it is that in the French experience collective violence has been a cause, effect, and constituent element of the political process. If that is the case, it makes little sense to imagine violent protest as a geyser newly erupting through a weakened but level surface – as an expression of either 'revolutionary propensities' or 'accumulated tension.' It then makes much sense, on the other hand, to suppose that if the nature of violent conflict changes significantly, other, much wider, changes in the political process must be going on. The rise of the food riot in the eighteenth century and the rise of the violent demonstration in the nineteenth signified far more general transformations of France's political structure. Perhaps the new features of the 1968 rebellion also signify more than an instant impulse.

Saying so, however, only poses the main questions more insistently. If there is some order to disorder, what is it? In the short run, how does the structure of non-violent social relations shape the structure of violence? In the long run, how do transformations of the social structure transform violent protest? And what, if anything, is peculiarly French about the French experience with these matters? These questions will guide the rest of our inquiry.

THE CENTRALIZATION OF POWER

Part of the answer lies in the broadest features of French political history. France has long stood out among nations for her centralizing verve. Although 'Absolutism' went much farther in theory than in practice (and the theory itself was a weapon fashioned in the long battle of the crown with provincial magnates), the centre prevailed. Tocqueville saw in the royal centralization of power, wealth, and population in Paris the roots of the Revolution and the origins of the subsequent fragility of democratic institutions in France. Much more recently, Hervert Luethy has commented that non-parliamentary institutions of modern French government represent

the state apparatus of the absolute monarchy perfected and brought to its logical conclusion under the First Empire. When the crowned heads fell, the real sovereignty was transferred to this apparatus. But it works in the background, unobtrusively, anonymously, remote from all publicity and almost in secret; a monarch, a monarch whose only surviving driving principle is routine. It is not so much a state within a state as the real state behind the facade of the democratic state.[11]

The French system has long subordinated local and regional authorities to direct national control. The departmental prefect is, of course, an agent of the central government. With the dissolution of the provincial National Guard units and the reduction of the Parisian Guard to ceremonial functions in 1852, the last legally armed forces not firmly under national control disappeared almost definitively – the deeply significant exception being 1870 and 1871. At about the same time as he tamed the National Guard, Louis Napoleon perfected an apparatus of spies, informers, and informants already assembled by earlier regimes. Later innovations in techniques of control – tanks, telephones, tear gas, automatic rifles – simply increased the technical advantages of the government over its challengers.

The administrative centralization promoted and fed on geographic centralization in Paris and its protuberance, Versailles. Paris has towered over all other French cities since there has been a France. The roads of France, and then the railroads of France, and then the airlines of France, grew up in the shape of a Parisocephalic octopus. Tocqueville entitled a pivotal chapter of *The Old Regime and the French Revolution* as follows: 'How in France, more than in any other European country, the provinces had come under the thrall of the metropolis, which attracted to itself all that was most vital in the nation.' (Indeed, a lexicon which permits 'province' to mean every part of the country but a single city would be fantastic almost anywhere else.) Marx saw Parisian dominance as a major political fact: 'If Paris, as a result of political centralization, rules France, the workers, in moments of revolutionary earthquake, rule Paris.'[12] Blanqui, writing in the waning months of the Second Empire, elevated the political reality into a doctrine:

A year of Parisian dictatorship in 1848 would have spared France and would have spared history the quarter of a century now drawing to a close. If it takes ten years of it this time, let us not hesitate. After all, the government of Paris is the government of the nation by the nation, and therefore the only legitimate one. Paris is not just a municipality entrenched in its own interests. It represents the nation.[13]

The sheer existence of such a doctrine illustrates the political centralization of France ... and gives point to the old fear that monstrous Paris will devour all the nation.

The work of centralization went on for centuries. It did not stop with the Revolution and Empire, but continued apace during the nineteenth century, as the state drew larger and larger parts of men's lives under its direct control through public education, univer-

11 Herbert Luethy, *France Against Herself* (New York: Meridian, 1955), pp. 19-20. Consider, in the same connection, that Louis Napoleon had only to tighten well-established procedures to produce the repressive regime of the early Second Empire: Howard C. Payne, *The Police State of Louis Napoleon Bonaparte* (Seattle: University of Washington Press, 1966).

12 Karl Marx, *The Civil Wars in France* (New York: International Publishers, 1935), p. 39.

13 Auguste Blanqui, 'La critique sociale' in *Textes choisis* (Paris: Editions Sociales, 1955), pp. 166-7.

sal military training, manhood suffrage, and programs of public welfare. Eventually the state seized control over substantial parts of the economy: railroads, airlines, radio, television, mines, utilities, important parts of banking, and automobile manufacturing. The great moment for that expansion came at the end of World War II. If Louis XIV declared, *L'Etat, c'est moi,* his successors announced, *L'Etat, c'est tout.* Today much of the debate about governmental reform in France concerns ways of reversing, or at least arresting, a centuries-old process of centralization.

THE NATIONALIZATION OF POLITICS

In addition to a centralization of power, the France of the last two centuries has seen a nationalization of politics. The two processes have depended on each other. Ordinary Frenchmen led fairly active political lives within their own communities and provinces long before the Revolution; they elected local officials, apportioned the local tax burden, wrangled over the expenses of the religious establishment. But they had only intermittent contact with national politics through privileged intermediaries – and even then more as subjects than as participants. The political reforms of 1787 and of the early Revolution actually restricted formal participation in community politics (by substituting an elected council for the assembly of all heads of households and imposing property qualifications for voting and office holding). On the other hand, the Revolution enormously increased the opportunities and incentives for ordinary people to participate in national politics through voting, holding office, joining clubs, adopting revolutionary styles, demonstrating, reading, arguing, volunteering.

The fashionable word for this drawing of people into intensive communication on a national scale is 'mobilization.'[14] After the early Revolution, the next great surge of political mobilization in France did not come until the Revolution of 1848. Then universal manhood suffrage, election campaigns, proliferating political associations, a relatively free national press, and a great acceleration of the movement of political information via telegraph and railroad drew men much farther into national politics than they had ever gone before. Centralization itself promoted this process of nationalization by placing more and more of the resources and decisions which really mattered in the national capital or the national government.

THE INSTABILITY OF REGIMES

The centralization and nationalization of French politics did not, to be sure, proceed smoothly and without hesitation. The French moved from regime to regime through revolutions and coups; 1789, 1799, 1830, 1848, 1851, 1870, and 1958 are only the largest markers. Even today French leaders and parties claim and contest the lines of descent from the eighteenth-century revolution with a passion resembling that of the Russians or the Chinese more than that of the Dutch or the English (to name four regimes of revolutionary genesis). Although the Radicals acquired a special position as protectors of secular republicanism under the Third Republic, no party has ever been able to establish a monopoly of revolutionary legitimacy, and few parties have avoided claiming one. As recently as the 13 May 1958 the insurgents who seized power in Al-

14 See J.P. Nettl, *Political Mobilization* (London: Faber and Faber, 1967).

giers, and ultimately brought down the Fourth Republic, sang the Marseillaise and formed ... a Committee of Public Safety.

Still 1958 is an exception in one crucial regard. It is the only occasion since 1799 in which the professional French military have taken an autonomous and fundamental part in the overthrow of a regime. Men who acquired their renown as soldiers have periodically come to power in France and have periodically appeared as threats to democratic continuity: Boulanger, Petain, and de Gaulle are the celebrated examples; the two Napoleons are the Men on Horseback with whom they are most often compared. Louis Napoleon did use the army with grim effectiveness in his 1851 coup. The question of civilian control over the military did almost tear France apart during the Dreyfus Affair. Yet the army as such has played only a small role in France's succession of revolutions and coups. In that respect, France's instability is unlike that of Spain or Brazil.

Under the Third and Fourth Republics, the quick turnover of cabinets combined with the memory of those coups and revolutions to give France a worldwide reputation for political instability. That French fickleness, as Raymond Aron points out, actually developed earlier than the Third Republic:

Instability at the top is ... less novel than the sociologists tend to think. In Tocqueville's time, during the July Monarchy, people joked about the same thing, and told the story of the ambassador who didn't know, when he left Paris, what ministry he would represent when he arrived at his post. The presence of a king, of an emperor or of a Charles de Gaulle temporarily removes the head of state from factional quarrels, but it does not do away with the quarrels. The head of state presides over our disputes more than he resolves them.[15]

Although by now a number of younger nations have thrown down serious challenges to France's supremacy in this line of endeavour, France's reputation for governmental discontinuity was well earned – with two important qualifications. The first is that the personnel of government, especially the state bureaucracy, persisted to a remarkable degree through changes of regime. Despite the sudden shift from heavy property qualifications for voting to manhood suffrage, a good half of the deputies elected in April 1848 had already served in pre-revolutionary Chambers. At the level of departmental councils, the continuity was much greater. Administrative personnel at all levels survived the change of regime with very little perturbation.[16]

The second qualification is that 'instability' does not equal 'violence.' The French have had plenty of violent moments, but so have most other peoples, regardless of

15 Raymond Aron, Immuable et changeante, *de la IVe à la Ve République* (Paris: Calmann-Levy, 1959), pp. 40-1.

16 André-Jean Tudesq, *Les Conseillers généraux en France au temps de Guizot* (Paris: Colin, 1967; Cahiers de la Fondation Nationale des Sciences Politiques, 157), pp. 85-102; *ibid., Les Grands notables en France* (Paris: Presses Universitaires de France, 1964; Publications de la Faculté des Lettres et Sciences Humaines de Paris, 'Recherches,' 21), II, 1065; George W. Fasel, 'The French Election of April 23, 1948: Suggestions for a Revision,' *French Historical Studies,* 5 (Spring 1968), 285-98.

whether they live under 'stable' or 'unstable' governments. England, the United States, Canada, and Belgium have all, in their times, experienced collective violence of the same general varieties as France's; their daily lives, over the long run, may even have been more violent than France's. Certainly the sheer amount of bloodshed does not account for France's contentious reputation. Over the period from 1930 to 1960, for example, about 100 Frenchmen died in political disturbances, mostly at the hands of the police. During the same period some 200,000 were killed in wars and 600,000 died in accidents. Obviously political disturbances create fear and trembling disproportionate to their toll in human life. France's distinction lies not in the amount of wounding and killing but in the frequency with which violent protests have brought down governments and regimes.

That special political experience has produced a special set of political attitudes. As Philip Williams puts it:

The Frenchman's approach to the problem of political authority is ... shaped by three factors: a political struggle which has always been waged with sectarian bitterness and thoroughness, sparing no sector of the country's organized life: an experience of governments abusing their authority to maintain their position: and an immensely powerful administrative machine, which provides a standing temptation to such abuse. There is a latent totalitarianism in the French attitude to politics, which makes French democrats fear the power of government, and regard it as a source of potential dangers rather than of potential benefits.[17]

No doubt most men are ambivalent towards the state. Frenchmen, more than most.

France's political history is to some extent an explanation, and to some extent a result, of the changing character of her collective violence. The centralization of government, the nationalization of politics, the barriers to independent political action by the army, the revolutionary heritage and the continuing vulnerability of regimes to challenge from the street give France a greater resemblance to, say, Italy than to England. A France with a more independent military might well resemble Spain or Argentina.

WEALTH

But only in some respects. The analogies of Italy, Spain, or Argentina lose some of their persuasiveness when it comes to matters of wealth, industrial structure, regional diversity and urban population. The history of collective violence in France depends not only on the country's formal political structure, but also on the great transformation of other features of the social structure.

Before the Revolution, France was one of the world's most prosperous, industrial, urban nations. Since that time a number of other countries have moved much faster than France along all of these dimensions. France still has a longer experience with comfortable levels of living than almost any other country in the world. With respect to income per capita, Holland and England no doubt pulled away from France as early

17 Philip Williams, *Politics in Post-War France* (London: Longmans, 1958, 2nd ed.), p. 2. Cf. Michel Crozier, *The Bureaucratic Phenomenon* (Chicago: University of Chicago Press, 1964), pp. 213-64.

FIGURE 1 *Estimates of changes in French National Income, 1810-1960*

as the seventeenth century. But the next-comers – Belgium, Germany, and the United States – did not pass her until fairly late in the nineteenth century.

All this is relative, of course. If we were to cast about the world of the mid-twentieth century for approximations of France's material condition at the beginning of the nineteenth century, we would have to seize on poor but civilized nations like Bulgaria, Yugoslavia, or Costa Rica. Even those analogies would touch on the grotesque; we would have to conjure up a Yugoslavia without railroads, without radios, without splashes of ultramodern industry, with a class of titled landlords still wresting their incomes from tenant farmers, and another class of merchants, bankers, industrialists, and officials just coming into their own, with even fewer of her people in big cities than in contemporary Yugoslavia, yet prevailing in a world of nations poorer and less powerful than herself. The France of that era has no counterpart in the Western world today.

Over the long run since the Revolution, the wealth of France has accumulated slowly and surely. One informed guess at the long-run rate of growth of per capita income in France puts it at 1.25 per cent per annum, about the same as England's.[18] Figure 1 presents three of the best known national income series for France since 1810.[19] They dis-

18 W.A. Cole and Phyllis Deane, 'The Growth of National Incomes' in *The Cambridge Economic History of Europe* (Cambridge: Cambridge University Press, 1965), vol. VI, part I, 12.
19 Sources for Figure 1: (1) Maurice Lévy-Leboyer, 'La croissance économique en France au XIXe siècle, Résultats préliminaires,' *Annales; Economies, Societies, Civilisations,* 23 (July-August 1968), 788-807. The statistic is an index number (1890 + 100) for 'global product' of agriculture, industry, and construction. It therefore excludes services, investment, government purchases, and net exports from among the items conventionally included in Gross National Product. (2) Colin Clark, *The Conditions of Economic Progress* (London: Macmillan, 1960), 3rd ed., pp. 123-229. The figures represent real income (including the imputed value of agricultural products produced and consumed outside the market) in billions of International Units. Up to 1913, the figures are annual averages for decades centred on the date shown. (3) Estimates of national income by Alfred Sauvy,

play a relatively steady growth throughout the nineteenth century. The twentieth century brought greater swings in income. According to these estimates, the most notable periods of decline were the depression of the 1870s, the two world wars, and the depression of the 1930s. World War II shows up as an economic disaster, even compared to the depression it followed. The periods of most notable growth (discounting the curious implications of Colin Clark's estimates) run from around 1855 to 1869, 1922 to 1930 and, incomparably, 1946 to 1960 and beyond. These dates correspond satisfactorily to what we know otherwise about the timing of industrial expansion. The curves register the steady increase of the older industries up to 1850, the spurting growth (relying increasingly on steel, railroads, and other new industries) of the 1850s and 1860s, and the tremendous expansion both of modern industry and of services since that time.

The increase of national income which occurred meant more to the average Frenchman than it would have to the average Englishman or American because the population of France grew slowly. Fewer persons shared the spoils. (Of course, it may well be – and has often been argued – that a higher rate of population increase would have accelerated France's economic growth.) France did not draw anything like the hordes of immigrants who sailed to Canada or Argentina. Her birth rate dropped steadily from the Revolution to World War II, generally faster than the death rate. In whole regions of Burgundy, Normandy, and Languedoc, families began limiting births rather stringently well before the Revolution. As a result, France's natural increase was slow and uncertain. The birth rate did tend to recover somewhat in prosperous days: the 1860s, the 1920s, and, sensationally, the 1950s. But war and depression actually produced substantial natural *decreases* in 1870-1, 1914-19, and 1936-55. Since World War II, on the other hand, with mortality still skidding down and fertility up to *fin-de-siècle* levels, Frenchmen have multiplied at rates unrivaled in at least two centuries. After a century of aging, this made the French population young again. Both demographically and industrially, the postwar change of pace far exceeded what happened earlier.

INDUSTRIALIZATION AND URBANIZATION

The same is true for the structure of employment. Figure 2 shows what a century and a half of industrialization did to the French labour force.[20] Some of the changes are factitious. The apparent decline of the total labour force after 1954, for example, resulted almost entirely from the application of stricter definitions to the agricultural population. Nevertheless, several facts come through:

1901-49 and, after 1949, extrapolation of Sauvy series at 1949, as reported in *Annuaire Statistique de la France, Résumé retrospectif,* 1966, Table 14, p. 556. The units are billions of 1938 francs. The estimates of production made by the researchers of the Institut de Science Economique Appliquée yield a somewhat different timetable for expansion and contraction, most notably in attributing greater growth to the decade from 1835 to 1844 than to the decade after 1854. See Jean Marczewski, *Introduction à l'histoire quantitative française de 1789 à 1964 - Conclusions générales* (Paris: I.S.E.A., 1966; Cahiers de l'I.S.E.A., AF, 7).

20 Source: J.-C. Toutain, *La population de la France de 1700 à 1959* (Paris: Institut de Science Economique Appliquée, 1963; Cahiers de l'I.S.E.A., AF, 3), pp. 135, 161.

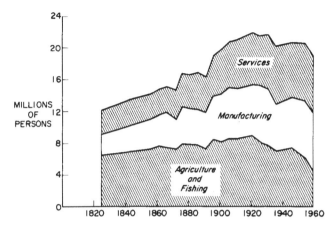

FIGURE 2 *The French labour force, 1825-1959*

1 Contrary to common notions of Revolutionary and post-Revolutionary France, close to half the labour force was already working outside of agriculture as early as 1825.
2 However, the absolute size of the agricultural population remained virtually constant for a century after 1825, began to slide after World War I, and has only fallen off rapidly since World War II.
3 As a consequence, France had an exceptionally high proportion of her labour force in agriculture, compared with other prosperous twentieth-century nations, right into the 1950s.
4 The shares of manufacturing and services grew constantly except around 1900 and during World War II. However, the pace of their growth depended on the general level of economic activity; the greater the prosperity, the faster the shift into manufacturing and services – and vice versa.
5 The shares of manufacturing and services have remained roughly equal over the entire period. France has not so far experienced the shift from secondary to tertiary industries supposed to characterize advanced industrial economies.

The period under examination, then, saw France transformed from a fairly poor, predominantly agrarian country to a prosperous industrial one, while a number of other countries travelled in the same general direction faster. Although in 1825 France already had long experience with traditional forms of manufacturing, the period since then is her essential time of industrialization.

France also urbanized. Revolutionary Paris, with its half-million inhabitants, was one of the world's great cities. For centuries Paris had been reaching out to control the men, mores, and markets of northeastern France; by the end of the eighteenth century, a vast area was pouring migrants and food into the city. Marseille, Lyon, Bordeaux, and Rouen, each with close to a hundred thousand people, dominated their own much smaller hinterlands. The great majority of Frenchmen, nonetheless, lived in villages.

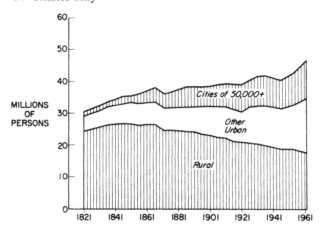

FIGURE 3 *Urban, rural, and total population, 1821-1962, etc.*

For French statisticians, the word 'urban' has traditionally singled out communes with at least 2,000 persons in the central settlement. By this criterion, about a fifth of the French population lived in urban places in 1820, about three-fifths in 1960. As Figure 3 shows, the rural population has been declining both absolutely and relatively since around 1850.[21] Big-city France, the France of places with 50,000 or more persons, has fed on that decline: only 4 per cent in 1821, 18 per cent in 1901, 25 per cent in 1962. The pace of urban growth was relatively even. Over the long run it comes, like per capita income, to about 1.25 per cent per year. The industrial expansion of the 1850s, the 1920s, and the 1950s, the slower industrialization from 1870 to World War I and during the Depression braked it; the two wars and the loss of territory to Prussia in 1870 dented the curve, but not for long.

If the French population in agriculture reached its peak, as we have seen, around the time of World War I, while the rural population began a steady decline around 1850, the two cannot have been the same. In fact, a good proportion – perhaps a third – of the so-called rural population of post-Revolutionary France was living from manufacturing, services, and other non-agricultural pursuits. The domestic textile industry (said in rural Meyenne, for example, to be the principle economic activity of the countryside before the Revolution) occupied far more people than its rivals, the woodburning forges, woodworking, tanning, basketry, pottery. All these industries quickly moved to the city during the nineteenth century, leaving a once-humming countryside more bucolic than it had been for centuries. Rural areas de-industrialized.

It looks as though hundreds of thousands of rural artisans hung on in small towns through the first half of the nineteenth century, living on half wages, seasonal work in

21 Sources: *Annuaire statistique de la France, Résumé retrospectif,* 1966, Table 3, p. 23; *Statistique de la France* (Paris: Imprimerie Royale, 1837), pp. 267-83. 'Urban places' are communes with 2,000 or more persons in the central agglomeration. The figures for 1821 and 1836 are estimates from the ratio communes 2,000+/communes 10,000+ for 1851, as applied to the actual total in communes of 10,000 or more in 1821 and 1836.

the fields, and dwindling hope for a return of the good old days. They and their descendants began to move off the land in growing numbers around 1850, as jobs in the new industrial centres became more plentiful, the railroads made travel to them easier, all rural industry expired, and traditional rights to glean, cut and hunt in common fields or forests disappeared before the advance of calculating, capital-intensive agriculture. So the 'rural exodus' so often deplored by French lovers of rustic virtue probably had three rather different, if overlapping, phases: (1) a draining of present and former workers in rural industry, peaking in the middle of the nineteenth century; (2) a tapping of 'extra' children of farm families, especially during the period of relatively high natural increase up to 1890 or so; (3) the movement of families displaced by the closing down and consolidation of farms since 1890, especially after 1930. The first movement had an air of desperation, the second offered a way out of poverty to several generations of young Frenchmen on the make, and the third went on rather smoothly except for the worst years of the 1930s. The three kinds of movement were bound to have very different impacts on agrarian protest.

The growth of cities and the draining of rural population were no more evenly distributed across the map of France then was the development of industry on a large scale. Let us call 'modern,' for the sake of simplicity, those areas with high per capita incomes, productive agriculture, large manufacturing establishments, high literacy, extensive means of communication, and so on. In these terms, the geographical distribution of modernity in France has followed a curvilinear path since the Revolution. Modernity was then already somewhat concentrated in Paris and its hinterland, plus much smaller regions immediately around a handful of other big cities. It grew even more unequal during the nineteenth century as those regions (and more generally, the northeastern quadrant of the country urbanized and industrialized. Slowly after World War I and rapidly after World War II the fruits of modernity – bitter and sweet alike – spread outside those regions of initial importance, and a degree of equalization occurred.

One rather surprising feature of this process shows up in agricultural yields.[22] From the beginning the hinterland of Paris has, under the stimulus of the metropolitan market, produced the highest yields per hectare. Regional disparities, especially the advantage of Paris, *increased* during the nineteenth century (despite the spread throughout France of new agricultural practices), only to give way to a much greater equalization during the twentieth.

Maps of road traffic in 1856-7 and 1955 identify two points in a very similar progression: inequality at the beginning, growing inequality with the industrial urbanization of the north, eventual spread of traffic to larger and larger portions of the country.[23] The traffic maps suggest the extent to which this twentieth-century spread of modernity is occurring through the expansion and convergence of existing urban regions: Lyon and Marseille linking arms and reaching around to Nice; Toulouse and Bordeaux building their own metropolitan network; Paris extending its alliances in every direction.

The process touches everyday life. In an Angevin country town:

22 Source: Paul-M. Bouju and others, *Atlas historique de la France contemporaine* (Paris: Colin, 1966), p. 56.
23 Source: *Ibid.*, pp. 72-3.

As the social networks in Chanzeaux have diminished in number, they have mostly because of the revolution in transportation, greatly increased their geographic spread. Whenever the people of Chanzeaux are not working, they are on the move, usually in order to visit friends, relatives, acquaintances of far-reaching networks. Eight years ago if we wanted to talk to a farmer, we would be sure to find him at home on Sunday afternoon, and our visit was welcome since he seemed to have nothing else to do. Now people are rarely at home when they have leisure time. If they stay at home, it is because they expect visitors. The traffic on all the roads of the Maine-et-Loire, especially the back roads leading to hamlets and farms, is surprisingly heavy on Sunday nowadays. Sometimes farmers – and townspeople – go even farther away for the weekend. Faligand visits his cousins in Paris. Bourdelle visits a friend with whom he has kept up since army days in Lille. The Massonneaus drive down from Paris to visit the Guitieres. Only the ill stay at home – and they have visitors. It used to be that on Sunday afternoon the Chanzeans who wanted to get away from home would walk along the Hyrome River to stop and drink with friends at the little wineshops along the way. Today one can walk the length of the path and see only an occasional fisherman. The people of Chanzeaux have broader contacts and interests.[24]

It is not so much that Frenchmen move *more* than they used to. Despite enduring myths to the contrary, rural communities in most sections of France have been experiencing rapid turnovers of population for at least a century. The big change is that the circles in which they travel, the networks they form, have spread and spread. This extension of social relations began with Paris and its hinterland, followed the growth of industrial metropolises in the nineteenth century, and has in recent decades been knitting all of France together.

I do not say the knit is smooth, regular, or harmonious. The French have shared a general experience of Western peoples: a shift of the crucial lines of division of wealth, prestige, power, social access, and solidarity from local to national. Division remains, the principles of division change. Particular attachments to this village or that, this family or that, even this faith or that, have lost much of their importance as promoters or inhibitors of collective action, however much sentimental value they may have retained. Positions in national systems of occupation and wealth have come to matter a great deal more.

CLASS STRUCTURE

Through the long years we are considering here, the urbanization and industrialization of France have transformed her class structure in four interdependent ways:
1 Control over liquid wealth, complex organizations, and the industrial apparatus has largely supplanted control over land as the central criterion of class position.
2 The numbers of persons working in large organizations under bureaucratic control (whether, through style of work and style of life, we call them 'working class' or 'middle class') has enormously and steadily expanded.

24 Laurence Wylie and others, *Chanzeaux* (Cambridge: Harvard University Press, 1966), p. 341.

3 As the French have moved cityward, position and acceptability within a particular community have lost much of their importance as determinants of individual or group behaviour; local notability, or notoriety, matters less and less as compared with position in the national occupational structure, membership in national associations, contacts and experiences outside the community.

4 Largely as a result of changing little while other things were changing much, positions as local representatives or interpreters of national structures - priest, notary, government functionary - have lost much of their prestige and power; by contrast, positions presuming technical expertise - scientist, engineer, doctor - have gained in lustre.

Familiar trends, all.

The hand of history has erased a France of peasants and artisans, of landowning local notables linked (although not always happily) with urban officials and financiers. It has written in their place a France of farmers, bureaucrats, technicians, and industrial workers, dominated by professional organizers in a variety of specialties.

With some disgust, Balac read the writing on the wall in the 1840s:

The three orders have been replaced by what are nowadays called *classes*. We have lettered classes, industrial classes, upper classes, middle classes, etc. And these classes almost always have their own regents, as in the *college*. People have changed big tyrants into petty ones, that's all. Each industry has its bourgeois Richelieu named Laffitte or Casimir Perier ...[25]

Just a few years later, Karl Marx wrote of the same transformations from a rather different perspective:

French industry is more developed and the French bourgeoisie more revolutionary than that of the rest of the Continent. But was not the February Revolution levelled directly against the finance aristocracy? This fact proved that the industrial bourgeoisie did not rule France. The industrial bourgeoisie can rule only where modern industry shapes all property relations to suit itself, and industry can win this power only where it has conquered the world market, for national bounds are inadequate for its development. But French industry, to a great extent, maintains its command even of the national market only through a more or less modified system of prohibitive duties. While, therefore, the French proletariat, at the moment of a revolution, possesses in Paris actual power and influence which spur it on to a drive beyond its means, in the rest of France it is crowded

25 Honoré de Balzac, 'Ce qui disparaît de Paris,' first published in *Le Diable boiteux* (1845-6) and reprinted in *Les Parisiens comme ils sont* (Geneva: La Palatine, 1947), p. 158. Four or five decades later, Edmond Goblot was to declare (prematurely, I believe) the end of the system Balzac had seen crystallizing: 'So we see all artificial inequality, as well as false equality, disappearing little by little, giving way to natural inequalities: intelligence, knowledge, talent, taste, virtue and vice. In short, personal merit is overcoming class distinctions. For there could not be a *class* of bright men, or men of good will, or men of good taste. A class can only survive by making others believe it is an elite, and cannot become an elite by ceasing to be a class. Thus it is remarkable that this condition of unstable equilibrium has been able to maintain itself for nearly a century.' *La Barrière et le niveau* (Paris: Alcan, 1930), p. 160.

into separate, scattered industrial centers, being almost lost in the superior numbers of peasants and petty bourgeois.[26]

The hand of history was, in short, busily producing a palimpsest.

Many traces of the old regime persisted into the twentieth century. That is what was special about France's version of a very general transformation of class structure in industrializing societies: in France, small-town life, marginal family farming, the family firm, and the small shop all hung on tenaciously, only losing their grip under the battering of the Depression and World War II. Politics grew to a national scale far faster, and far more decisively, than did routine social life. The result was the disparity between the nationalization of politics and the segmentation of solidarity which Stanley Hoffmann considers the foundation of the 'stalemate society' of France under the Third Republic.[27]

ORGANIZATION FOR COLLECTIVE ACTION

Hoffmann also argues that the poverty of French associational life also contributed to the stalemate. On that score, I am not so sure. Throughout the interdependent transformations of demographic, economic, political, and class structures we have been reviewing, Frenchmen turned increasingly to complex organizations, including associations in the narrow sense of the word, as the means of getting their work done. The trend is obvious in the worlds of industry and government. The history of voluntary association for political and economic ends is more elusive, because successive governments from the Revolution to the beginning of the Third Republic set ponderous barriers in the way of private association. They did it selectively, so that employers long had the organizational advantage in dealing with their workers. Nevertheless, even under the forbidding eye of the Minister of the Interior, French workers, peasants, bourgeois, and political activists persisted in forming clubs, secret societies, *compagnonnages*, associations for mutual aid, rudimentary trade unions, and parties. As Henry Ehrmann says:

... the legal obstacles were frequently ignored; many categories did not wait for the change in legislation to form groups and to constitute in fact the 'partial societies' condemned by Rousseau. But the necessity of achieving this by subterfuge was nevertheless bound to shape group practice and to spread doubts about the legitimacy of group activities.[28]

The proof that associational life was far from extinguished lies in the energy with which the spies of the Interior Ministry eavesdropped and infiltrated during regimes of relatively strict control like the Restoration and the Second Empire, and the startling speed with which such associations proliferated - or came out into the open - in times of relative freedom like the spring of 1848.

26 Karl Marx, 'The Class Struggles in France, 1848-1850' in Karl Marx and Friedrich Engels, *Selected Works* (Moscow: Foreign Languages Publishing House, 1958), I, 148-9.
27 Stanley Hoffmann, 'Paradoxes of the French Political Community' in Stanley Hoffmann *et al., In Search of France* (Cambridge: Harvard University Press, 1963), pp. 1-117.
28 Henry W. Ehrmann, *Politics in France* (Boston: Little, Brown, 1968), p. 171.

Now, it appears that the pace, scale, and complexity of formal organization in France all increased rapidly as France urbanized and industrialized after 1840. The evidence is uncertain precisely because so much of the new organization took place in the shadows. Tocqueville did not detect it when writing *Democracy in America* in the 1830s; on the contrary, he considered the absence of associations a prime reason for the weakness of democratic institutions in France. Yet in his own time the Saint-Simonians, Fourierists, Blanquists, and other sects teetering between reform and revolution had gone into frenzies of organization. As early as October 1831 a report of Paris's prefect of police, summarizing the reports of his spies, gives some of the flavour of organization in the capital:

The society of *Amis du Peuple* is vigorously continuing its organization of *decuries*. They reproduce, under another name, the *ventes* of the Carbonari ... The *Société des Amis de l'Egalité* into the *Amis du Peuple*. Both of them are counting heavily for new recruits on the return of the students; but generally speaking the young people coming back from the provinces appear little inclined to rejoin the popular societies.[29]

At Lyon, mutual aid societies began to flourish in the late 1820s, and came angrily to light in the insurrections of 1830 and 1834. In general, Paris preceded the other big cities in the nurturing of association, the big cities preceded the towns, and the towns preceded the countryside.

It was not, however, a simple function of industrialization, at least not in any narrow sense of the word. The workers in the new, expanding, factory-based nineteenth-century industries – steel, railroads, cotton textiles – organized slowly.[30] The industries breeding extensive organization were older, more artisanal, smaller in scale, with the egregious exception of mining. Four main conditions promoted organization, in industry and elsewhere: (1) the absence of hereditary memberships in community, family and the like as bases for collective action; (2) a good-sized population in daily contact over a long period of time; (3) an accumulation of common lore, grievances, and political experience; (4) the visible presence of an antagonist. These conditions first obtained in traditional small-scale industries like typography and silk weaving. Eventually they developed in factories and even among agricultural workers. Thus over the nineteenth century the principal loci of working-class organization shifted from shops to factories with a lag of several decades behind the shift of the labour force from one to the other.

Politics and industry set the standard for religion, sociability, and intellectual life; the Third Republic brought France into its golden age of association. Napoleon III had speeded the process, or at least conceded to it gracefully, by openly tolerating workers' associations throughout the 1860s, legalizing the strike in 1864, and considerably relaxing restrictions on public assembly in 1868. The real spate of organizing and joining came, however, after the French rid themselves of Napoleon III.

It is true that Frenchmen have perpetuated a myth to the contrary. Confronted with the evidence of ubiquitous semi-secret lodges, sodalities, and religious associations in

29 Archives Nationales F^{1}cI 33, report of 14 October 1831.
30 Peter N. Stearns, 'Patterns of Industrial Strike Activity in France during the July Monarchy.' *American Historical Review*, 70 (January 1965), 371-94.

the south during the eighteenth and nineteenth centuries, Maurice Agulhon has postu-
lated a *sociabilité méridionale* peculiar to that region.[31] In fact, we have no good reason
to limit that 'sociability' to the south. In our own time, French rural communities are
reputed to resist voluntary association. But when calm observers look carefully, this
turns out not to be the case. In the small, and ostensibly backward, French villages he
studied, Laurence Wylie found fire companies, multiple church-based association, political parties, *classes* of all young men eligible for conscription in a given year, and other
special-purpose organizations to be active participants in community life. Robert T.
Anderson and Barbara Gallatin Anderson, studying a village sixteen kilometres from
Paris, found voluntary associations proliferating from late in the nineteenth century:

The decades on either side of the turn of the century saw four voluntary associations
introduced and sustained: a hunting society, an unemployment–funeral insurance (mutuality) society, a musical society, and a voluntary fire-fighting society. We are more
concerned here with the last four decades of abrupt change when, under the impact of
primary urban–industrial change, approximately forty associations were founded.[32]

The Andersons go on to note how regularly the formal associations parallel and grow
from older, existing groups in the community: the shop, the farm, the family, the
church, and the community as a whole. In a sense, the organization was already there;
the association simply crystallized and formalized it.

In those times when the state blocked the formation of distinct special-interest associations (which means most of the time before 1901, plus most of that during World
War II), the French tended to overload whatever existing, tolerated means of assembly
and collective action they had at hand. During the Revolution church services were
often the occasions for agitation, argument, and action. Under the Restoration and the
July Monarchy, not only church services, but funerals and theatrical performances, became important contexts for demonstrations of political sympathies. About a year
after the July Revolution, for example, the Parisian public attending the provocatively
titled *Voyage de la liberté* (including medal-holders from the Revolution itself, who
were deliberately seated together by the management) took the many veiled political
allusions in the play as their opportunity to stomp, hoot, cheer, and otherwise display
their opposition to the regime.[33] Often the crowd went further than that; the insurrection of 1832 began with the funeral of the popular General Lamarque. At the same
time, Frenchmen were busily forming secret societies for mutual aid and political
action. They seized whatever organizational means were at their disposal.

Two things are deceptive about French organizations: (1) they often form as off-
shoots of organizations already in existence – the Catholic church, the Communist
party, and so on; (2) while coherent and active, many of them do not quite acquire
formal, legal existence. Both conditions contribute to the illusion of under-organization

31 Maurice Agulhon, *La Sociabilité méridionale* (Aix-en-Provence: La Pensée Universitaire, 1966),
2 vols.
32 Robert T. Anderson and Barbara Gallatin Anderson, *Bus Stop for Paris* (Garden City: Doubleday,
1965), pp. 224-5.
33 Archives Nationales F^{1c}I 33, report of 20 July 1831.

in France. The state's long resistance to formally constituted voluntary associations of any kind, the consequent tendency to form such groups in the shadows, the consequent unwillingness of the state to collect and publish information on voluntary associations (even political parties) add to the illusion.

The long concentration of the French population in rural communities probably did slow the creation of autonomous voluntary associations. And Frenchmen probably are more loath to form *community-wide* associations, but more eager to form associations serving *particular interests,* than other people. Duncan MacRae points out that, while on the whole joining was less common in the France of the 1950s than in the United States, France differed little from Britain and Germany in that respect. Then he goes on to suggest that '... organizations that reinforced existing social divisions were more typical in France, while those that cut across other divisions and made decisions at the community level were more characteristic of the United States.[34] So the history we are reviewing is peculiarly a history of special-interest associations. From the later nineteenth century forward, craftsmen, students, teachers, winegrowers, farmers, big businessmen, veterans, professional women, and innumerable others devised new formal organizations to pursue their interests on a national scale.

THE CHANGING STRUGGLE FOR POWER

This vast series of change in French social structure reshaped the struggle for political power in three fundamental ways. First, position in the national structure of power came to matter far more, for practically every purpose, than local position did. Second, the struggle increasingly took the form of contention or coalition among formal organizations specialized in the pursuit of particular interests; communal groups virtually disappeared from politics. Third, new contenders for power emerged as the class structure and the organizational structure of France evolved. The rise of organizations speaking for segments of the industrial working class was the most important single movement, but other bids for power came from representatives of assorted groups of peasants, of youths, of schoolteachers, of Catholic employers, of government employers, of shopkeepers. Even when old established wielders of power like landholders and churchmen contended for power, they adopted the new associational style.

As in other Western countries, the political parties which emerged to full activity in Third Republic France compounded diverse interests. The Radicals, the Socialists and, for that matter, the Radical Socialists long represented curious melanges of the French electorate. As compared with her neighbours, nevertheless, France always had a remarkable susceptibility to party fragmentation, an exceptional openness to new parties representing new or old but separate political interests, a considerable tendency for parties to slim down to a single major interest. The Parti Ouvrier Français, the Parti Social Français, the Boulangists, the Christian Democrats, the Communists, the Poujadists represent different phases of this specialization of parties. Fragmentation was the normal condition of French parliaments, alliance among fragments the parliamentary

34 Duncan MacRae, Jr., *Parliament, Parties and Society in France, 1946-1958* (New York: St. Martin's, 1967), pp. 29-30. See also Orvoell R. Gallagher, 'Voluntary Associations in France,' *Social Forces,* 36 (December 1957), 153-60.

game. Genuine threats to the parliamentary system came less from this kind of splintering than from the occasional appearance of an important political force acting outside the parliamentary arena: the Ligue des Patriotes, the Croix de Feu, Algerian nationalists, sometimes the Gaullists or the Communists. Inside or outside parliament, the twentieth-century political struggle pitted associations representing relatively narrow segments of the population against each other, and aligned them with or against the regime. Interest-group politics emerged in France.

Our France, the France of 1830 and after, never stopped transforming herself. Our review of social change in France has pointed up spurts of industrialization, urbanization, and demographic transformation after 1850, after 1920 and, pre-eminently, after 1945; they contrast with crises and reversals at the times of the Franco-Prussian War, the two world wars and the depression of the 1930s. These are but ripples in a fast-flowing stream. An urban–industrial class structure built on liquid rather than landed wealth, separating owners and managers of large formal organizations (factories, governments, schools) from their employees, emphasizing position in the national labour market over local attachments, giving exceptional rewards to technical expertise, gradually emerged from a class structure based far more on land and locality; periods of urban-industrial growth accelerated this transformation of the class structure. The centralization of politics through the growth of a massive and powerful state apparatus continued trends already established centuries earlier, although the advent of Louis Napoleon after 1848 and the extension of controls over the economy in the 1940s speeded the process. The nationalization of politics through the shift of power and participation to an arena far larger than local went on more or less continuously, but the political mobilization of 1848, of the early Third Republic, of the Popular Front and of the years just after World War II probably drew men into involvement in national politics faster than at other times. The shift of collective action – both political and non-political – from communal to associational bases proceeded inexorably over the entire period, especially during those same periods of political mobilization. These changes transformed the struggle for power, and thus transformed the character of collective violence.

BACK TO VIOLENCE

How? Most immediately by changing the collective actions characteristically producing violence. Remember that group violence ordinarily grows out of collective actions which are not intrinsically violent - festivals, meetings, strikes, demonstrations, and so on. Without them, the collective violence could hardly occur. People who do not take part in them can hardly get involved in the violence. The groups engaging in collective action with any regularity usually consist of populations perceiving and pursuing a common set of interests. And collective action on any considerable scale requires co-ordination, communication, and solidarity extending beyond the moment of action itself. Now the urbanization and industrialization and political rearrangement of France from the Revolution onward utterly transformed the composition of the groups capable of collective action, their internal organization, their interests, their occasions for collective action, the nature of their opponents, and the quality of collective action itself. The transformation of collective action transformed violence.

Again, how? It is easy to illustrate and hard to analyse. The classic French tax rebellion, for example, took two forms, singly or in combination:

1 A group of taxpayers attacked the matériel of tax collection, typically by smashing toll gates and burning assessment records.

2 Many of the residents of a community greeted the tax collector by blocking his way, by beating him, or by running him out of town; if he brought an armed force, the villagers fought them.

A typical small version of the tax rebellion occurred at St. Germain (Haute-Vienne) in August 1830. The local tax collectors stopped a carter to check his load and collect their toll. A crowd of men, women, and children 'armed with picks and with stones' surrounded them, shouted against the tax, and led away man and wagon from the helpless revenue men.[35] This elementary form of resistance sometimes expanded into widespread and grave rebellion, as in the years before the Fronde, during the early Revolution, and (for the last time) in 1849. Although the sheer difficulty of paying when times were hard certainly had something to do with this common form of resistance to the state, it is important to see how regularly and directly it centred on the very *legitimacy* of the tax. Not long before the Revolution of 1830, the procureur general of the judicial district of Poitiers reported that 'seditious posters' had been appearing in the city of Fontenay (Vendée); 'the content of the posters is always to forbid the payment of taxes before the ministers who voted the budget are brought to trial.'[36] The same sort of campaign was gathering strength in other parts of France at the same time, and continued through the Revolution, often operating secretly and without violence, but now and then showing up in a public confrontation. The tax rebellion rose in the sixteenth century, flourished in the seventeenth, continued through the eighteenth into the nineteenth, recurred in 1789, 1830 or 1848 as new revolutionary officials sought to reimpose the state's authority; it vanished after 1849. Its history traced the government's long struggle to secure obedience and income.

Gabriel Ardant has identified the general conditions for waves of fiscal revolts in France: a sharp increase in the central government's demands for cash, a sharp decrease in the market for products of rural industry or agriculture (and hence in the ability of villagers to convert their surplus into cash) or, more serious still, both at once. He has also pointed to their clustering in areas of 'closed economy' – not necessarily poor, but little involved in production for the market, typically composed of largely self-sufficient farms. As he sums it up for the Massif Central:

The proportion of the population in agriculture remains relatively large. No doubt some industries have grown up in the Massif Central near the coalfields, but the coalfields themselves are less productive than those of the North and the East. Furthermore, the factories do not have the advantage of channels of communication comparable to the networks of rivers and canals in the North and the East. In any case, industries like agriculture are far from the important markets of the North, the East and the Parisian re-

35 Archives Nationales BB[18]1186, 14 August 1830.
36 Archives Nationales BB[18]1181, report of 3 February 1830.

gion. From all this comes a larger tendency than elsewhere to live in a closed economy. Thus we can explain that the regions of the Massif Central have been perpetual zones of fiscal rebellion, that movements like those of the Croquans have periodically reappeared in Limousin, Perigord and Quercy, that in 1848 and 1849 the resistance to taxation developed in these same provinces. In our own time the Poujadist movement started out from Haut-Quercy (now the department of Lot), and the first departments affected were the adjacent ones, the locales of fiscal sedition under the old regime.[37]

Tax revolts grouped together in time and space, largely because the changes in national policy which incited them affected many localities sharing common characteristics at more or less the same time. The largest nineteenth-century bursts of tax revolts came in 1830, when the officials of the new monarchy sought to reimpose taxes on the provinces, in 1841, when the new Minister of Finance tried a special census as a step to wards reorganizing the whole inequitable tax system, and – last and most – in 1848 and 1849, when another revolutionary government tried to put its fiscal affairs in order.

The tax rebellion often succeeded in the short run. The tax man fled, the toll gates fell. Its success, its timing, its personnel, its very form, however, depended on the solidarity of small, local groups of taxpayers and on the vulnerability of a system of control which relied on agents dispatched from cities into treacherous hinterlands. While Frenchmen have shrewdly finagled and dissimulated to avoid taxes up to our own day, their capacity for *collective* resistance to the tax collector sank fast after the middle of the nineteenth century. When anti-tax movements did revive with winegrowers after 1900, small distillers in the 1930s, or shopkeepers in the 1950s, the groups that joined the combat were no longer the taxpayers of a single commune, then of the next, but specialized regional and national associations responding to centralized direction. Marcelin Albert's Comité de Défense Viticole (in the first period), Henri Dorgére's Comités de Défense Paysanne (in the second), and Pierre Poujade's Union de Défense des Commerçants et Artisans (in the third) all adopted the defensive stance of earlier tax rebels, right down to their titles; all left violence aplenty in their wakes; but in these cases the defensive actions and the violence came after the deliberate, strenuous organization of protest groups through substantial sections of small-town France.

That comparison provides a necessary clue. Around the middle of the nineteenth century, the scale and organizational complexity of the collective actions normally producing violence – and hence of violent action itself – both increased rapidly and decisively. That happened for two related reasons: (1) the scale and organizational complexity of the groups already contending for power increased rapidly and decisively; the expanding organization of industrial workers in the most notable case; (2) communal groups dropped out of the struggle as the new associations, and new groups organized associationally, joined it. The organizational revolution reorganized violence.

There is something more, something the tax rebellion alone cannot reveal. Take the point of view of the state for a moment. From that perspective, the predominant forms of collective violence in France during the first half of the nineteenth century

37 Gabriel Ardant, *Théorie sociologique de l'impôt* (Paris: SEVPEN, 1965), II, 784.

were *defensive*: tax rebellions fending off state employees, food riots beating back outside merchants' attacks on machines repelling technical innovations. The demonstrations, strikes, and rebellions which grew in importance over the century had a much
larger *offensive* component; their participants reached for recognition, for a larger share,
for greater power.

The crux of the contrast is the relationship of the participants to organization at the
national scale: the national market, the national culture and, pre-eminently, the national state. In the earlier, defensive phase, most of the participants were *resisting* the
claims of national structures, especially the state; in the later, offensive phase, most of
the participants were bidding for power over the operation of those national structures.
In between, the nation won out.

We can be more exact. The nationalization of politics and economic life in France
actually divided the major forms of collective violence into three main categories, which
waxed and waned successively. The first we may call *primitive* collective violence. Primitive conflicts include the feud, the violent rivalries of adjoining villages, the recurrent
ritual brawls of competing groups of artisans. They are the most visible form of the constant contention among communal groups within small-scale, local political systems.
They predominated – at least in the statistical sense – in France before statemakers like
Mazarin and Colbert began pressing the claims of the national state and the national
economy over local commitments and resources.

That bitter struggle of the statemakers for control promoted defensive, resistant,
backward-looking conflicts between different groups of local people, on the one hand,
and agents of the nation, on the other. The word *reactionary* sums them up. The tax
rebellion, the food riot, violent resistance to conscription, machine-breaking, and invasions of enclosed land rose and fell in their own rhythms. They often occurred in the
course of transfers of power which our comfortable retrospect permits us to treat as
progressive revolutions. Yet they had in common a tendency to involve communal
groups jostled and outraged by the commotion of state-making.

The French state triumphed eventually over the major varieties of resistance to its
claims. From that point on, what we may call *modern* forms of collective violence predominated. The deliberate attempt to seize control of the state qualifies. So does the
demonstration, or the strike, which leads to a violent encounter. They differ from the
reactionary forms of collective violence in several important ways: in pivoting on attempts to control, rather than resist, different segments of the national structure; by
normally involving relatively complex special-purpose associations rather than communal groups; through a greater articulation of objectives, programs, and demands. These
characteristics imply further contrasts with reactionary conflicts. One is a lesser de-
pendency on natural congregations like markets, church services, and festivals in favour
of deliberate assemblies and shows of strength (since special-purpose associations rarely
draw all their members from the same round of life, but are often effective at calling
together a diverse membership at crucial moments). Another is a tendency of the disturbances to be large and short; communal groups, once committed to a conflict, rarely
mobilize large numbers of men, rarely have leaders with the authority to negotiate
quick compromise settlements, and rarely can call off the action rapidly and effectively;
associational groups, on the other hand, tend to become involved in violence as an out-

growth of brief, co-ordinated mass actions which are not intrinsically violent. Still another is a prevalence of indignation about the loss of specific rights and privileges in reactionary disturbances, as compared with a greater emphasis, in modern disturbances, on rights due on general principles.[38]

Two features of the shift from primitive to reactionary to modern forms of collective violence stand out: the change in *organization* of the participants, the change in *locus* of conflict. First, the groups taking part in collective violence became bigger, more complicated, more bureaucratized, more specifically committed to some public program or ideology, more open to new members prepared to support the group's special goals; earlier I called this a transfer from communal to associational bases for collective action. Second, the locus of the conflicts involved moved away from the purely local towards the national, and even the international, scale; although Frenchmen were already making national revolutions and demonstrating in support of Poland in 1830, the great bulk of the violent conflict of the time aligned essentially local issues; by the 1930s national issues and national antagonists took precedence. From a national perspective, this change seemed to involve a politicization of conflict. The trouble with that way of putting it is the fact that the primitive and reactionary forms of collective violence also grew out of well-developed struggles for power, out of political conflicts, on a smaller scale. The tax rebellion, the food riot, the invasion of fields and even the artisans' brawl pivoted on local questions of rights, duties, and power. For that reason, we would be better off speaking of a nationalization of conflict, integrally related to the nationalization of political life. In our own day we may have to speak of a further stage of internationalization.

It will not quite do, however, to picture primitive, reactionary, and modern collective violence as three distinct, exclusive stages. That image has two defects. First, some communal groups gradually acquire associational characteristics, and retain their capacity for collective action throughout the process; a city's traditional elite joins a national pressure group, a religious community becomes a corporation. During the transformation their characteristic *forms* of collective action, and thus of collective violence, change as well. Second, the modern forms of collective violence emerged early in those sectors of French society in which the national structures also emerged early: major cities, areas of advanced industry, the hinterland of Paris, and so on. At the centre of the centralized French system, men had already begun struggling for control of the state and the national market centuries before their brothers at the periphery stopped fighting the expansion of the state and the market.[39] The rapid nineteenth-century transition from predominantly reactionary to predominantly modern forms of collective violence resembled the movement from one terrain to another rather than the passage of a guarded frontier. We might imagine the statistical distribution shown in Figure 4.

---

38 I have discussed and documented these contrasts at much greater length in 'The Changing Place of Collective Violence' in Melvin Richter (ed.), *Social Theory and Social History* (Cambridge: Harvard University Press, forthcoming) and 'Collective Violence in European Perspective' in Hugh Davis Graham and Ted Robert Gurr (eds.), *Violence in America* (Washington: U.S. Government Printing Office, 1969), pp. 5-34.

39 Sylvia Thrupp has pointed out to me that the typology also leaves no place for the extraordinary role that simultaneously communal and associational groups of the type of sworn brotherhoods played in the collective violence of the European Middle Ages.

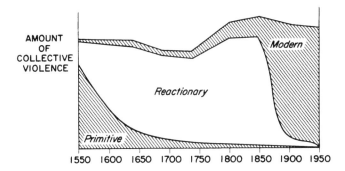

FIGURE 4 *Hypothetical evolution of collective violence in France*

In the absence of reasonable criteria for the amount of collective violence and of reasonable data for the period before the nineteenth century, the exact shapes of the curves represent nothing but informed speculation. The biggest speculation is that the volume of reactionary collective violence swelled rapidly during the heroic state-making of Louis XIII and Louis XIV; we know that popular rebellions of a reactionary form abounded at that time, but too little work has been done on conflicts well before and well after the Fronde to make the general timing sure. Figure 4 rests on a much firmer factual footing in illustrating that reactionary disturbances grew up to a nineteenth-century peak, instead of gradually diminishing.[40] The real point of the diagram, however, is to portray the slow displacement of primitive by reactionary collective violence as the French state extended its claims, and the rapid displacement of reactionary by modern collective violence during the nineteenth-century nationalization of the struggle for power. Only on the latter do we have much systematic information.

After the Revolution, the major periods of widespread collective violence in France were these: 1830-2, beginning with the antecedents of the July Revolution and ending with a great miscellany of rebellions touching the whole range of French politics; 1846-51, running from the last great round of food riots, through the February Revolution and the June Days of 1848, on past another mixture of tax rebellions, machine-breaking, and other conflicts, all the way to the angry, unavailing response to Louis Napoleon's coup; 1869-71, starting with massive, violent strikes and ending with the putting down of the Commune; 1934-7, with its great, rowdy demonstrations and strikes of all varieties; 1947-8, encompassing a wide range of postwar struggles for power; and, finally, the revolution (or coup, depending on your perspective) of 1958. The Chronology provides more details on the kinds of events making up each of these clusters of collective violence.

Several features of the calendar of violence deserve attention. First, the major bursts of violent conflict accompanied the largest realignments of the French political system, and vice versa; violence and political change depended on each other to an important

40 I have put considerable evidence on this point into 'How Protest Modernized in France, 1845-1855,' an unpublished paper presented to the Conference on the Application of Quantitative Methods to Political, Economic and Social History (University of Chicago, June 1969), of which a revised version is to be published in a volume edited by Robert Fogel.

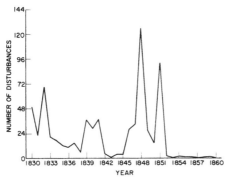

FIGURE 5 *Number of disturbances,*
1830-60

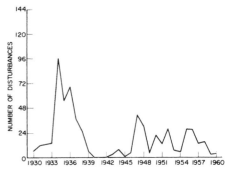

FIGURE 6 *Number of disturbances,*
1930-60

extent. Second, the surprising durability of the superficially unstable Third Republic from 1870 to 1940 shows up again in its relative freedom from major crises of violence except at its birth and death; the 1890s and the early 1900s were turbulent years, but their incidents did not cumulate like those of the 1840s or the 1930s. Third, there was no particular tendency for violent protests to concentrate during or after the principal surges of urban expansion or industrial growth; the calendar offers no support for the idea that the pace of urbanization and industrialization itself determines the amount of protest. Fourth, the turbulence of 1846-51 was the last in which reactionary collective violence played a large part; after that, the tax rebellion, food riot, machine-breaking, and similar events virtually disappeared. Fifth, despite all the fluctuations, France remained violent in the twentieth century, as she had been in the nineteenth; advanced industrialism did not bring domestic peace. To be sure, the transformations wrought by industrialization changed the contenders, the style of conflict, and the prizes to be gained in French politics. But the rhythm of collective violence itself depended very little on the timing of population movements, changes in the organization of work, or the introduction of technological innovations; it depended very much on the shifts in the struggle for political power.

Figures 5 and 6 offer a closer look at the fluctuations in collective violence in France over two thirty-year segments, 1830-60 and 1930-60. In this case, a disturbance is any event in which at least one group of fifty persons or more took a direct part in an action in the course of which some persons or property were damaged or seized over resistance; the figures represent the numbers of such disturbances encountered in a day-by-day reading of two national newspapers over the entire period.[41] (The average size and duration of disturbances is sufficiently constant from one year to the next to permit the making of general inferences about the total amount of time and numbers of persons involved from these curves.) More clearly than the simple chronology can, the curves bring out

41 Important qualification: the enumeration excludes acts of war with an external enemy, and thus distorts the actual level of violence in the territory of France during 1870 and 1940-44.

the wide contrast among adjacent blocks of years, the presence of some periods (especially periods of extensive repression like the 1850s) with almost no collective violence at all, and the rough correspondence of major bursts of collective violence with major crises of the French political system. They also show that, although 1848 topped every other year in this series, the massive strikes and demonstrations of the 1930s produced as large a set of violent incidents as any comparable segment of the nineteenth century. The postwar period was less turbulent in this respect than the 1930s, but far from calm. Collective violence did not trail away with modernization.

A ROUGH CHRONOLOGY OF
COLLECTIVE VIOLENCE IN FRANCE, 1830–1960

NOTE: This is neither a complete nor a representative list of incidents. It characterizes the violence of the most turbulent years, and mentions the largest *clusters* of disturbances. In fact, almost every single year produced at least a few violent incidents.

1830 After few, small, and scattered disturbances during the first half of the year, the July Revolution in Paris, with immediate repercussions in Nantes, Bordeaux, Toulouse, Nîmes, and a few other places; later, tax rebellions, food riots, workers' protests, and violent demonstrations through many parts of France

1831 Continuation of smaller disturbances, many attacks on machines (e.g. St. Etienne, Bordeaux, Toulouse), multiple violent demonstrations in Paris and a few other big cities, silk workers' insurrection in Lyon

1832 Major rebellions in Paris, minor ones in a number of other cities, food riots in the east and southwest, large Legitimist protests at several points in the south, and an even larger Legitimist insurrection through important parts of the west

1834 Amid the usual small disorders here and there, another silk workers' rebellion in Lyon, with significant responses in St. Etienne and Paris

1839–40 Frequent food riots, invasions of forests, several large conflicts in Paris, notably the abortive Insurrection of the Seasons (May 1839)

1841 Some tax rebellions and closely related resistance to the census, concentrated in the southwest

1846–7 Exceptionally widespread food riots and similar conflicts, in a great semicircle around Paris

1848 February Revolution (especially Paris, but with a much wider response elsewhere than in 1830), continued rioting and agitation up to the June Days; attacks on machines and railroads, resistance to tax collectors, anti-Semitic violence, attacks on convents and châteaux through many parts of France

1849–50 More tax rebellions (the Forty-Five Centime Revolt), forest disorders, and similar small-scale events, recurrent fighting between government forces and demonstrators, including one serious attempt at a coup, in Paris and a few other cities

1851 Armed resistance to Louis Napoleon's coup in almost a third of France's departments

1869-70 Major strikes, leading to battles with police and troops, most bloodily at St. Etienne and Aubin

1870-1 Insurrection in Alsace, revolution after the French defeat at Sedan beginning in Paris, with strong responses in Lyon and Marseille, further disturbances during and after the siege of Paris, followed by the Commune; similar but smaller rebellions in Marseille, Lyon, Toulouse, Limoges, Le Creusot, St. Etienne

1880 Numerous violent strikes

1891-4 Many violent strikes and much terrorism attributed to Anarchists, including the assassination of President Carnot in Lyon, 1894

1900-1 Turbulent, insurrectionary strikes in Belfort, Monteau-les-Mines, Marseille, and elsewhere

1906-7 Many violent strikes involving struggles with troops or retaliation against non-strikers and bosses; winegrowers' protests in the south

1911 More violent confrontations of strikers, non-strikers, owners, troops

1919-20 Attempted general strikes and national workers' demonstrations leading to fights with troops, police, other workers

1934-5 Large demonstrations of both Right and Left leading to frequent clashes among demonstrators, counter-demonstrators, and forces of order; attempted general strikes, violent meetings of peasant organizations

1936-7 Great sit-down strikes, clashes between adherents of political extremes, particularly Communists and extreme right-wing organizations

1944 Extensive Resistance activity, including a few large demonstrations and strikes

1947-8 Violent resistance to fiscal controls; frequent rioting and conflicts with police based on protest demonstrations and on meetings of political extremes; insurrectionary strikes, including the occupation of railroad stations and public buildings, throughout France

1950-2 Numerous clashes beginning with strikes, demonstrations or political meetings, focusing on French and American foreign policies (e.g. violent demonstrations against Eisenhower in 1951), coupled with bombings and other terrorism directed mainly against Communists

1955-6 Turbulent meetings, demonstrations, and street battles, featuring Poujadists and partisans of various policies in Algeria

1958 Coups in Algeria and Corsica, attempted coups elsewhere followed by street battles in Paris and other cities, eventuating in de Gaulle's coming to power

The curve of disturbances for the thirty-one years from 1830 through 1860 has three high points: 1832, 1848, and 1851. Historians do not conventionally treat 1832 as a major crisis, yet it produced collective violence running from an unsuccessful insurrection in Paris to tax and food riots in many regions to widespread guerrilla action in the counter-revolutionary west. We already recognize 1848 as a revolutionary year. Yet many of the year's disturbances were food riots, tax revolts, and similar events coming well after the February revolution and not belonging in any obvious way to the same action. The disturbances of 1851 occurred mainly in the course of the resistance to Louis Napoleon's *coup d'état*; 76 of the year's 92 disturbances came in December.

After that, under the watchful eye and iron fist of the imperial police, collective violence on any scale virtually disappeared from France for over a decade.[42]

World War II breaks the second three-decade period in half. That violent interlude appears calm in the graph because I have excluded acts of international war, and because most of the terror and counter-terror of Occupation and Resistance involved very small, if deadly, groups of men. The great years for open, violent confrontation were 1934 (a year of constant demonstrations and of street fights growing out of them) and 1947 (a year of massive, often insurrectionary, strikes). The largest series of disturbances actually run from 1934 to 1937, and again from 1947 to 1952. In the first period, Frenchmen were battling over the place of labour and its representatives in the structure of power. In the second, an even more complex struggle over the form, strength, composition, and policy of French government was raging.

Summing up for each decade, I estimate the total number of persons taking part in these disturbances as:

1830–9	300,000
1840–9	500,000
1850–60	100,000
1930–9	750,000
1940–9	250,000
1950–60	750,000

If these numbers are approximately accurate, they mean that the number of people taking part in collective violence rose substantially over the century of modernization. A breakdown of these totals appears in Table 1. The table uses statistics similar to those commonly employed in the reporting of strikes. They show the disturbance rate in most decades to have run around seven or eight per million population (while strikes in contemporary countries like France, Britain, or Italy tend to be four or five times as frequent. They also show a considerable rise in the mean number of participants, a drop in the mean days the average participant spent in a disturbance and, as a result, a fluctuation without trend in the total man-days spent in disturbances. With due allowance for the repeaters who returned for encounter after encounter, the figures make it appear possible that as many as one Frenchman out of a hundred took part in a collective action producing violence at some time during the average decade. If we took only adults, and only towns in which disturbances actually occurred, the figure would be more like one in twenty. In either case, a small minority, but not a negligible one.

The figures show that from the nineteenth to the twentieth century the typical disturbance became shorter, and bigger. As a consequence, the number of man-days absorbed by the average disturbance changed relatively little. To be sure, the decades

42 Comparisons of newspapers with major police series (notably BB[18] in the Archives Nationales indicate that some of the apparent damping of violence in the 1850s was due to reduced reporting of conflict in the press. A number of brawls between Piedmontese and French railroad workers, for example, escaped notice in the national papers, as did a substantial peasant rising in the Beauce in December 1854 (BB[18]1537). Nevertheless, the archives also register a huge drop in the frequency of collective violence after 1851, lasting well into the 1860s.

TABLE 1

The volume of collective violence in France, 1830-60 and 1930-60

Period	Number of disturbances	Disturbances per million population	Mean participants	Man-days per participant	Participants per million population	Man-days per million population
1830–1839	259	7.7	1,150	1.6	8,700	13,900
1840–1849	202	8.2	1,750	1.9	14,300	27,300
1850–1860	114	3.2	950	1.6	3,000	4,700
1930–1939	333	7.9	2,200	1.0	17,500	17,500
1940–1949	93	2.3	2,400	1.0	5,500	5,500
1950–1960	302	7.1	2,200	1.0	15,600	15,600

varied considerably in the number of disturbances, and therefore in the *total* man-days they brought into violent action. As a glance at the figures will show, the ten years from 1840 through 1849 produced the greatest volume of disturbances as measured by total man-days, but the 1930s produced a larger number of disturbances. The total energy flowing into collective violence and the kinds of particles in which the energy was emitted varied somewhat independently of each other.

We are actually dealing with two interlocking processes, one determining the shape of the typical disturbances, the other determining the frequency of disturbances. The long, slow process of association, the move from communal to associational bases for political action, lies behind the change in shape of the *typical* disturbance. In the 1830s, the typical disturbance (whether invasion of fields, tax rebellion, or food riot) would bring men, women, and children from the same small area out in anger for a day, and then another, and then perhaps still another. By the 1930s, the typical disturbance was the political party's one-day show of strength in a major city: a demonstration which often attracted determined counter-demonstrators, and frequently led to scuffles, or pitched battles, with the police. Associations came to be the important mobilizers of collective action, and thus the important participants in collective violence.

The other process affected the *number* of violent incidents at any particular time. It was (and is) a complex political process, governing, first, the occasions on which differ-ent contenders for power take collective action to assert their strength, defend their rights, or vent their anger and, second, the frequency with which such collective actions produce violence. The two questions are separate. A repressive government like that of Vichy holds down collective violence by making collective action of any sort difficult and costly. Whether repressive or not, a government faced with strikes, sit-ins, demon-strations, or other collective actions which, if illegal, are not intrinsically violent, has a considerable choice of tactics for dealing with them. Some tactics lead to frequent kill-ing and wounding.

On the other side, when new contenders for power are appearing or old ones are losing their places, the frequency of collective action rises; the possibility of violence rises with it. And as associations become more prominent in the struggle for power, the men who lead them gain a certain ability both to move their followers around and to calculate the probability that one action or another will lead to violence. They therefore acquire some of the same control over the frequency of violence that the state ordinarily possesses. So the number of disturbances at a given point in time is a function of the intensity of the political struggle and the tactics of the contenders.

A similar pair of interlocking processes – one organizational, the other broadly political – seems to have determined the evolution of strike activity in France.[43] From the 1880s, when the first really comprehensive data on strikes became available, to World War II, the mean strikers per strike rose irregularly from 200 to around 700. After remaining around five or six days for decades, on the other hand, the median duration fell precipitously to a single day some time during or after the massive unionization of the Popular Front. Strikes also became big, but short. The timing is different from that of the transformations of collective violence, but the processes are surely related. In both cases, complex organizations not only capable of mobilizing men for protest, but also fairly effective in demobilizing them once the issue is decided, assumed a larger and larger role in the preparation of encounters between contenders and the authorities. The *number* of strikes at any given time and place, on the other hand, has fluctuated enormously in response to the intensity of grievances and the negotiating tactics of both labour and management. Over the very long run, aggregate strike activity has risen enormously in France as the labour force has industrialized, but within the industrial labour force itself the rate has tended neither up nor down. Industrial conflict and collective violence have a lot in common. In both cases, the form of the individual conflict depends on the organization of the contenders, and changes with that organization, while the frequency of conflicts depends more directly on the give-and-take of the struggle for power.

There is also a rough parallel in timing between strike activity and collective violence.[44] The evidence on strikes is mixed. Before 1855 we have fragmentary reports on strikes and fuller reports of persons criminally charged with striking; from 1885 on we have relatively complete enumerations of strikes. From this evidence, the outstanding moments for strike activity were 1830-4, 1847-8, 1852-6(?), 1890-4, 1899-1912, 1919-20, 1936-8, and 1947-53, with the last period breaking all records for the sheer amount of time spent in strikes (see Figures 7 and 8). Those periods fit the calendar of disturbances to some extent. The flurry of criminal charges in the 1850s may be due to Louis Napoleon's clamping down at the beginning of his regime. The years before the Commune do not mark the statistics very heavily, but, in fact, there were great strikes in 1869 and 1870, centring on St. Etienne, Mulhouse, and Le Creusot, many of whose authors escaped prosecution. Tentatively, we may conclude that there has been some tendency for industrial conflict and collective violence to occur together; indeed, at times they have been indistinguishable from one another.

43 These statements summarize some of the findings of an analysis of strike activity conducted by Edward Shorter and myself at the University of Toronto, the first report of which appears in an as yet unpublished paper by Shorter and Tilly, 'The Shape of Strikes in France, 1830-1968' (University of Toronto, 1969).

44 Sources: François Simiand, *Le Salaire, l'évolution sociale et la monnaie* (Paris: Alcan, 1932), III; Jean-Pierre Aguet, *Les Grèves sous la Monarchie de Juillet (1830-1847)* (Geneva: Droz, 1954); Direction du Travail, *Statistique des grèves et des recours à la conciliation*, 1893-1936; Direction du Travail, *Notices et comptes rendus*, nos. 3 et 7, 1890-92; Ministère du Travail, *Bulletin*, 1937-9; I.N.S.E.E., *Annuaire statistique de la France, résumé rétrospectif, 1966*.

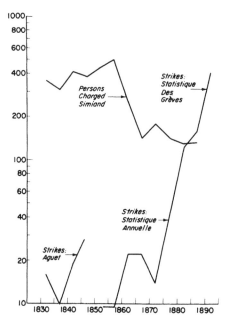

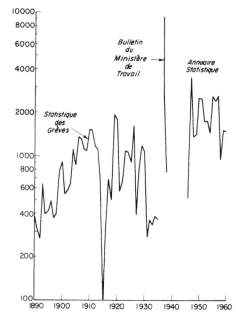

FIGURE 7 *Number of strikes and num-*
ber of persons charged for strike activity,
1825-94 (five-year sums)

FIGURE 8 *Number of strikes, 1890-1960*

However, it is *not* true that either strikes or collective violence ebbed and flowed in response to the pace of structural change. We might look back to the signs we have already inspected. The great periods of economic expansion in France came between 1855 and 1870, 1920 and 1930, 1945 and 1960; the first period started quiet and ended raucous, the second produced little violent protest after a turbulent first year, the third an alternation of insurrectionary years with merely disorderly ones. The years of substantial downswing and depression were roughly 1870 to 1875, 1914 to 1920, 1931 to 1945 (with some small relief just before the war). The first period began, of course, with one of France's great revolutionary moments; the second, after the external disorder and internal order of World War I, ended with nationwide protests; and the third might have been continuously turbulent if a brutal war had not diverted French attention both inward and outward from the national political arena. One might possibly argue a complex connection between economic *contraction* and protest, with the immediate proviso that war counteracts even that connection. But the interdependence between collective violence and the timing of economic growth is clearly very weak, very complicated, or both.

During the period before 1860 there was some small correspondence between price swings and collective violence, mainly due to the rise of food riots in years of high prices. Figure 9 presents two composite price series for the years 1825-60.[45] The score

45 Source: *Annuaire statistique de la France, résumé rétrospectif, 1966.*

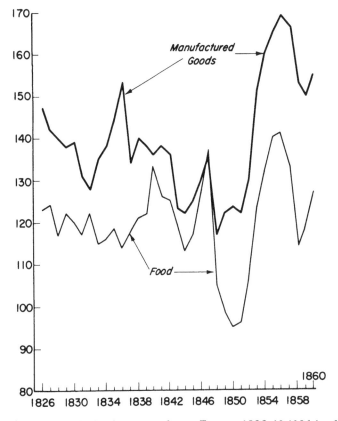

FIGURE 9 *Wholesale price indexes, France, 1825-60 (1914 = 100)*

is about fifty-fifty: the high prices of 1838-41 and 1846-7 did correspond to the secondary bursts of protest in those years, and the lower prices of the mid-30s and early 40s did coincide with periods of relative peace, but neither 1830 nor 1848 was an especially high-priced year, and the great leap upward in prices of the 1850s may have distressed many people, but it did not lead them into collective violence. (In fact, a last scattering of food riots occurred in 1853 and 1854, but they were small and few by comparison with 1847 or 1839.) In short, this comparison produces little more evidence of any straightforward determination of protest by economic fluctuation.

Since the timing of mechanization, of new industrial employment, of technical innovation, and even of urban growth followed approximately the same calendar as that of overall economic expansion, the conclusion is a more general one. If there is a connection between the pace of structural change and the frequency of violent conflict, it is not a direct, mechanical one. Fast social change does not, for all its bewilderments, incite disorder immediately or reliably. The relationship does not resemble that between the flushing of a toilet and the pulling of the handle. A better analogy might be the relationship between the performance of automobiles and the stamping of the dies used in making their parts: indelible but indirect.

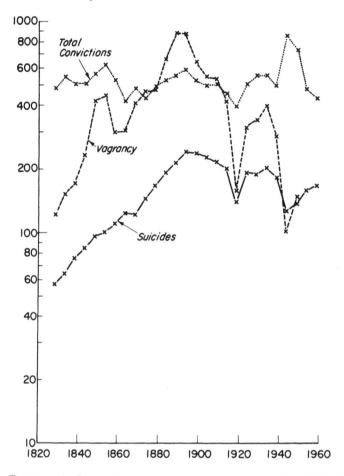

FIGURE 10 *Criminal convictions, vagrancy, and suicide, 1826-1960*

Of course, it could still be true that collective violence, as one type of disorder, appears with other signs of social disintegration, and thus reflects a general weakening of social cohesion and control. Do the variations of conventional indexes of social disorganization in France correspond to those of violent conflict? We can at least examine fluctuations in reported suicide and crime (Figure 10).

Since Emile Durkheim wrote his famous *Le Suicide,* sociologists have ordinarily been willing to accept the frequency of suicide as an indicator of the extent of social disintegration. France has long had an exceptionally high rate of suicide, a fact which seems to dovetail with her tendency to lapse into political chaos. But what of fluctuations in the reported rate?[46] During the nineteenth century, the rate of suicide marched inexo-

46 Sources: *Annuaire statistique de la France, Résumé rétrospectif, 1966.* Tables 4 and 5, pp. 124-7, Tables 3-9, pp. 161-6. Emile Levasseur, *La Population française* (Paris: Rousseau, 1889-93), II, p. 126. Maurice Halbwachs, *Les Causes du suicide* (Paris: Alcan, 1930), p. 92. 'Total convictions'

rably upward, almost heedless of political transformations; during the twentieth, it has been relatively steady, except for the declines in suicide at the times of the two world wars. The all-time peak in the rate came near 1890, about the time Durkheim began his study of the phenomenon. Since then, Frenchmen have destroyed themselves (or, at least, have been reported as destroying themselves, the incompleteness of suicide reporting being considerable) less often. At this level there is not detectable correspondence between suicide and collective violence. Does crime come closer?

Criminal statistics have some of the same weaknesses as suicide statistics. They ordinarily describe actions of the state – arrests, convictions, incarcerations, and so forth – rather than actions of its citizens. They therefore vary with the repressive powers and proclivities of the government. In the case at hand, the statistics include some of the direct responses of various French governments to political disturbances. In any case, the figures for total criminal convictions in France fit the temporal pattern of collective violence only a trifle better than the figures for suicide do. The maxima come around 1833, 1852, 1894, 1912, 1934, and 1942, which are at least in the vicinity of considerable clusters of violence. Their distribution might possibly justify the inference that repression tends to *follow* major upheaval, rather than that outbreaks of crime and political disturbances come together. However, the violent portions of the 1860s and 1870s were actually low points for criminal convictions, the turbulent period from 1944 to 1948 produced a significant decline in convictions, and the record crime levels of World War II surely had more to do with the repressive policies of Vichy and the Nazis than with any tendency for disorder to run rampant through France.

As for arrests for vagrancy, which one might expect to have some connection with the availability of insurrectionary masses, they did rise dramatically before 1848 and again before 1870, as well as less emphatically in the early 1930s. They reached their greatest height, on the other hand, around 1890, not the century's vintage year for violence. And they remained exceptionally low in the troubled years after World War II. So if there is a connection there, it is mediated and attenuated by other factors.

These negative conclusions clear the way for an assessment of the actual connections between modernization and changes in the character of conflict in France. The assessment must take the form of an argument – incompletely documented, but generally consistent with the evidence already reviewed. First, the conglomerate changes thrown together in the bin labelled 'modernization' had no uniform effects whatsoever on the level, locus, form, or timing of political conflict in France, although some of the processes that observers ordinarily have in mind when using the sweeping term did have some well-defined effects. Second, rapid urbanization and industrialization alike generally depressed the level of conflict in the short run, because they destroyed various contenders' means and bases of collective action faster than they created new ones. Peasants who moved to cities, for example, ordinarily left settings in which they were sufficiently organized and aware of common interests to throw up repeated resistance

sums convictions in Cours d'assises, Tribunaux correctionnels and (after 1952), Cours d'appel; the figure is an annual average rate per 100,000 population over the five-year interval centring on the date shown. 'Vagrancy' represents arrests for *mendicité* and *vagabondage*; it is also an annual average rate per 100,000 population over the same five-year intervals. 'Suicide' is reported cause of death, calculated as an annual average rate per 10,000 population over the same five-year intervals.

to taxers, drafters, and grain-buyers; in the industrial city it commonly took them and their children a full generation to form the new organization and the new consciousness essential to renewed collective action. Third, urbanization and industrialization, nevertheless, directly stimulated political conflict when they diverted resources and control over resources from established groups which retained their internal organization; food rioters fighting the shipment of grain from their villages to cities, and urban craftsmen fighting the threat of mechanization are two cases in point. When these changes proceeded faster than the dissolution of existing organization (which appears to have been the case in the 1840s, for example) the effect was actually to raise the level of group conflict. Fourth, the emergence of industrial capitalism, the development of a class structure organized around relations to a national market and the means of industrial production, the rise of bureaucracies and other formal organizations as the principal means of accomplishing collective ends combined to transform both the identities and the interests of the major contenders for power, and the form of their concerted action as well. Since conflict, including violent conflict, grows out of concerted action, the transformation of the contenders transformed the nature of contention in France. That series of transformations has occupied most of this paper's attention.

But what determined how *much* conflict there was? In those general terms, my inquiry into the French experience has produced no answer at all; without firmer establishing of types of conflict, and equivalencies among them, there is no way to rule out the possibility that conflict is constant in human life, and that only its visage is variable. If we restrict our attention to the public, collective forms of conflict which commonly lead to violence, however, then we can see how much their frequency and outcome depends on the operation of the state.[47] The nineteenth-century centralization and nationalization of politics, as the state crushed its local rivals, incited widespread protest and durably shifted the focus of violent conflict. State repression of collective action by contenders for power diminished the frequency of violent conflicts during the 1850s and the two world wars, whereas the relaxation of that repression in the 1860s or the later 1940s permitted the contention to come back into the open. Throughout the two centuries, the state resisted the bids of new contenders for power in the name of those who already had established places in the structure of power; the tactics selected by the agents of the state (for example, in controlling hostile demonstrations) strongly determined the extent of violence. As a consequence, new contenders for power tended to pass through a cycle going from quiet organization to violent contention to conquest of a position within the structure of power to involvement in violence mainly through the proxies of police and soldiers. Enough new contenders came along, however, and enough of them were rebuffed to keep the level of violence high. Today, students, intellectuals, and technical workers seem to be hammering at the gates.

Samuel Huntington has interpreted part of this experience as a nineteenth-century peculiarity:

47 The argument to follow resembles in many respects that laid out by William Gamson in 'Stable Unrepresentation in American Society,' *American Behavioral Scientist,* 12 (November–December 1968), 15-21.

In the nineteenth century in Europe and America industrial labor was radical and at times revolutionary because industrialization preceded unionization, the dominant groups in society often vigorously opposed unions, and employers and governments did what they could to resist the demands of labor for higher pay, shorter hours, better working conditions, unemployment insurance, pensions, and other social benefits. In these countries, the mobilization of labor easily outran the organization of labor, and consequently radical and extremist movements often gained support among the alienated working class before unions became strong. When unions were organized they were of this new class. Communist and other radical groups were strongest in labor movements which were denied legitimacy and recognition by the political and economic elites ... All these conditions are much less prevalent among countries industrializing later.[48]

The experience of France does not support the contention that 'the mobilization of labor easily outran the organization of labor.' Mobilization actually came as a consequence of organization. The French experience does, on the other hand, fit Huntington's implicit argument that recognition and legitimation diminish a contender's involvement in violent conflict. In his argument, Huntington stresses the mollifying effect of (a) legitimate means for the expression of demands and grievances, (b) the direct control which 'institutionalization' gives governments over contenders. There is more to it than that. I would say it is also because recognition opens up new means to the accomplishment of the contender's ends, because recognition brings with it some control over the state's existing resources, because recognition tends to commit the leaders to the maintenance of the structure they have entered, because recognition was part of what they were seeking in the first place, and because recognition restrains the state's repressive agents from reacting violently to the new contender's displays of strength.

QUESTION: is this a peculiarity of the nineteenth century, or of France alone? The peculiarity, it seems to me, resides in the greater readiness of the twentieth century's new states to pre-empt, co-opt, and even stimulate organization among emerging contenders for power as a means of keeping them under control.[49] As it happens, the new

48 Samuel P. Huntington, *Political Order in Changing Societies* (New Haven: Yale University Press, 1968), p. 284.

49 In this connection, it is interesting to note that by far the most powerful factor in Ted Gurr's analysis of civil strife in 114 polities, 1961-5, was 'social and structural facilitation,' which combines measures of internal geographic accessibility, legitimacy of the Communist party, and the extent of external support for the initiators of strife (the first two being negatively related to the extent of strife, the third positively related to it), and most of the other significant variables have to do with the relations between the state and its citizenry, rather than, say, the extent of economic hardship or the prevalence of religious barriers within the population. As proportions of the total variance explained, the factors are: persisting deprivation 24%, short-term deprivation 12%, 'institutionalization' (which really has to do with the representation of interests within the polity) 1%, legitimacy 11%, coercive potential 4%, social and structural facilitation 48%. Ted Gurr, 'A Causal Model of Civil Strife: A Comparative Analysis Using New Indices,' *American Political Science Review*, 62 (December 1968), 1104-24. See also his 'A Comparative Study of Civil Strife,' in Hugh Davis Graham and Ted Robert Gurr (eds.), *Violence in America* (Washington: U.S. Government Printing Office, 1969), II, pp. 443-95.

states often fail, and violent conflict is widespread among them. The underlying processes producing collective violence in those countries have much in common with those at work in nineteenth-century France.

In the twentieth century as well, France's collective violence shares a number of traits with the collective violence of other industrial countries. It probably shares causes as well. For example, the nearly simultaneous swelling of separatist movements, student protests, and other strident demands for autonomy and release from state control in a wide variety of Western countries, including France, probably tells us that both individually and collectively they are undergoing similar political transformations. Marshall McLuhan, in an interview for a popular magazine, made an interesting stab at analysis:

PLAYBOY: On what do you base your prediction that the United States will disintegrate?
McLUHAN: Actually, in this case as in most of my work, I'm 'predicting' what has already happened and merely extrapolating a current process to its logical conclusion. The Balkanization of the United States as a continental political structure has been going on for some years now, and racial chaos is merely one of several catalysts for change. This isn't a peculiarly American phenomenon; as I pointed out earlier, the electric media always produce psychically integrating and socially decentralizing effects, and this affects not only political institutions within the existing state but the national entities themselves.

All over the world, we can see how the electric media are stimulating the rise of ministates: in Great Britain, Welsh and Scottish nationalism are recrudescing powerfully; in Spain, the Basques are demanding autonomy; in Belgium, the Flemings insist on separation from the Walloons; in my own country, the *Québecois* are in the first stages of a war of independence; and in Africa, we've witnessed the germination of several ministates and the collapse of several ambitiously unrealistic schemes for regional confederation. These ministates are just the opposite of the traditional centralizing nationalisms of the past that forged within one national boundary. The new ministates are decentralized tribal agglomerates of those same ethnic and linguistic groups. Though their creation may be accompanied by violence, they will not remain hostile or competitive armed camps but will eventually discover that their tribal bonds transcend their differences and will thereafter live in harmony and cultural cross-fertilization with one another.[50]

I beg leave to doubt that 'the electric media' lie behind the new minification. I lack McLuhan's confidence in a harmonious future. I miss, in this statement, some sense of the prevalence of communal, autonomist longings *outside* the traditional ethnic and linguistic groups. Yet the notion that the domestic troubles of our own time depend in an important way on a realignment of the international structure of politics – and, more exactly, on the national state's loss of power and autonomy – strikes me as worth serious consideration. Perhaps the emergence of huge blocs of states like those dominated by the United States or the Soviet Union, and those which show some signs of forming in Europe and around China reduces the room for manoeuvre of the men who

50 'Playboy Interview: Marshall McLuhan,' *Playboy* (March 1969), 68.

run any particular state, and thus simultaneously diminishes the value of membership in the national political system and encourages those who have their strongest invest-ment in some smaller unit to throw off the weight of the state. If so, a new transforma-tion in the character of political conflict is occurring. And, as before, the transformation nonetheless continues processes of change which began long before. That such a trans-formation should occur by no means follows ineluctably from the logic of this paper's argument. But it is the *kind* of transformation we have been discussing.

Ultimately, to be sure, much of the argument comes down to an awesome tautology. Political conflict changes as a consequence of changes in the political system. Since 'the political system' is itself a name for the regularities in a series of conflicts and reso-lutions of conflict, the proposition comes close to reading: political conflict changes as a consequence of changes in political conflict. That apparently self-defeating result has more value than is evident. It calls attention to the intimate dependence on central po-litical processes of protest, riots, and movements (like machine-breaking and tax rebel-lions) which have frequently been considered non-political and have commonly been portrayed as direct responses to the strains of economic change. It points up the con-tinuity between the violent and non-violent forms of political contention. It opens the way to the examination of the effects of different forms and degrees of state control of collective action on the character of political conflict, including the most violent forms of conflict. It finally leads to reconsideration of a crucial question barely raised in this paper: how does the nature of the conflict affect the distribution, or redistribu-tion, of power?

For men articulate, advertise, and sometimes achieve their interests through conflict. That includes violent conflict. Ordinary Frenchmen, by rioting, force the authorities to hold down the price of bread. The great demonstrations and sit-down strikes of the 1930s did solidify the place of organized labour in the structure of power. Mass action did help produce significant transfers of power in 1789, 1830, 1848, 1870, and 1958. The use of the special word Revolution for most of these dates should not obscure the fact that the collective action involved in the events shared the characteristics of the much larger number of collective actions of their own eras which did *not* produce transfers of power. The great bulk of the actions we now sum up as the Revolution of 1789 were, in fact, food riots, tax rebellions, and similar conflicts of exactly the same variety as prevailed in France for a century before 1789 and another half-century after then. The continuities are so great as to indicate that those theorists of revolution who ask themselves how so rare a collective action as revolution could come about are chasing a will-o'the-wisp. What we call revolutions in retrospect are whole chains of collective actions, many of them at cross-purposes. In the French experience, at least, they deeply resembled other collective actions far removed from revolution. The real question is why only a few of a large number of similar actions result in transfers of power.

Barrington Moore, Jr., has theorized that the main conditions for revolution are:

1 the development of a widespread challenge to prevailing modes of thought and to the predominant explanations or justifications of human suffering;
2 the emergence of acute conflicts of interest within the dominant classes;
3 the elite's loss of unified control over army, police, and other instruments of violence;

4 the mobilization of a revolutionary mass either from the urban plebs or (more likely) the peasantry, which is most likely to occur with 'a sudden increase in hardship coming on top of quite serious deprivations, together with the breakdown of the routines of daily life - getting food, going to work, etc. - that tie people to the prevailing order.'[51]

The first three conditions have to do mainly with elite control over the political apparatus and its justifications; only the fourth refers directly to mass action. Moore distinguishes sharply (and, I believe, rightly) between the conditions under which regimes are vulnerable and the conditions under which ordinary men act against regimes. Only the convergence of the two makes revolution likely. Here I have dealt almost entirely with the second sort of question: the conditions for mass action. At best that amounts to only half the problem of accounting for 1789, 1848, or 1958.

If my analysis is correct, the immediate stresses and strains of technological changes, population movements, and other such components of 'modernization' play a rather small part in the promotion of collective action. Nor does material hardship as such, or even the sudden increase of material hardship, seem to have had a primary role in France. The crucial exception is that when (as in the standard food riot) someone else appears to be creating or profiting by the new hardship and doing so through violations of his own duties and other people's rights, ordinary men often strike at the presumed profiteers in the name of justice. But it is justice - and conflicting conceptions of justice, at that - which is at the heart of violent conflict. That means violent conflict remains close to politics in origin as well as in impact. In that respect, France resembles other European nations.

Nonetheless, France has a particular history, and that history affects her political conflicts. The foundation of all her modern regimes on one version or another of a revolutionary tradition has, paradoxically, justified the government's taking on of exceptional powers when it could declare *la patrie en danger.* That has probably produced greater fluctuations in repression, and sharper distinctions between 'ins' and 'outs' in times of repression, in France than in most other Western countries. Likewise, the enormous centralization of power within the French system has probably defined more different kinds of struggles in France than elsewhere as confrontations between the state and its enemies - and as struggles the state could not afford to lose. Before broadcasting conclusions from French political history throughout the world, we must begin to treat these two features, the presence or absence of a revolutionary tradition and the degree of centralization of power, as major variables. That done, we have much to learn about modernization in general from the modernization of political conflict in France.

In the France of the last two centuries, political conflict did modernize, in the sense of shifting towards larger-scale, more highly organized forms of collective action. The changing relations of Frenchmen to a state which over at least half that period was increasing its hold over their everyday lives set one of the major rhythms: the change

51 Barrington Moore, Jr., 'Revolution in America?' *New York Review,* 30 January 1969, 6-12. Moore draws one conclusion which runs counter to the general argument of this paper: 'Though the influence of prior forms of social organization, pre-existing habits, and general outlook is a topic that requires further investigation, I have come to suspect that it too plays a much less important role than immediate circumstances in creating a revolutionary mass.' *Ibid.,* 8.

from primitive to reactionary to modern forms of collective violence. At the same time, men's everyday organization for collective action changed slowly as France urbanized and industrialized; the reorganization of everyday life transformed the character of collective conflict; that long-run reshaping of solidarities, rather than the immediate production of stress and strain, constituted the most important impact of structural change on political conflict. In the shorter run, the state's tactics of repression and accommodation strongly affected the intensity, form, locus, and outcome of conflict. Throughout the two centuries, the struggle to acquire or maintain established places in the structure of power, and thus to gain control over the conditions of their own existence, most regularly brought different groups of Frenchmen into violent conflict with one another. Even in modern France, the struggle continues.

S.D. CLARK

Rural migration and
patterns of urban growth

In this paper I want to pursue the topic of suburban society. As cities grow, they push outwards from the centre. The country is made into the city in the process of transformation of the whole urban area.

There is a large literature in sociology dealing with the general pattern of urban growth and development. There is no need here to make any detailed reference to it. What does need mention is the fact that much of this literature reflects the North American experience of urban development as it took place in the early years of the twentieth century. North American cities grew in those years largely by recruiting an immigrant population from overseas. The entrepreneurial skills and capital required for the urban economy were provided by the local population. The overseas immigrant provided the much needed work force. In this manner, such cities in Canada as Montreal, Toronto, Hamilton, Windsor, and Winnipeg developed as important industrial centres in the years after the turn of the century. New cities, growing out of the industrial development of the north after 1920, for example, Sudbury, Timmins, Kapuskasing, Noranda, and Dolbeau, became even more dependent, in the early years of their growth, upon overseas immigration for their work force.

Growth of the city through the recruitment of an immigrant population resulted in that pattern of development made so familiar by the sociological literature. The immigrant from Europe crowded into the central areas of the city. It was here he could most readily maintain his ethnic associations, and secure, momentarily, shelter from the disruptive influences of the urban environment. What the European immigrant, in effect, re-created in the very heart of the North American city was the village society he had left in his homeland. The shifting land-use patterns of the downtown urban area offered the opportunity for the immigrant to build a non-urban-type society within the enclaves of a highly urbanized area.

Numerous sociological studies of ethnic colonies in North American cities attest to the stability of the society the immigrant built for himself. Herbert Gans's urban villagers, Italians located in central Boston, could maintain their ethnic heritage for a considerable time, protected from urban influences.

Yet the very location of these ethnic colonies made their eventual disintegration inevitable in the growing city. The downtown urban area is truly a transitional area. Its inherent character as a downtown area denies survival to any form of occupation. The immigrant was attracted by this transitional character and consequently was ultimately and inevitably pushed out. In being pushed out, he was pushed up.

Thus have been joined together in the sociological literature the two processes of ecological growth outwards and assimilation. Urbanization has been made to mean the continuous spreading out of the urban community from its centre and the continuous assimilation of the population to an urban way of life. The downtown urban area, by its very nature became a melting pot. Looked at from this vantage point, the most urban elements of the population appeared to be those residing farthest from the centre of the city. Movement of the population from the central areas of the urban community to the suburbs involved, or so it seemed, a rise in the social hierarchy from lower class to middle class and a shift from the values of a non-urban ethnic culture to those of an urban society. In such a conception of the process of urbanization, the suburban society has been made to represent the fully urban society. Here those barriers to social movement which operate in the older areas of the city to preserve cultural differences tend to break down almost completely. In moving out of the city, the suburban resident becomes possessed of all the attributes of mobility of the completely urban man.

In this conception of the process of urbanization, however, the question may be raised whether sufficient account has been taken of the patterns of settlement of all the various types of people who have found their way into the city. In the Canadian city, for instance, the immigrant from the United Kingdom located himself in a manner very different from that of the immigrant from the continent of Europe. In the years between 1900 and 1940, heavy concentrations of British immigrants were to be found in such outlying residential areas of Toronto as Riverdale, across the Don River from the city, and in York Township, beyond the city's borders. Such areas assumed very much the character of working-class districts and could be explained ecologically in these terms. But it would appear evident that it was not solely the working-class character of the population that determined its location. It was also due to its origin in the United Kingdom.[1] In coming to Canada, the British immigrant had no feeling of settling in a strange land. Therefore, in his search for cheap living space, he tended to settle on the outer edges of the city rather than in the downtown area. The result was that he could remain undisturbed in his place of residence for a great number of years, despite urban growth. As late as World War II, a substantial part of the population of Riverdale and York Township consisted of the original settlers of these areas, immigrants from the United Kingdom.

To what extent this pattern of settlement retarded the 'assimilation' of the British immigrant into Canadian urban society is not our concern here. What is of interest is the fact that the British immigrant did not locate in the Canadian urban community in the manner of the immigrant from continental Europe. In considering the effect

1 The immigrant from the United Kingdom had, of course, a socio-economic background different from that of the immigrant from Europe, particularly from eastern and southern Europe. He came from urban centres in Britain, and brought with him the skills required to enter factory or clerical employment.

upon urban development, it has been the settlement of non-English speaking immigrants which has attracted most attention. Yet in the development of the Canadian city in the early 1900s, the British immigrant figured much more prominently than did the immigrant from the continent of Europe.

If little regard has been paid to the British immigrant, even less regard has been paid to the rural migrant to the city. Much has been written, it is true, about rural–urban migration, but these writings relate more to the migration of people out of rural areas and the effect of that migration upon the rural society than upon the migration of rural people into urban areas and the effect upon the urban society. In the case of the European immigrant, in contrast, the concern has been with his movement into the urban community. The reason for this difference in emphasis is not hard to understand. The European immigrant can be readily identified, and his movement into the city and from one part of the city to another examined without great difficulty. He shows up in the census, if not in wholly accurate fashion. But the rural migrant, once he leaves the rural community, is almost wholly lost to view. Once he has settled in the city, his numbers can be determined only in the roughest way. There is no way of determining from the census where he locates in the city, or where he moves after he locates there. No population figures of an urban census tract will reveal his existence.

It is our contention that the concentration upon the settlement of the European immigrant in the urban community, to the neglect of the settlement of the rural migrant, has led to an undue emphasis upon the pattern of development of the urban community from the centre outwards and thus to an exaggeration of the process of urbanization. The migrant from the farm does not locate in a colony near the centre of the city, in contrast to the immigrant from outside the country. Rather, he seeks to locate wherever in the urban community he can find accommodation he can afford, without regard to whether he will have fellow 'countrymen' as his neighbours. Very often, and especially if cheap accommodation must be found, he locates beyond the city's borders, in areas not yet built up.

This has always been the course followed by the rural migrant to the city, but until recent years such migration has not been important in the development of our cities. It is only when we turn to other parts of the world - Egypt, India, Venezuela, or Japan, for instance - that the effects of rural migration upon the past development of urban communities can be seen clearly. There, cities have tended to develop by the process of forming, on their outskirts, what have the appearance of rural towns or villages. The urban community assumes the shape of a string of rural villages bordering on one another. The original city constitutes the urban centre, but there is no discernible pattern of development from this centre outwards. The process of urbanization here takes on a very different meaning.

In Canada, with its large numbers of immigrants from Europe in the years since World War II, attention has continued to focus upon the manner in which the newcomer locates in the central areas of the urban community and the old resident moves to the outskirts. The central city of Toronto, in comparison with the neighbouring municipalities, has changed in the past quarter century from a community with a population predominantly Anglo-Saxon in origin to one with a population predominantly non-Anglo-Saxon. Yet the great urban growth that has taken place in Canada in recent years is due as much to rural–urban migration as to European immigration, and sociological analysis of the pattern of urban development must take account of how the rural migrant, as well as the European immigrant, has fitted himself into the urban community.

Where the movement of population has been from prosperous farm communities or small towns, the impact upon the urban society has not been great. A middle-class population moving out of rural areas joins readily a middle-class population moving out of the city into the suburbs. Indeed, to a very large extent, this movement has been one of young people trained for urban occupations. Farm families, as such, where agriculture is a prospering industry, do not move out of rural into urban areas. The Canadian city, in contrast with a city like Caracas in Venezuela or Calcutta in India, could grow by drawing upon a large reservoir of young people from farm communities where economic conditions are such as to make possible their being equipped with the skills to make their way in an urban working world.

Not all rural–urban migration in Canada, however, has involved the movement of population out of prospering rural areas. Increasingly, in the years since World War II, the movement has been out of economically and socially depressed farm and fishing areas of the country, in Newfoundland, eastern Nova Scotia and New Brunswick, Northern Ontario and Quebec, north-central Manitoba, northern Saskatchewan and Alberta, and various other parts of the country where there are small pockets of countryside unsuited for farming but which in early days were occupied by a farming population. Among the migrants from such areas have been many young people, denied in the occupation of farming or fishing opportunities for economic advancement, large numbers of families as well. It is the effect of this migration upon the development of the urban community that is the primary concern of this paper.

This effect can be seen most clearly in the way in which the northern industrial cities of Ontario and Quebec have developed. These cities grew in their early years by the recruitment of a work force from overseas. By the end of the nineteen twenties large immigrant populations were to be found in Sudbury, Timmins, Noranda, and other northern cities. In characteristic fashion, this immigrant population located in the central areas of each community.

The growth of these communities in the years after 1930 might have been expected to follow the normal pattern. To some extent it did. There was a pressing out from the central area, a penetration of the outer borders of the community by the upper income groups of the population. But this pattern was only barely perceptible. The very great growth that took place after 1930 led not to an extension outwards of the boundaries of the established community but rather to the creation of whole new communities outside the existing one. Thus Rouyn developed outside Noranda; Mistassini outside Dolbeau; Brunetville and Val Albert, as well as Moonbeam and Fauquier, outside Kapuskasing, and a community not so clearly identifiable stretching into Mountjoy Township outside the old boundaries of Timmins.

What happened in the development of these northern industrial communities was a shift from the recruitment of an immigrant population from overseas to the recruitment of a population from those farm areas of Northern Ontario and Quebec which had been opened up for settlement after the turn of the century. It is not possible here to examine in detail the nature of this movement of population into the northern industrial community. Census figures indicating the number of abandoned farms in large areas of the north, and the decline in the number of farms, tell part of the story. Already, by 1941, as reported by the census, there were 513 abandoned farms in Abitibi, 269 in Lake St. John East and West, 1,130 in Cochrane, 172 in the Quebec census division of Timiskaming, 286 in the Ontario census division of the same name, 255 in Chicoutimi, and 439 in Sudbury. Between 1941 and 1961, in spite of the fact that new farm settlement continued until the mid nineteen fifties, the total number of operating farms in Abitibi declined from 7,317 to 3,439, in Cochrane from 3,000 to 900, and in Lake St. John West from 3,118 to 2,008. There was, after 1941, a massive shift of population out of the farm areas of the north.

A very large part of this population settled in the industrial communities of the north, and started steadily to replace the European immigrant population as the main source of labour. In Timmins, for instance, in 1941, the immigrant population totalled 5,831, but of this total 3,100 had entered the country in the 1921–31 period. Only 808 immigrants arrived in Timmins between 1931 and 1941. Yet in these ten years the population of Timmins grew from 14,200 to 28,790. In the other industrial communities of the north the change in the composition of the population was equally striking. It can be measured most readily by the increase in the proportion of French-speaking people. As the development of the north took place, the industrial centres had come to be occupied by a population predominantly non-French, while the rural areas in both Northern Ontario and northern Quebec had been settled by a population overwhelmingly of French origin. Thus Noranda, for instance, located in the centre of a large farming area wholly settled by French-speaking people, had a population in 1931 only 23 per cent of which was French-speaking. By 1961, its French-speaking population comprised 60 per cent of the whole.

It was not, however, within the borders of the industrial community of the north but outside these borders that the great increase in the proportion of French-speaking population took place. Noranda, growing from a population of 2,246 in 1931 to 11,477 in 1961, showed a rise in its French-speaking population from 513 to 6,907. During these same years, immediately adjacent to Noranda, the community of Rouyn grew from 3,225, 57 per cent French-speaking, to 18,716, 90 per cent French-speaking. Much the same pattern of development occurred in Kapuskasing, where the large increase in population after 1941 came outside the town's borders through the development of new communities predominantly French-speaking. Brunetville and Val Albert, and, farther out, Moonbeam and Fauquier, in 1961 had a population dependent almost wholly upon employment with the Spruce Falls Pulp and Paper Company of Kapuskasing, and this population, larger than that of Kapuskasing itself, was almost wholly of farm background.

There were special factors in the development of the industrial community of the north which favoured the settlement of new population groups outside the community's borders. The northern industrial community developed largely as a company town. It was a community which from its beginning was almost wholly planned. Developments within the community's borders were rigidly controlled, particularly in the case of such industrial centres as Kapuskasing. There was here, as a consequence, no large deteriorating area in the central parts of the community where, because of its transitional character, cheap housing was available for newcomers to the city. On the other hand, land in the surrounding areas had very little value, and, with rough lumber readily available, it was easy for those farm families moving into the industrial community to provide themselves with the necessary housing outside the central core. The skills required for house-building were the skills acquired on the farm. Thus there could develop in the north, in a way not possible in older Canadian urban communities, large and heavily populated shack-town communities outside the industrial centre, housing a population very largely of rural origin.

But the factors which favoured this settlement in the north of new population groups outside the community's borders were not wholly absent in the development of our older urban centres, particularly in the years immediately after World War II. Outside most Canadian cities, scattered here and there, were to be found, up to at least the end of the nineteen fifties, pockets of land which, while unsuitable for agricultural purposes, were not favourably located for middle-class residential development. Here cheap land could be obtained for cottage-type housing developments. It was not the fact that pockets of cheap land existed beyond the borders of the urban community, however, that accounted solely for this type of residential development. It is noteworthy that the large immigrant populations which moved into the industrial communities of the north in the early years of their development did not locate on the community's outskirts. What changed the pattern of development of the northern industrial community was the shift from the recruitment of an immigrant population to the recruitment of a population from the surrounding poor farm areas. It would appear that many of the residential developments beyond the borders of our old established urban communities also resulted from the movement of population into the urban community from poor farm areas beyond.

This is a fact not easy to document with respect, for instance, to such a city as Toronto. The census will reveal, with respect to the changing population structure of the Toronto community in the years after World War II, that the farther one moved out from the centre of the city the more predominantly did the population show an Anglo-Saxon and Protestant background. The stereotype of suburbia as an area housing the old settled middle-class elements of the urban population, Anglo-Saxon and Protestant, appeared amply confirmed by the census data. But the census data did not tell the whole story. It was, indeed, a predominantly Anglo-Saxon and Protestant population that moved out from the city to the suburbs, but it was also, in the case of a city like Toronto, a predominantly Anglo-Saxon and Protestant population that moved out of poor farm areas into the urban community.

It is only thus by a detailed examination that it is possible to determine where in fact the population of the suburbs came from, whether out of the older settled areas of the city or the country. A comparison of two residential areas outside Toronto, Thorncrest Village and Riverdrive Park, reveals strikingly the differences in the background of two population groups, both of which were suburban and both of which were predominantly Anglo-Saxon and Protestant. All the residents of Thorncrest Village were people who had moved to this suburban community from older established urban areas, whether in Toronto or other Canadian cities. These were people who would have been described by Whyte as 'organization men.' They could very accurately be described as highly urban.

On the other hand, a good part of the population of Riverdrive Park was one which had never been incorporated in an urban society. A large number of the people in this community had come from small towns or rural areas. Now, dependent on employment in the urban community, they had settled there, but on its very outskirts.

Riverdrive Park was far from constituting an exceptional case. It is true that with respect to the overall development of the Canadian urban community after World War II the preponderant movement of population was from the central areas of the city to the suburbs. The postwar society was an affluent one. There was a great shift of Canadian people up into the middle class. This broadening of the base of the Canadian middle class was reflected in the rapid growth of the suburban population. But, because of the preponderance of the movement of population from the central areas of the city to the suburbs, it is easy to overlook the importance of the very different kind of movement that took place from the country to the city. The pattern of development of the northern industrial community showed up clearly, particularly in the case of such communities as Kapuskasing and Noranda-Rouyn, because of the ethnic difference. As already noted, the population moving in off the farms was French-speaking. Montreal, for the same reason, offered a clearer picture of the effect upon the pattern of development of rural migration than did Toronto. Very early here, the settlement of French-speaking people on the eastern outskirts of the city gave to Montreal something of the character of an urban community to which was attached a great sprawling village reaching eastward into the country.

It would be a mistake, however, to conclude that it was the ethnic background of the population which accounted for the kind of development that took place in Montreal, or in Kapuskasing, or Noranda-Rouyn. The community of Mistassini, growing up beyond the borders of Dolbeau, had a population hardly more French-speaking than that of Dolbeau itself, yet the people of these two communities came from two very different social worlds. The Dolbeau population was one that had moved there from older urban areas. The Mistassini population was drawn almost wholly from the poor rural parishes of the Lake St. John region.

The ethnic factor assumed importance only because the French-speaking element constituted such a large proportion of the people being forced out of poor farm areas into the urban community. It was not its ethnicity that accounted for the manner of its settlement in the urban community but its rural background. Wherever farm families, as distinguished from single individuals, migrated from the country to the city they tended, where possible, to locate on the city's outskirts. What occurred was a sort of half way or partial movement. When the European immigrant moved from his homeland to the land that was now to become his home, a total commitment was involved. He could in no easy way turn back. The rural family, in contrast, made no clear commitment. In many cases, indeed, a shift from the occupation of farming to an urban occupation occurred well before there was any change in the family's place of residence. Employment, often of a part-time sort, may have been found first in the nearby town. The move of the family to the town followed, and then to other towns, and finally to the larger industrial centre where greater opportunities for employment were offered. But in all this moving of the rural family there occurred scarcely any break from the rural society. The rural family moved to the urban community without making itself a part of the urban society. It camped, so to speak, on the urban community's outer edges.

Where urban growth was very great, it is true, the urban community reached out and ultimately engulfed those elements settled beyond its borders. The shack town was razed by the subdivision developer's bulldozer, and the small town and rural village, harbouring many of the families moving out of farm areas, were made part of the city. But these were developments that took place only after a long interval of time, and, indeed, if urban growth slowed down, never took place at all. By the very nature of their establishment, many of the communities forming outside the borders of the urban community lay far beyond its reach. They tended to grow up in those areas least suitable for urban residential development, and once thus occupied they discouraged occupation in a different form. Therefore, as the urban community grew outwards, it tended to by-pass those residential developments which could not easily be incorporated within it. Growth of the industrial centre of Dolbeau led to the development of smart new residential subdivisions south of the town, whereas Mistassini across the river continued to recruit its population from the rural countryside. Riverdrive Park, beyond the borders of Toronto, settled in 1950, remains now, almost twenty years later, scarcely disturbed by the growth of the Toronto urban community.

Rural people, lacking the means and the skills, and even more the social outlook, to make their way in an urban environment sought to shelter themselves by locating in that no-man's land between city and country. This was a land easy to move into. The abandoned summer colony, the small town suffering economic depression from its location now too near the big city, the farm burdened with mounting taxes and able to produce a profit only by the sale of building lots along the country road, offered to the family from the farm a means of providing itself with cheap housing in a social environment not much different from that left behind.

But if these were areas easy to move into, they were, on the other hand, areas hard to move out of. The European immigrant, settling in the central areas of the urban community, soon became caught up in the forces of urban growth. He was made a part of the urban society. The rural migrant, in contrast, by settling beyond the reach of the forces of urban growth, continued for a long while to live outside the urban society. In not being pushed out, he failed to be pushed up.

Though not so clearly apparent, this is the case even when the rural migrant has been forced to settle farther in, nearer the centre of the city. Not all migrants from the country to the city managed to locate in outlying areas, beyond the urban community's boundaries. Indeed, as cities have continued to grow, and urban developers and planners have reached farther and farther afield, the 'soft' pockets for cheap residential developments beyond the urban communities have begun to shrivel and disappear. Increasingly, in recent years, the population moving into the city from the country has scattered itself throughout the urban community. But the pattern of settlement remains very different from that of the European immigrant. There is no clustering of rural migrants in particular areas. There is no settling alongside their 'countrymen.' The nature of settlement of the rural migrant shows up most clearly in the case of the Indian moving in off the reserve. It is not in the city that the Indian seeks ties of community and neighbourhood. He already possesses such ties back in his reservation. For him, the city becomes a place to camp. There is something of this character in the settlement of all impoverished rural migrants in the city. It is on the back streets of the city, so to speak, that such migrants locate, not as groups but as single families or individuals. Without the ties of community that group settlement provides, the settlement of the rural migrant in the city takes the form of 'camping' on the edge of the urban community, with the only real ties of community remaining in the community left behind.

Much has been said and written in recent years about the problem of poverty in our society. For a long time the easy explanation could be found in the economic difficulties faced by the recent immigrant to the country. The impoverished state of the thousands of Irish immigrants of the 1840s and 1850s offered a striking early example of the problems of economic adjustment encountered by new arrivals. The sociological literature in the years before World War II became largely caught up in the problem of the assimilation of the European immigrant. Because heavy immigration to Canada from Europe continues, there remains even today in Canadian sociological work a distinct emphasis upon the place occupied by the immigrant in our urban society. Yet it is increasingly apparent that the really serious divisions in Canadian society bear little relation to the presence in this society of large numbers of European immigrants. Indeed, they have shared fully in the economic prosperity of post-war Canada. The gulf between rich and poor develops out of very different divisions in the Canadian society than that between immigrant and non-immigrant, and these are divisions much deeper and more persistent. Today we are paying the price of a public policy which for more than two centuries persisted in encouraging the settlement of people on land which was not fit for farming. That policy was carried furthest, and as a result has had the most disastrous consequences, in French Canada, where as late as 1955 thousands of families were still being settled in new farm areas in northern Quebec. In no part of the country, however, were there not to be found large areas of farm settlement (or settlement based on the fishing industry) where only the barest of a livelihood could be gained. The struggle of the native Indian population to eke out an existence on land set apart for its occupation offers only an extreme example of the disastrous consequences of a public policy developing out of the philosophy that life in the country is the good life.

Rural people, caught in a situation that progressively impoverishes them, almost completely lose the capacity to move. There does not occur, until the pressures become very great indeed, a migration out of the rural area, and then it is of a very halting sort. The attributes of immobility, acquired within the rural situation, are carried by the population into its new urban situation, and there, because of the nature of its settlement in the urban community, these attributes persist. The poor of our urban society, of course, are not only the people moving into the urban community out of farm areas whose rural background has failed to equip them to make their way in an urban world. The hazards of urban living impose a heavy cost upon those who fail to make their way in the competitive struggle. But to far too great an extent we have directed our attention to the fate of those people who have become the casualties of this competitive struggle to the neglect of examining the fate of those people who, in effect, have had no opportunity to become involved in the struggle. Functional theory has committed the sociologist, taking his lead from the anthropologist, to view the disturbing forces of an urban society in a state of rapid growth as a bad thing. Yet it was because he could not escape the impact of these disturbing forces that the European immigrant has made such a successful adjustment to the urban society of America. Today, in the United States, the colour of a large proportion of the recent migrants to the city introduces a new and very serious impediment to the integration of the American urban population. In Canada, the issue of race assumes little importance, but that of ethnicity gains prominence in the strained relations of French- and English-speaking Canadians, and, though the problem extends beyond that of the disadvantaged position of a people of a heavily rural background caught in an urban situation, it is their rural background that renders disadvantaged the position of a large element of the French-speaking population. The ethnic division only gives emphasis to the much deeper and more widespread division within the urban society arising out of the failure of certain elements of the population to become integrated into the society.

EDWARD SHORTER

Sexual change and illegitimacy: the European experience

Sex has gotten into everything nowadays but the study of modernization. While scholars have investigated how political institutions, social structure, economic systems and
family life have been transformed by the social changes of modernization, they have
left the realm of sexual behaviour and values pretty much unexamined. Only in the
plastic-wrapped volumes of the 'dirty' bookstores may one find a set of explanatory
hypotheses and an accumulation of evidence bearing on sexual change.

The failure of social scientists to study sex in the context of modernization is puz-
zling to a European historian. One of the signal changes in popular life in Europe during the last two centuries has been a revolution in sexual mores. European society has
passed from the rigid prudishness which hallmarks traditional life to the hedonistic self-
indulgence characteristic of modern sexual attitudes. Indeed, the much discussed 'sexual revolution' of our own times is, I would argue, merely the most recent development
in a process of secular change two centuries old. The rapid evolution of sexual values
and behaviour which both Europe and North America – although only the former will
be discussed here – experienced starting around 1750 is the subject of this paper.

To be more precise, only one of the manifestations of sexual change will occupy us
here: a rapid increase in the rate of illegitimate births between the mid-eighteenth and
mid-nineteenth centuries. I shall make the case that this explosion in illegitimacy is one
sign that sexual attitudes and behaviour were changing swiftly, becoming 'modernized,'
if one will. We may bring to bear other kinds of evidence as well upon sexual history,
such as the observations of contemporaries, various 'medical' surveys of the population
conducted by the cameralist governments of western and central Europe, court records
on sexual crimes and aberrancies, or the study of pornography. And in an investigation

Reprinted from *Modern European Social History,* edited by Robert Bezucha, with the kind permission of the publisher, D.C. Heath and Company.
Glen Jones and Joan Baker assisted in preparing the data on which this article is based. Among those
who suggested changes in earlier drafts are Rainer Baum, Natalie Davis, David Hunt, Peter Laslett,
W.H. Nelson, Paul Robinson, Ann Shorter, Lawrence Stone, Charles Tilly, Mack Walker, Barry Well-
man, and E.A. Wrigley.

currently in progress I am studying these kinds of data as well in an effort to illuminate changing sexual patterns. However in this paper I wish to present the evidence of illegitimacy alone.

First potential objections to illegitimacy data as a measure of real sexual attitudes and practices are examined; second, the dimensions of the increase in illegitimacy between the mid-eighteenth and mid-nineteenth centuries are discussed briefly; third, a review of some current theories about sexual behaviour and illegitimacy is in order; fourth, a general model linking modernizing forces to sexual change and illegitimacy will be proposed; finally, empirical data will be presented, confirming some of the linkages in this model from a region of central Europe which participated in the illegitimacy explosion – the Kingdom of Bavaria.

I

Clearly one may use the incidence of illegitimacy to study sexual behaviour only with some important reservations in mind. What we are really interested in is the level of premarital intercourse, a substantial increase in which is central to sexual change in western Europe.[1] And many factors can intervene between the action of premarital coitus and the birth of an illegitimate child, duly registered as such by the state authorities.

One stumbling block is the possibility that premarital intercourse may not lead to conception, or rather that the chances of its doing so will vary over time on the basis of the practice of contraception. We may be dealing with a situation in which young people are engaging in intercourse as much as ever, yet fewer girls are becoming pregnant because they have begun to employ contraceptive devices or to follow the 'rhythm' method intelligently. This objection, I believe, commands caution in attributing a *fall* in illegitimacy to changing sexual behaviour, but would not apply to the rise we are concerned with here. One cannot argue that around 1750 the European population started to forget an accumulated lore of contraceptive information.

A more important objection to using illegitimacy data as an index of sexual behaviour is the possibility that many children conceived out of wedlock will be born legitimate because their parents got married in the interim period. In other words, one might argue that the level of premarital intercourse in a society is really more or less constant, and that changes in illegitimacy are merely a function of changes in the marriage rate. This, of course, is a weighty objection. Ideally, one would consult the incidence of pre-bridal pregnancies to find out about premarital intercourse. Yet such information becomes available only through detailed monographic studies of individual parishes and towns, and clearly is not to be found among published aggregate statistics.

There are several reasons why one should not seek to explain illegitimacy primarily in terms of the inability of the couple to get married. If we ask: why didn't the parents

1 Other quantitative changes, such as an increase in extramarital intercourse or in homosexuality, must also be considered in chronicling the revolution in sexual behaviour, as must such *qualitative* shifts in the kinds of sexual things people do as oral intercourse or fetishism. At this stage in my researches I have little concrete evidence on these matters, however, and so limit the discussion to premarital heterosexual relationships.

wed before the child was born? we have probably made two implicit assumptions about the situation of its conception. Either we assume that the couple are a devoted pair whom fate, in the form of bad harvests or financial penury, prevented from sanctifying their relationship at the altar; or we assume that the girl was, for some reason or another, unable to *compel* her seducer to wed her. A scholar who thought illegitimacy could best be studied through the negative question of 'why no subsequent marriage? ' would, therefore, attempt to account for the illegitimacy explosion in terms of a change over time in either economic conditions or in the social controls which the fallen woman and her family could exert upon the seducer.

I argue that these two assumptions do not exhaust the possibilities. We may envision a situation where the couple is not at all a stable, devoted pair but rather two people who casually cohabit and then go their separate ways. Getting married later would not have occurred to them, high grain prices or not. And even after the girl became pregnant, forcing the man to wed her would have appeared either undesirable or unrealistic. This third assumption about the background of the premarital conception defines, I think, the situation that came to predominate in Europe. Part of the mechanism of sexual change there is a certain unlinking of sex and marriage, the creation of a value system which prizes sex for the sake of physical or romantic gratification and which does not see all sexual actions in marital terms. This means that in theory we may account for changes in illegitimacy with arguments that have little bearing upon the ability of the parents to get married.

In practice, the marriage and illegitimacy rates, observed over time in various areas of Europe, are not correlated in any neat inverse way. During the 1840s, for example, a time of poverty and disaster for much of Europe's population, the marriage and illegitimacy rates simultaneously fell. One would have expected a decrease in marriage to have produced an *increase* in illegitimacy, if illegitimacy were a smooth function of marriage. The opposite, in fact, happened.[2]

Just as there is little evidence that marriage delayed for economic reasons produced illegitimacy, there is no evidence that normally high ages at marriage resulted in illegitimacy. E.A. Wrigley points out that historically in Europe no association has existed between late marriage and illegitimacy. Rather it was probably the other way around: 'Where early marriage was widely countenanced, extramarital intercourse was often also common and the percentage of illegitimate births rather high, whereas if a community set its face against early marriage illegitimate births were nevertheless usually few in number.'[3] (If we assume that knowledge of contraception was minimal, at least among the lower classes, we may only conclude that in *traditional* society people remained continent until marriage.) This further suggests that we should not try to write a history of illegitimacy as a history of marriage customs alone.

2 See the data presented by Friedrich Lindner, *Die unehelichen Geburten als Sozialphänomen: Ein Beitrag zur Statistik der Bevölkerungsbewegung im Königreiche Bayern* (Leipzig: A. Deichert, 1900), p. 57. The Thüringen Statistisches Bureau noted this inverse correlation between falling illegitimacy and rising grain prices during the late 1860s. 'Zur Statistik der unehelichen Geburten in den Thüringenschen Staaten,' *Jahrbücher für Nationalökonomie und Statistik,* 22 (1874), 337-8, especially p. 346.
3 The Wrigley citation is from *Population and History* (New York: McGraw-Hill, 1969), p. 119.

Another point: it may be demonstrated that relatively few of the couples who produced illegitimate children did, in fact, marry later. In Europe only one-third of the illegitimate children born each year were later legitimated by the subsequent marriage of their parents.[4] Now, if illegitimate children are the work of young people devoted to each other but who, for some economic reason perhaps, are unable to get married just then, one would expect the legitimation rate to be much higher.

State marriage laws also help to make illegitimacy a useful indicator of premarital sexual activity, not just of difficulty in getting married. Until the last half of the nineteenth century, government restrictions in central Europe made marriage a difficult goal for the lower classes to attain: if they did succeed in winning official authorization for marriage it was only after a long, arduous battle with officialdom. The central European governments were obliged by municipal officials to impose these curbs on marriage. The local authorities feared that, were the lower orders permitted to marry freely, their numerous families would swamp local poor-relief resources in the event of bad times. So for many people marriage became possible only as they advanced towards middle age, when communal consent could finally be obtained. These restrictions themselves helped skyrocket the illegitimacy rate, which is part of the story.[5] The point is

---

4 The legitimation rate varies considerably over time and place. In Bavaria on the average between 1857 and 1862 some 15 per cent of illegitimate births were subsequently legitimated. (Note that this statistic merely relates the number of children legitimated in a year to the number born illegitimate; it does not say how many of a year's crop of bastards were themselves later legitimated.) See 'Bewegung der Bevölkerung, 1857/58 bis 1861/62,' *Beiträge zur Statistik des Königreichs Bayern,* 11 (1863), 87. Results for Saxony and Austria around the turn of the century point to a legitimation rate of around 30 per cent. But unlike the Bavarian data, these figures exclude from consideration the illegitimate children who died before legitimation. See Ludwig Elster (ed.), *Handwörterbuch der Staatswissenschaften,* 4th ed., vol. 8 (Jena, 1928), 394-5. In Dresden during the 1890s around 60 per cent of the illegitimate children who survived until age five were legitimated. See Eugen Würzburger, 'Zur Statistik der Legitimationen unehelicher Kinder,' *Jahrbücher für Nationalökonomie und Statistik,* 3rd ser., 18 (1899), 94-8. According to the statistician Bertillon, in Paris one quarter of the illegitimate children were soon 'recognized' by their natural fathers in 1880, which is perhaps the functional equivalent of legitimation. Cited in Louis Chevalier, *Classes laborieuses et classes dangereuses à Paris pendant la première moitié du XIXe siècle* (Paris: Plon, 1958), p. 381, n. 1.

5 On these marriage and settlement laws see Karl Braun, 'Das Zwangs-Zölibat für Mittellose in Deutschland,' *Vierteljahrschrift für Volkswirtschaft und Kulturgeschichte,* 20, iv (1867), 1-80; Eduard Schübler, *Die Gesetze über Niederlassung und Verehelichung in den verschiedenen deutschen Staaten* (Stuttgart, 1855); John Knodel, 'Law, Marriage and Illegitimacy in Nineteenth-century Germany,' *Population Studies,* 20 (1966-7), 279-94; Mack Walker, 'Home Towns and State Administrators: South German Politics, 1815-30,' *Political Science Quarterly,* 82 (1967), 35-60; and Edward Shorter, 'Social Change and Social Policy in Bavaria, 1800-1860,' Harvard Diss., 1968.

A government official explained in the Bavarian legislature in 1840 how such laws caused premarital conceptions to become illegitimate births. He said that an elderly man had approached him in his office, desperate 'because he had the misfortune to see his only child, his daughter, dishonored. To be sure, the seducer was prepared to marry her, but the communal officials had thundered against him with their veto.' After the official explained that the royal government could not possibly overturn the communal decision, the old man 'collapsed in desperation, tearing his hair, beating his head against the wall, and threatening to kill himself.' Bavaria. *Verhandlungen der Kammer der Abgeordneten des Königreichs Bayern, 1840,* vol. 4, 428-9.

that even if a girl were to become pregnant, official regulations made a quick, honour-saving marriage out of the question. And so her child would be illegitimate. As long as these regulations prevailed, and variations in the severity of their administration did not take place, we may assume that many premarital conceptions among the poor and working classes would lead to illegitimate births.

A final objection which could be offered to using illegitimacy data as a reliable measure of behaviour is the quality of the reporting of such statistics. More particularly, might one not interpret the increase in illegitimacy from 1750 to 1850 as a statistical artefact resulting from an improvement in the official collection of demographic data? If illegitimacy appears to have risen, is that not partly because people became more meticulous about recording such births? I think some improvement in the reporting of vital statistics did take place during this period as a consequence of increasing governmental centralization and awakened interest in gathering reliable social statistics. Yet I think that whatever sharpening in official observation of illegitimacy occurred would contribute only marginally to the tripling and quadrupling of illegitimacy commonly found. Possibly such reporting improvements might account for a leap in illegitimacy rates just as official statistical services are established. But it is difficult to maintain that, once established, the European statistical offices dramatically increased their reporting reliability as the nineteenth century progressed. In the course of a thorough study of census reporting and data gathering in one European state – the Kingdom of Bavaria – I found no hint in the administrative correspondence that the actual determination and registration of which births were illegitimate might be a problem. Either these officials were obtuse, which I doubt, or the quality of official illegitimacy statistics in Bavaria after 1825 was excellent.

Having dealt with these potential objections to illegitimacy as a valid and reliable indicator in the evolution of sexual behaviour, I again state the main case I wish to make: the rapid increase in illegitimacy, between around 1750 and 1850, measured as the number of illegitimate children born each year per 100 total births, suggests that the populations of Europe, and of North America as well, were undergoing a revolution in the sexual attitudes of young people towards one another, a revolution manifest in a great increase in premarital sexual intercourse.

II

The scattered illegitimacy data available for Atlantic society since the eighteenth century show an explosion of illegitimate births taking place in virtually every country from Prussia to the American colonies. Past scholarly inattentiveness to illegitimacy means that few compilations of aggregate statistics exist; fewer still are the local studies which present time-series data on bastardy. Our survey of the development of illegitimacy over time, then, rests upon a wide variety of sources.

Yet these various sources reveal marked similarities in the historical development of illegitimacy in western society. Before the eighteenth century relatively few children were born of unwed mothers. The illegitimacy rate was perhaps one per cent of the total births. Then a great increase in prebridal pregnancies and illegitimate births began sometime during the eighteenth century in every region or society for which demographic data have become available, accelerating during the years of the French Revolution and the Napoleonic Wars. Illegitimacy continued to rise throughout the first half of the nineteenth century, peaking in the 1850s and 60s. Then the trend reversed itself, a universal decline of some percentage points setting in until the early twentieth century. From the beginning of this century until the 1960s the illegitimacy rate has remained more or less constant in most western countries. Finally, during the 1960s a second substantial rise in illegitimacy, not unlike the eighteenth-century explosion, has been noted in northern Europe and in the Anglo-Saxon countries.[6]

Thus the secular pattern followed by illegitimacy in modern times has been a universal increase from roughly 1750 to 1850, to take two convenient dates; a slight dropping off in the last half of the nineteenth century; a stabilization at a fairly high level during the first half of the twentieth century; and what may prove to be the beginning of another major upward thrust in the 1960s (or possibly just a minor undulation).

Let us examine the development of rates country by country, going clockwise around Europe. Illegitimacy data available for long periods of time have been reproduced in Figure 1. They are calculated as a percentage of total births.[7]

In Sweden and Germany bastards were an infinitesimal number before the eighteenth century: on the whole less than one per cent of all births in seventeenth-century Frankfurt-em-Main, less than 2 per cent in Lychen, Erfurt, and Halle. Then in the eighteenth century the increase began: a jerky upward movement in Frankfurt started in the 1720s, peaking at 19 per cent in the Napoleonic era and at 23 per cent in the 1860s. The increases in Sweden, Leipzig, Hamburg, the countryside around Halle, Chemnitz, and Styria were roughly similar, the take-off and peak decades different from one case to another, but everywhere the pattern of rapid late-eighteenth- and early-nineteenth-century increase. German illegitimacy then paused in the last quarter of the nineteenth century, rose substantially in the first decades of the twentieth, and has declined sharply since the Great Depression. Swedish illegitimacy, in contrast to German, has climbed sharply since World War II.[8]

6 The sources for illegitimacy data by country since 1906 are: Henri Bunle, *Le mouvement naturel de la population dans le monde de 1906 à 1936* (Paris: Editions de l'Institut National d'Etudes Démographiques, 1954), pp. 73-7; United Nations, *Demographic Yearbook: 1959*, pp. 218-38 for 1949-58; *Demographic Yearbook: 1965*, pp. 516-30 for 1959-64. These have been used for all countries in Figure 1 after 1906; the data are for five-year periods.
7 It makes little difference whether one takes live births or total births – stillbirths included – as the denominator in these calculations, for although the stillbirth rate among illegitimate children was generally higher than among legitimate, the difference will affect our figures only marginally.
8 The source of Swedish data is Gustav Sundbärg, *Bevölkerungsstatistik Schwedens, 1750–1900: Einige Hauptresultate*, 2nd ed. (Stockholm: P.A. Norstedt, 1923), p. 117. Data represent five-year averages. Sundbärg also makes available the optimum illegitimacy statistic: the number of illegitimate children as a percentage of the number of unmarried and widowed women, ages 20–45. This is a more refined measure, preferable to calculating illegitimacy as a gross percentage of total births, because a population in which fertility in general is low can appear to have a misleadingly high illegitimacy rate. Yet demographic data on unmarried women in the population are seldom available in historic situations.
   Pre-1900 data for individual German cities and regions come from W. Hanauer, 'Historisch-statistische Untersuchungen über uneheliche Geburten,' *Zeitschrift für Hygiene und Infektion-*

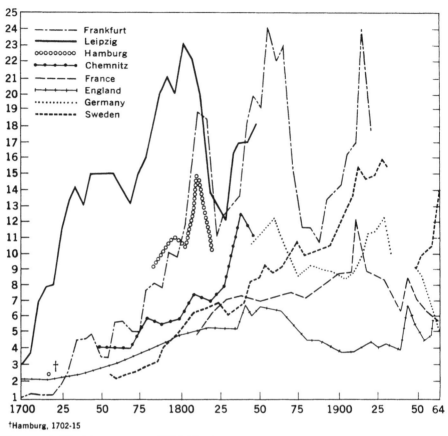

FIGURE 1 *Illegitimacy rates, 1700-1964; 5-year averages in most cases*
(*number of illegitimate births/total number of births × 100*)

Serial data on Italy appear only in the last quarter of the nineteenth century. The figures of that time and the shards of information for earlier periods are highly unreliable because of the Mediterranean custom of making unwanted children foundlings. The Italian foundling rate is extremely high, and one does not know how many of these abandoned children are illegitimate. In any event, published figures put Italian illegitimacy at around 7 per cent late in the century, at 2 or 3 per cent since World War II.[9]

I have seen no time-series data on illegitimacy for eighteenth-century France, but isolated reports of the rate in one village or another at various fixed points in time

skrankheiten, 108 (1927–8), 656-84; German national data for the nineteenth century are from the Federal Republic of Germany, Statistisches Bundesamt, *Statistisches Jahrbuch für die Bundesrepublik Deutschland, 1965,* p. 58; data are for single years taken at five-year intervals since 1875.

9 Italian data before 1900 come from Alexander von Oettingen, *Die Moralstatistik in ihrer Bedeutung für eine Socialethik,* 3rd ed. (Erlangen: A. Deichert, 1882), pp. xxxv and 303.

indicate that the Old Regime knew very little of it. Several authors attribute this to a strictness of morals in rural France, where both illegitimacy and premarital conception rates appear to have been very low. Yet premarital sexual activity, as measured by the incidence of prebridal conceptions at least, was quite high in some *urban* places. In Sotteville-lès-Rouen, with minimal illegitimacy, the incidence of premarital conceptions was sometimes 30 per cent of all first births. A great increase in foundlings in Paris from 1709 to 1789 may also point to rising urban illegitimacy, most foundlings being of illegitimate parentage; yet that measure must be used with caution. Finally, in urban Bordeaux, bastardy increased from 4 per cent early in the seventeenth century to 20 per cent in 1784, to 35 per cent in 1840. Official statistics indicate that by the first decade of the nineteenth century French illegitimacy, following the widespread pattern, had risen to 5 per cent, fluctuated then at around 7 per cent until the turn of the century, and has declined since.[10]

The Anglo-Saxon world too participated in the illegitimacy explosion late in the eighteenth century. Although data are scarce (the American and English administrations not sharing the central European penchant for collecting social statistics), some intriguing local results emerge. P.E.H. Hair, after studying a number of different parishes, concludes that bridal pregnancy increased considerably in England after 1700.[11] Before the eighteenth century perhaps one-fifth of all brides were pregnant, thereafter two-fifths. This result is particularly interesting in view of the general superiority of premarital pregnancy to illegitimacy as an index of sexual activity. By studying a sample group of parishes, E.A. Wrigley and Peter Laslett have discovered a temporary upturn in bastardy early in seventeenth-century England. As in other countries, a major rise then took place in the course of the eighteenth century, levelling off at a high

10 For a few lonely statistics on eighteenth-century France, see Etienne Gautier and Louis Henry, *La population de Crulai: Paroisse normande: Etude historique* (Paris: Institut national d'études démographiques, 1958; cahier no. 33), p. 67, which data, in fact, show an increase in bastardy during the last half of the century; Pierre Girard, 'Aperçus de la démographie de Sotteville-lès-Rouen vers la fin du XVIIIe siècle,' *Population,* 14 (1959), 485–508, and especially 494; M. Terrisse, 'Deux monographies paroissiales sur la population française au XVIIIe siècle. I, Un faubourg du Havre: Ingouville,' *Population,* 16 (1961), 285–300; Ingouville had an average illegitimacy rate of 6 per cent in 1774-90. Pierre Goubert comments on the low level of bastardy in France, mentioning 'a certain strictness of morals, particularly in the countryside.' 'Recent Theories and Research in French Population between 1500 and 1700,' in *Population in History: Essays in Historical Demography*, D.V. Glass and D.E.C. Eversley (eds.) (London: Edward Arnold, 1965), pp. 457-73 and particularly p. 468. For foundling data on Paris, see Marcel R. Reinhard, *et al., Histoire générale de la population mondiale,* 3rd ed. (Paris: Eds. Montchrestien, 1968), p. 268; M.-Cl. Murtin, 'Les abandons d'enfants à Bourg et dans le département de l'Ain à la fin du XVIIIe siècle et dans la première moitié du XIXe,' *Cahiers d'Histoire,* 10 (1965), 135-66. Bordeaux data come from private information with which Robert Wheaton has kindly supplied me, and from a notice in the *Annales de Démographie Historique, 1968,* p. 182. Nineteenth-century illegitimacy data are summarized in Wesley D. Camp, *Marriage and the Family in France since the Revolution: An Essay in the History of Population* (New York: Bookman, n.d.), p. 108; data are for ten-year averages. The yearly number of illegitimate births are published in France. Institut National de la Statistique et des Etudes Economiques, *Annuaire Statistique de la France, 1966: Résumé rétrospectif*, pp. 66-75.
11 P.E.H. Hair, 'Bridal Pregnancy in Rural England in Earlier Centuries,' *Population Studies,* 20 (1966-7), 233-43, especially 237-40.

plateau throughout much of the nineteenth.[12] Official British statistics show that illegitimacy declined from these heights to a constant level of 4 per cent or so from the 1870s to the 1950s. In the 1960s British illegitimacy has again been on the increase.[13]

In the United States the eighteenth century was also a period of increasing illegitimacy and prebridal pregnancy. John Demos has pointed out that no couple in Bristol, Rhode Island, had a child within eight months after marriage between 1680 and 1720; between 1720 and 1740, 10 per cent of the newlyweds did; between 1740 and 1760, 50 per cent did! Demos attributes this dramatic increase to a 'significant loosening of sexual prohibitions as the eighteenth century wore on ...' Furthermore, 'It is my own guess that when the subject of American sexual behavior is more fully explored, the middle and late 18th century may prove to have been the most "free" period in our history.'[14]

Finally, a quick look at the growth of illegitimacy in Bavaria is required, for we shall shortly return to that country for a more detailed empirical examination of some of the assertions presented in this article. Bavaria followed a pattern common in Europe: acceleration of bastardy from almost nothing to perhaps a fifth of all births by the 1850s, a brief slackening off during the last quarter of the nineteenth century, then maintenance of illegitimacy at a constant level during the twentieth.

The source of Bavarian illegitimacy data for the years before 1825, when official reporting of such statistics began, is the baptismal registers of sixteen rural communes in the province of Oberbayern, 1760–1825.[15] The statistics are displayed in Figure 2. These selected communes had a relatively low, constant level of illegitimacy in the mid-eighteenth century: 4 per cent in 1760 and 1770. With the 1780 data, when illegitimacy soared to 12 per cent of all baptisms, a rise commences. Between 1795 and 1825 bastardy climbs in an unbroken progression from 5 to 18 per cent.

In 1825 official statistics begin, revealing that the rate for Bavaria as a whole was similar to that of these sixteen selected communes, as Figure 2 further indicates. Between 1825 and the early 1850s Bavarian illegitimacy hovered near the 20 per cent mark, a final dramatic peaking of 24 per cent taking place around 1860. The decline

12 Mr. Laslett kindly communicated these findings to me in a letter. For a preliminary report of Laslett–Wrigley illegitimacy data, see also the revised French edition of Laslett's *World We Have Lost* (*Un monde que nous avons perdu* [Paris: Flammarion, 1969], p. 149).

13 Data for England and Wales after 1840, which I have turned into five-year averages, are from B.R. Mitchell and Phyllis Deane, *Abstract of British Historical Statistics* (Cambridge: At the University Press, 1962), pp. 29-30, and from United Kingdom, Central Statistical Office, *Annual Abstract of Statistics*, no. 102 (1965), pp. 20-1. D.E.C. Eversley finds a 'marked increase' in illegitimacy in a group of Worcestershire parishes after 1789, peaking in 1815-19. 'A Survey of Population in an Area of Worcestershire from 1660 to 1850 on the Basis of Parish Registers,' in *Population in History*, Glass and Eversley (eds.), pp. 394-419, especially p. 413. On recent developments, see Shirley M. Hartley, 'The Amazing Rise of Illegitimacy in Great Britain,' *Social Forces*, 44 (1966), 533-45. K.H. Connell discusses the low Irish rate in 'Illegitimacy before the Famine,' in his *Irish Peasant Society: Four Historical Essays* (Oxford: Clarendon, 1968), pp. 51-86; an absence of time-series data makes it impossible to say if Ireland participated even hesitantly in the original illegitimacy explosion.

14 'Families in Colonial Bristol, Rhode Island: An Exercise in Historical Demography,' *The William and Mary Quarterly*, 3rd ser., 25 (1968), 40-57, especially 56-7.

15 I am indebted to Dr. Michael Phayer, O.S.B. for these data. Dr. Phayer spent many hours culling church records in the archive of the episcopal chancellery of the archdiocese, and most generously made the results of his researches available to me.

FIGURE 2 *Bavarian illegitimacy rate, 1760-1897*
(*number of illegitimate births/total number of births* X 100)

commenced in 1868/9, with the repeal of legislation which made marriage for the
lower classes dependent upon municipal consent. By the end of the century the rate
had stabilized at around 14 per cent. Bavarian illegitimacy in the 1960s, although still
the highest in West Germany with the exception of West Berlin, was 7 per cent of all
births.[16]

I do not wish to extend this recitation of statistics into the tedious. The point is that
all the regions of western and central Europe, the United Kingdom, and colonial America seem to have experienced a similar explosive increase in illegitimacy, starting sometime in the eighteenth century and levelling off late in the nineteenth. Of course, further investigation will turn up considerable variation in what now appears to have been

16 The official statistics are summarized in Lindner, *Uneheliche Geburten*, p. 217. Data for 1963 are
reported in *Statistisches Jahrbuch für die Bundesrepublik Deutschland, 1965*, p. 61.

a uniform, homogeneous process: important differentials in the timing and pacing of the increase will emerge, or factory industrial, cottage industrial, and agricultural districts will turn out to differ in significant ways. At this point we note merely that an extraordinary quantitative change in illegitimate births occurred around the time of the Democratic revolutions.

III

We may make sense of these transformations in illegitimacy rates only if we are able to construct hypotheses linking modernization with sexual change. And in this area the existing literature in the social sciences is weak. Until now scholars have pursued the social dimensions of sexual questions haphazardly, and no clearly defined body of literature provides a theoretical core of hypotheses from which future research might depart. Here work on the illegitimacy explosion may prove useful, for the historical facts I have just recounted suggest a model which will take us from fundamental modernizing social changes such as urbanization and industrialization to changes in sexual behaviour and values. First, we shall examine current sociological theories about sex and illegitimacy, going on from there to present a tentative model.

Recent research emphasizes a common thread of social class in accounting for differences in sexual behaviour. Stratification influences may make themselves felt in the form of differentials by class in the need for ego gratification and assurance of status. One researcher tells us that among the upper and middle classes sex is thought of as a means of self-enhancement and personality development.[17] Ira Reiss points out that differences in sexual behaviour are traceable to class differences in family and courtship patterns, these latter factors being the true variables which determine sexual behaviour. Reiss also observes that whatever libertineness may exist among the lower classes does not result from the 'disorganized atmosphere of poverty,' an assertion shortly to be of relevance to us.[18] Other well-known research links social class to sexual behaviour via class differences in role segregation between husband and wife: in lower-class families the functions of husband and wife are usually highly 'segregated.' A negativeness or indifference to sexual relations among lower-class women, for example, is associated with this rigid compartmentalization.[19] The only recent sociological study of sexual patterns without a class emphasis is Harold Christensen's work on international differences in sexual permissiveness: Christensen thinks cultural differences are strategic.[20]

These are useful findings, for they permit us to see that variations in sexual behaviour are not distributed in some random way among the population, and to reject the notion

17 Clark E. Vincent, *Unmarried Mothers* (New York: Free Press, 1961), p. 92 and passim.

18 Ira L. Reiss, *The Social Context of Premarital Sexual Permissiveness* (New York: Holt, Rinehart and Winston, 1967), pp. 177-8.

19 Lee Rainwater, 'Some Aspects of Lower Class Sexual Behavior,' *Journal of Social Issues*, 22, ii (April 1966), 96-108; see also his *And the Poor Get Children: Sex, Contraception, and Family Planning in the Working Class* (Chicago: Quadrangle, 1960).

20 Harold T. Christensen, 'Cultural Relativism and Premarital Sex Norms,' *American Sociological Review*, 25 (1960), 31-9.

that such matters do not vary from group to group. Rather we realize that sexual mores are systematically linked to such basic and familiar forces as social class. What previous research does not permit us to do is relate social change to the realm of sex. We need to know how modernization *changes* sexual practices, not merely how such practices are found among already 'modern' populations.

A more substantial literature on the specific subject of illegitimacy will help to formulate hypotheses on the history and socioogy of sex. During the nineteenth century, when illegitimacy first became a major social problem, a number of writers gathered statistics and speculated on the causes of the phenomenon. And in the 1970s, when events taking place within the black ghettos again cause illegitimacy to emerge as a signal concern, a second round of writings on the subject appears. Two different theoretical approaches to illegitimacy may be discerned in existing writings.

One group of authors sees illegitimacy as the product of enduring common-law-type unions within the context of a stable culture. For one reason or another, the culture does not demand that all those who live and sleep together get married, and so an informal style of marriage, perfectly durable and sanctioned by the society, may come to be the dominant form of cohabitation. Of course, the children born of these unions are legally registrable as illegitimate, but that doesn't mean their conception resulted from some kind of social pathology. The point is that the parents of these illegitimate children either think of themselves as married for most intents and purposes, or they shortly do in fact get married. William J. Goode, while rejecting this 'stability' interpretation in general, applies it to the peasant cultures of northwestern Europe. An instance of it has been found in the numerous prebridal pregnancies of Denmark. And one sociologist interprets Caribbean illegitimacy in light of the 'consensual union' hypothesis.[21] It says, to sum up, that there is nothing pathological about illegitimacy, no aura of social disorganization around its apparition. Rather bastardy is a statistical artefact, arising solely from the fact that the parents, who represent a stable union within a stable culture, have not yet decided to legalize their intimate relationship.

An alternate group of writers takes a diametrically opposed position: illegitimacy is a product of social disorganization. It occurs when the normal processes which regulate courtship and family life break down, when social disaster hits the society and things start to fall apart. This view is in line with classical sociological theories which emphasize the disintegrating effects of social change, predicting that modernization will result in instability and disorientation, social alienation, and individual anomie. It is when people lose a sense of what is right, of what manner of behaviour society expects from them, that they begin to have premarital sex – which, of course, eventuates in illegitimacy. This point of view characterizes the 'moral statisticians' of the nineteenth century, such as Alexander von Oettingen and Georg von Mayr. And it characterizes such twentieth-century observers as Louis Chevalier as well, who in his study

21 William J. Goode, 'Illegitimacy, Anomie, and Cultural Penetration,' *American Sociological Review,* 26 (1961), 910-25, especially 912; Sydney H. Croog, 'Aspects of the Cultural Background of Premarital Pregnancies in Denmark,' *Social Forces,* 30 (1951-2), 215-19; Hyman Rodman, 'Illegitimacy in the Caribbean Social Structure: A Reconsideration,' *American Sociological Review,* 31 (1966), 673-83.

of the 'dangerous classes' in Paris of the early nineteenth century attributed an upsurge in illegitimacy to the disorganizing effects of social change.[22]

A persuasive, sophisticated version of this thesis is advanced by William Goode, who argues that high Latin American illegitimacy rates may be explained in terms of the disorganization arising from the clash and interpenetration of two different cultures. A breakdown in community creates some anomie, and the ensuing confusion about cultural values leads to premarital intercourse, and thence to illegitimacy.[23] In a similar vein Daniel Patrick Moynihan, in his famous report on the Negro family, argued that the social disorganization black people experience in northern industrial cities has devastated family life, causing illegitimacy to become almost the norm.[24]

Within the general social disorganization explanation of illegitimacy there is a subgroup of authors who see economic deprivation and the ruin of the workingman's life brought about by industrial capitalism as chiefly responsible for illegitimacy. This interpretation goes back to Friedrick Engels, who noted in the industrial slums of England a trend to 'sexual license' among the working classes. But the writers who indict capitalism and industrial society for producing illegitimacy are by no means all Marxists: many conservative nineteenth-century observers claimed that the working classes were both demoralized and impoverished by industrial growth, thus unwilling and unable to marry. Hence illegitimacy.[25]

The social disorganization approach to illegitimacy is important because it represents the only cluster of theories within the area of sex research able to connect sexual evolution with social change. As we have seen, current sex research has a timeless quality about it, and is unconcerned with how large-scale societal changes operating over time alter sexual behaviour. The social disorganization school, at least, hooks up the two by claiming that modernization causes traditional moral values and stable behavioural patterns to break down, with the consequences of libertine sexual mores and illegitimacy.

Can we not combine the two approaches? The stable-union theorists rightly point out that the presence of illegitimacy need not betoken social disorganization, as it may

---

22 Oettingen discusses illegitimacy in *Moralstatistik*, pp. 289-346; Georg von Mayr, *Statistik und Gesellschaftslehre*, vol. 3: *Sozialstatistik* (Tübingen: J.C.B. Mohr, 1909), pp. 127-50; Chevalier, *Classes laborieuses*, pp. 380-97; Chevalier takes up illegitimacy within a section entitled 'un état pathologique.'

23 'Illegitimacy, Anomie, and Cultural Penetration.'

24 See the original report and comments on it in Lee Rainwater and William L. Yancey, *The Moynihan Report and the Politics of Controversy* (Cambridge, Mass.: MIT Press, 1967), pp. 39-124. Moynihan's views are, of course, in a tradition dating back at least to E. Franklin Frazier, who thought illegitimacy a consequence of social disorganization and a cause of personal demoralization. On Frazier, see Charles A. Valentine, *Culture and Poverty: A Critique and Counter-Proposals* (Chicago: University of Chicago Press, 1968), pp. 20-4.

25 Friederick Engels, *The Condition of the Working-Class in England in 1844* (London: Allen and Unwin, 1892), p. 128; see Pierre Pierrard's discussion of worker concubinage and illegitimacy in a French industrial city: *La vie ouvrière à Lille sous le Second Empire* (Paris: Bloud et Gay, 1965), pp. 118-35; for a typical conservative account linking industrialization to 'immorality' and illegitimacy, see Ernst Fabri, *Der Notstand unserer Zeit und Seine Hebung* (Erlangen, 1850); some of the popular polemical writing in mid-nineteenth-century Germany on this subject has been summarized in Edward Shorter, 'Middle-Class Anxiety in the German Revolution of 1848,' *Journal of Social History*, 2 (1969), 189-215.

arise from 'normal' conditions, from integrated societies with unchallenged value systems. The social disorganization people rightly see social change as resulting in illegitimacy, a fact we know historically to be true because during a time of great turmoil western illegitimacy rates did indeed soar. Might one argue that modernization has fostered illegitimacy in western society by creating new social groups or subcultures which look benignly upon the permissive sexuality from which illegitimacy springs?

IV

Let us for a moment climb down from these arid theoretical plateaux and consider the situation of a young girl deciding whether to sleep with a young man. Understanding this microscopic situation will permit a better specification of the macro-sociological forces which bear upon it.

The young unmarried woman, contemplating having sex with her boyfriend, will probably ask three questions: (1) who will know? (2) who will be hurt? (3) what will my friends say? She will probably not start sleeping around if the local parson or Mom and Pop will find out about it; she will be loath to have premarital sex if becoming pregnant would mean disappointing family expectations in her forthcoming arranged marriage with Farmer Huber's lad; and she will not have intercourse if her girlfriends would strongly disapprove and think her deviate, a cheap little hussy as one used to say. On the other hand, she probably will shed her qualms about premarital sex if the questions were answered the other way: if she can keep her activities secret from those who know her well; if becoming pregnant would not mean ruining the elaborate economic arrangements about land inheritance and dowries predicated upon her arranged marriage; if her friends would either be indifferent to, or actually applaud, the boldness in shaping her own life and the readiness to develop her personality she has expressed by going to bed with Laborer Meier's son. This third question is necessary because even if anonymity and innocuous consequences were guaranteed, religion, and other internalized value systems would make her pull back from 'sin' unless her peers approved as well.

The answers to these questions do not remain constant over the years, but instead change on the basis of changes in the worldview and social situation of young people. Accordingly, the level of premarital sex in society is not steady, but varies with varying answers to these questions. Assuming for the moment that these propositions hold, we go on to determine what large-scale social changes might alter the willingness of this young girl, and millions like her, to participate in sex before marriage.

We now raise our sights to a macro-societal view. These three questions suggest that premarital intercourse and illegitimacy will be furthered by social changes which do three kinds of things: (1) which enhance anonymity, making it possible for young people to do as they please without the censuring eyes of parents or social authorities upon them; (2) which create a propertyless proletariat among whom need not apply the rigid familial controls on sexual behaviour which prevail among burgher and peasant populations (personal skill and talent, rather than family position, become the means through which the lower classes advance themselves, if at all, in the world); (3) which re-orient value systems from 'traditional' to 'modern,' creating specifically a youth subculture

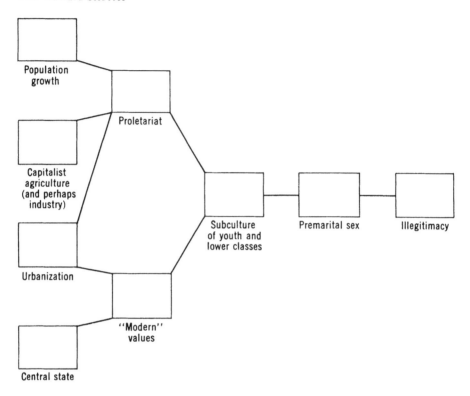

FIGURE 3 *A model linking modernization to sexual change in Europe, 1750-1850*

in which qualities like self-expression, ego development and individuality are prized. I shall argue that the forces which bring out these three conditions are those primarily responsible for the sexual revolution and its accompanying illegitimacy explosion.

How may these considerations be linked together in a model which will explain the course of events in Europe? Figure 3 traces the rough steps which get us from modernization to illegitimacy. Various modernizing social changes, to be more closely identified below, altered the structure of traditional society in several critical ways. For one thing, the European population in the late eighteenth and early nineteenth centuries was both much larger and much younger than ever before. For another, the class structure was swiftly changing during this time, owing to the accumulation of great numbers of landless labourers in both urban and rural areas, in short owing to the growth of a proletariat. Thirdly, the centre of gravity of Europe's population began to shift from the countryside to the city. And finally, the tentacular growth of the modern state altered the structure of society, as government bureaucrats, emissaries of centralist rule, began to weaken the authority of the traditional local elites.

Next step in the model: these structural changes lead to the growth among the young and the lower classes of a new subculture, different from the traditional culture in its devotion to 'modern, specifically urban values. This new value system exalts individualism, opening the door for romantic love, at the cost of traditional values of obedience to the dictates of the family and of the communal social authorities, agencies which command sexual abstinence before marriage.[26] Further step: the values of this new subculture lead to a great increase in premarital intercourse, now sanctioned as a legitimate means of ego development ('true love'). Final step: this higher incidence of coitus leads to an explosion in illegitimate births.

Before the particular developments which 'modernizing social change' entails are specified, an earlier warning about the role of poverty and marriage in this matter should be reiterated. It is a mistake to say that immiserization caused the original illegitimacy explosion by making the founding of a family more difficult. Instead, I suggest that young people participate in intercourse for reasons having little to do with the prospect of later marriage. There are positive cultural reasons why they might engage in such activities. The lack of correlation between economic disaster and illegitimacy, or of one between illegitimacy and marriage rates, are empirical reasons for being cautious in linking together poverty, marriage, and illegitimacy. My model finds the critical relationships in the area of new social classes and new value systems, not in that of economic crisis and postponed marriage.

Four major kinds of social change proved strategic in transforming European patterns of sexual behaviour: the growth of population, the advent of capitalist agriculture and industry (both domestic and factory), the growth of cities and the ensuing diffusion of urban values into society as a whole, and finally the spread of the modern, centralist, bureaucratic state. We now consider the impact of each of these.

The turbulent growth of Europe's population, beginning around 1750, stimulated illegitimacy by creating a landless proletariat. The traditional agricultural system was based upon the single family farm, which is to say upon peasant subsistence agriculture. And the traditional family demanded chasteness of its daughters in order to marry them off in a way economically advantageous to the family. Thus economic exigencies made the peasant family an agency of rigorous sexual control. The need for sure controls vanished with a rising population, as more and more people appeared for whom no individual holding could be made available. Landless labourers, they could behave sexually as they wished: it was a matter of indifference to the family.[27]

26 In using such expressions as 'lower-class subculture,' I follow Walter B. Miller, who has demonstrated how juvenile delinquency, commonly considered pathological, is accepted, normal behaviour among the strata from which most delinquents come. 'Lower Class Culture as a Generating Milieu of Gang Delinquency,' *Journal of Social Issues*, 14 (1958), 5-19. In employing 'individualism' I have Robert A. Nisbet in mind, who restated the thesis that western man's growing sense of individuality sent the institutions of traditional society into disrepair. See *Community and Power* (formerly *The Quest for Community*) (New York: Oxford University Press, 1962; Galaxy edition), passim.

27 Of the enormous literature on social life under subsistence agriculture several titles may be mentioned by way of example: Pierre Goubert has defined the peasant morality of small-farm areas in *Beauvais et le Beauvaisis de 1600 à 1730: Contribution à l'histoire de la France du XVIIe siècle*, 2 vols. (Paris: SEVPEN, 1960); Goubert previewed some of his findings in 'The French Peasantry of the Seventeenth Century: A Regional Example,' *Past and Present*, no. 10 (Nov. 1956), pp. 55-77; on England, see Peter Laslett, *The World We Have Lost* (New York: Scribner's, 1965); Laslett notes the probity of rural sexual mores, and comments: 'If the shape of the society was to be maintained, Pauline morality had to be enforced' (p. 130). The fact of Europe's enormous population growth requires no citation. A recent challenging treatment of the subject is by William Langer, 'Europe's

Agricultural capitalism, another of the great historic forces which upset traditional European society, also promoted illegitimacy by further breaking down the peasant family farm. The engrossment of fields into unitary market-oriented holdings meant the displacement of the cottagers and the yeoman smallholders. Formerly independent peasants lost their holdings and became landless labourers in the employ of the modernizing agriculturalists.[28] So here again the economic considerations which formerly had induced sexual restraint disappeared.

Industrial capitalism must also be counted an important variable, but the linkage between industrial growth as such and illegitimacy is still indistinct. One circumstance commands caution: the availability of non-agricultural employment would have made the founding of a family easier than it had been in purely pastoral societies, particularly in those where agricultural inheritance was not partible. So in the long run industrialization should have reduced illegitimacy.

In the short run, however, the rise of industry probably boosted illegitimacy in two ways. One, by providing an alternative to staying down on the farm or in the craft shop under the father's watchful eye, industry offered young people a means of physically liberating themselves from the controls upon their lives inherent in traditional occupations. Two, by promoting 'modern' value systems among the population caught up in this mode of production, industry – and especially the domestic system or 'putting-out' system – encouraged sexual adventure. Rudolf Braun has demonstrated how the outworking population in the Zurich highlands became more open to individualism, to the gratification of personal desires as an acceptable social goal, in consequence of finding work in the putting-out system.[29] A similar transformation of traditional peasant value systems seems to have gone on in other places as well where cottage industry spread. Whether factory industry will prove to be related to the spread of illegitimacy is a separate question which only further research will clarify.

Urbanization, the third of the great forces bearing upon European society, stimulated sexual change, and therewith illegitimacy, by several means. Urban growth meant the sheer physical transplantation of much of the agricultural population into the cities. There, where industrial or commercial work was available, the migrants were definitively removed from the sexual controls and property considerations of the peasant family

Initial Population Explosion,' *American Historical Review,* 69 (1963), 1-17, who argues that the cultivation of the potato stimulated the subdivision of land, therewith the founding of new families, all of whose offspring constituted the population explosion. It seems clear that when farm sizes dropped beneath a certain level, inheritance and chastity would no longer be social problems: the holdings were simply too tiny. On the social consequences of population growth, see also Wrigley, *Population and History,* pp. 135-43.

28 E.J. Hobsbawm and George Rudé have shown recently how agricultural capitalism proletarianized England's rural labourers in *Captain Swing* (New York: Pantheon, 1968), especially pp. 11-93. Helmut Bleiber traces the social impact of capitalist agriculture in a region of Germany in *Zwischen Reform und Revolution: Lage und Kämpfe der schlesischen Bauern und Landarbeiter im Vormärz, 1840-1847* (East Berlin: Akademie-Verlag, 1966), especially pp. 57-81.

29 *Industrialisierung und Volksleben: Die Veränderungen der Lebensformen in einem ländlichen Industriegebiet vor 1800 (Zürcher Oberland)* (Erlenbach-Zurich: Eugen Rentsch, 1960), passim; a companion volume takes the story into the twentieth century: Braun, *Sozialer und Kultureller Wandel in einem ländlichen Industriegebiet (Zürcher Oberland) unter Einwirkung des Maschinen und Fabrikwesens im 19. und 20. Jahrhundert* (Erlenbach-Zurich: Eugen Rentsch, 1965).

and of the local village authorities. So to the extent that people moved to the city we should expect to see illegitimacy increase, up to a point.[30] But the quality of urban life itself, the values of the city, also stimulated illegitimacy. A city is a place where anonymity lets the individual experiment with his life, strike out in new directions if he wishes. It is a place where a premium is placed on individual freedom and the cultural values which accompany this personal liberation, as Georg Simmel pointed out. Thus the city is a place where the pastor's censuring eye does not extend, and where true love flourishes.[31]

But the city changed the worldview not only of the people who moved to it: the urban way of life reached out in the nineteenth century to permeate the countryside as well. Urbanization means not merely the physical growth of cities, it means the spread of 'urbanism' to the entire society. In Europe great cities like London and Paris - and Munich in Bavaria - represented nodal points for communication. Most activities came to be channelled through them, which meant that sooner or later news of the urban way of life would penetrate to the most distant hinterland village.[32] Between 1750 and 1850, as a result of increased circulation of goods and people, of the exposure to the wider world through military service, or of the widespread distribution of popular magazines and novels, the cultural horizon of the agricultural village expanded to reach the black smokestacks and busy wharves of Europe's great cities. And the swelling proletariat in these villages liked the image of urbanity newly offered to them.

The last of the great social changes which directly influenced illegitimacy was the rise of the modern state. The liberal, rationalistic, bureaucratic colossus grew up everywhere between 1750 and 1850, sending into the hinterland tax officials, subprefects, forestry agents, gendarmes, and a host of other officials, who now would be close to local populations which formerly had only the most ephemeral contacts with deputies of the state. At the hands of these men the structure of moral society in the villages suffered a devastating blow. Everywhere the secularization of church property and

30 Adna F. Weber, *The Growth of Cities in the Nineteenth Century: A Study in Statistics* (New York: Macmillan, 1899; Cornell reprint, 1963) is still the standard quantitative treatment of Europe's urbanization. Of recent research on the growth of European urban populations, Wolfgang Köllmann, 'Zur Bevölkerungsentwicklung ausgewählter deutscher Grosstädte in der Hochindustrialisierungsperiode,' *Jahrbuch für Sozialwissenschaft,* 18 (1967), 129-44; and Philippe Pinchemel, *Géographie de la France,* 2 vols. (Paris: Colin, 1964), especially, II, 560-640, may be mentioned.

31 Simmel's 'The Metropolis and Mental Life' is conveniently reprinted in *Classic Essays on the Culture of Cities,* Richard Sennett (ed.) (New York: Appleton-Century-Crofts, 1969), pp. 47-60. J.A. Banks, in a recent important article, argues that urban migration took place because of the cultural attractiveness of English cities for young people: the city became a site for individual emancipation and personality development. He rejects the horror-story approach to urbanization in England, arguing instead that countrymen flocked to the city for positive reasons. Banks's insight is akin to my assertion that one should not attempt to explain the illegitimacy explosion as a consequence of the economic deprivation and social disorganization which accompanied the industrial revolution. 'Population Change and the Victorian City,' *Victorian Studies,* 11 (1968), 277-89.

32 See E.A. Wrigley, 'A Simple Model of London's Importance in Changing English Society and Economy, 1650-1750,' *Past and Present,* no. 37 (July 1967), 44-70; '... A city like London in the later seventeenth century was so constituted sociologically, demographically and economically that it could well reinforce and accelerate incipient change' (p. 54).

other forms of anti-clericalism damaged the status of the regular and secular clergy who formerly had great influence. The bureaucratic state, with its notions about civil liberties, equality before the law and the like, abolished such administrative paraphernalia of sexual control as the 'fornication penalties' and sartorial regulations, which had been of such utility to the local authorities. The local reeves and aldermen now saw their administrative authority curbed by a straightjacket of government regulations and possibilities of appeal to higher authorities.[33] I would argue that their ability to control sexual behaviour – either by penalizing premarital intercourse or by compelling the seducer to wed the hapless girl – suffered grievously through the expansion of the central government.

This, then, is a model which may serve to explain how the various social changes Europe experienced between 1750 and 1850 resulted in a transformation of patterns of sexual behaviour, and therewith in a surge of illegitimate births. The model is, to be sure, still highly tentative and under-elaborated, doubtless failing to take note of many nuanced relationships or forces for change. Perhaps it will be drastically modified in the course of future research. Yet it may be the beginning of understanding.

V

These general speculations receive some empirical confirmation in the Kingdom of Bavaria, which had one of the highest illegitimacy rates in Europe. We examine briefly the experience of that state in the nineteenth century in order to demonstrate that the model proposed above fits the facts in at least one instance.

Until 1871, when the kingdom joined Bismarck's new German Empire, Bavaria was an independent state, the third largest after Austria and Prussia in central Europe. The kingdom combined within its own borders much of the social and economic diversity found in Europe as a whole. 'Old Bavaria,' the former electoral state of the eighteenth century, was part of the country between the Danube and the Alps, largely agricultural with farms of considerable size on which laboured live-in farmhands (*Dienstboten*) and day labourers (*Taglöhner*). The great city of Munich dominated this part of the country, a focus for all commerce and transportation. During the Napoleonic era parts of the regions of Swabia and Franconia had been added to the old electoral state, and the new political construct became in 1806 the Kingdom of Bavaria. In contrast to Old Bavaria, these provinces to the north and west were rich in industry. During the eighteenth century the putting-out system had infiltrated much of the Franconian countryside, with its centre around the city of Hof. And, in the nineteenth century, factory industry appeared in the artisanal cities of Nürnberg, Würzburg, and Augsburg. This meant that

33 On this process in Germany, see Mack Walker, 'Napoleonic Germany and the Hometown Communities,' *Central European History*, 2 (1969), 99-113. Charles Tilly sees the penetration of the centralized state into the most backward hinterland and the most routine areas of daily life as profoundly important in European social history; he argues specifically that the sprawl of central authority altered the nature of collective violence in the course of the nineteenth century from a 'primitive' pattern to a 'reactionary' one. 'Collective Violence in European Perspective,' in *Violence in America: Historical and Comparative Perspectives*, H.D. Graham and T.R. Gurr (eds.) (New York: Bantam Books, 1969), pp. 4-45, and especially pp. 16-24.

a 'modern' population involved in commerce and industry would be mixed in among the peasant subsistence farmers of Franconia and Swabia.[34]

Bavaria was well known to the moral statisticians and philosophers of nineteenth-century Europe for its great illegitimacy, which amounted at its height, as we have seen, to a quarter of all births. This high level was probably due to two factors: the kingdom's strict regulations for marriage and practicing a handcraft, and the 'impartible' inheritance system in agriculture, which meant the family farm would not be subdivided among the children, passing intact to the eldest instead. (The younger children would be bought off with money payments, and either stayed around as farm help or drifted away.) Both circumstances worked to stimulate illegitimacy. Young journeymen would be denied for years the right to marry and to set up an independent livelihood as master craftsmen because the municipal authorities who rejected their requests feared the burden of poor relief if these men, together with their new families, were to require assistance. Also the existing master craftsmen, who spoke a powerful word in the town halls, feared added competition, and so encouraged the rejection of young journeymen. In agriculture the non-partible nature of inheritance meant that the younger sons of a peasant could not acquire sufficient land to become 'independent,' and lacking such independence they were kept from marriage by both rural custom and law. As a result of these laws, then, both urban and rural proletarians were consigned to bachelorhood, and sired hordes of illegitimate children.[35]

But these facts do not explain the original upturn in illegitimacy. And in order to understand the change over time, which we observed above, we must seek out other factors. Here the general model already outlined will be of service. One may observe how well the relationship it identifies holds up in reality by looking at Bavaria's experience between 1750 and 1850.

Late in the eighteenth century Bavaria had to face the problem of surplus rural population, people for whom no farmstead could be found. The problem of the rural poor, of course, had always been present there, as in all of Europe. Yet the first stirrings of population growth exacerbated it. While the population of Old Bavaria seems to have stagnated throughout much of the eighteenth century, several local studies have demon-

34 For an introduction to Bavarian economy and society in the nineteenth century, the reader is referred to: M. Doeberl, *Entwicklungsgeschichte Bayerns,* vols. 2, 3 (Munich: Oldenbourg, 1928-31); Wolfgang Zorn, 'Gesellschaft und Staat im Bayern des Vormärz,' in *Staat und Gesellschaft im deutschen Vormärz,* Werner Conze (ed.) (Stuttgart: Ernst Klett, 1962), pp. 113-41; Zorn, *Kleine Wirtschafts-und Sozialgeschichte Bayerns, 1806-1933* (Munich-Pasing: Verlag Bayerische Heimatforschung, 1962).

35 On these laws, customs, and their consequences for illegitimacy, see Knodel, 'Law, Marriage and Illegitimacy in Nineteenth-Century Germany'; Shorter, 'Social Change and Social Policy in Bavaria'; and Lindner, *Uneheliche Geburten.*

Large-scale agriculture had traditionally prevailed in many regions of Bavaria, and with it a rural proletariat of farm labourers. And while the numbers of such people increased during the first half of the century in consequence of general population growth, their ranks were not augmented by the specific process of agricultural capitalism. On the lack of market orientation before 1850, see Christoph Borcherdt, *Fruchtfolgesysteme und Morktorientierung als gestaltende Kräfte der Agrarlandschaft in Bayern* (Kallmünz/Regensburg: Michael Lassleben, 1960), p. 31. On the rural labouring classes, see Hanns Platzer, *Geschichte der ländlichen Arbeitsverhältnisse in Bayern* (Munich, 1904).

strated significant population increases in Franconia towards the end of the century. And certainly during the first half of the nineteenth century the Bavarian population everywhere increased at a rapid clip, rising from an estimated 3,060,000 around 1812 (excluding the Palatinate) to 4,029,000 in 1860, an increase which averages out to seven-tenths of a per cent growth per year. One must keep in mind that perhaps a quarter of the gross increase in population during this time was siphoned off by emigration, so the growth is all the more impressive.[36]

Meanwhile, cottage industry was transforming the countryside. Starting in the 1790s, cottage cotton weaving became an important means of subsistence in much of rural Oberfranken, and other provinces too shared in the expansion of the domestic system.[37] So late in the eighteenth century a rural underclass was rising outside the framework of traditional peasant subsistence agriculture. Itself landless, this proletariat would not be subject to the constraints upon sexual experimentation which the peasant family normally imposed.

Another of the social changes responsible for illegitimacy which made itself felt both in Europe as a whole and in Bavaria was urbanization. It is impossible to attribute the original impetus for sexual change to the shift of population from the countryside to the city, for urban migration became a substantial force for change only after 1830. And Bavaria did not become an urbanized land, in the quantitative use of the term, until the twentieth century, for in 1855 only 14 per cent of her population lived in communities composed of more than five thousand people.[38]

Yet amidst Bavaria's torpid urban burghs was the dynamic city of Munich, which experienced accelerated growth starting with the Napoleonic era. Munich's population doubled from an estimated 63,000 around 1812 to 132,000 in 1852 – a quarter of the land's urban population. And the city's importance in society as a whole increased at an even faster pace, for Munich became in the early nineteenth century the national market-place, and the centre point for culture, communications, and transportation. The spread of Bavaria's government bureaucracy out from this state capital also enhanced the city's importance. I would argue that Munich did much to spread 'urban' values through the Bavarian population by virtue of its central position alone.[39] These

36 Friedrich Lütge, citing Schmelzle's study of Old Bavaria, claims the eighteenth-century population of the electoral state did not increase. *Die Bayerische Grundherrschaft: Untersuchungen über die Agrarverfassung Altbayerns im 17.-18. Jahrhundert* (Stuttgart: Piscator, 1949), p. 10. But various authors find evidence of substantial population growth in Franconia in the eighteenth century. See Valentin Steinert, *Zur Fräge der Naturalteilung: Eine Untersuchung über die bäuerlichen Verhältnisse des fränkischen Grabfeldgaues,* in the series Wirtschafts- und Verwaltungsstudien ... Bayerns, 23 (1906), 53; Wieland Kindinger, *Beiträge zur Entwicklung der Kulturlandschaft in der zentralen Rhön vom Dreissigjährigen Krieg bis 1933* (Würzburg, 1942; Fränkische Studien, NF 4), pp. 86-91; Ludwig Schmidt-Kehl, 'Wandel im Erb und Rassengefüge zweier Rhönorte, 1700-1936,' *Archiv für Bevölkerungswissenschaft,* 7 (1937), 176-99, especially 179; Carl Hofmann, *Die Hausweberei in Oberfranken* (Jena: Gustav Fischer, 1927), p. 22; Friedrich Kästner, *Die Oberfränkische Handweberei* (Diss. Munich, 1918), p. 7. For national population growth data, see 'Geschichte der neueren bayerischen Statistik,' in *Beiträge zur Statistik des Königreichs Bayern,* 86 (1914), 269.

37 See Hofmann, *Hausweberei,* and Kästner, *Handweberei.*

38 Bavaria. Königliches Statistisches Landesamt, *Bayerns Entwicklung nach den Ergebnissen der amtlichen Statistik seit 1840* (Munich: K. Statistisches Landesamt, 1915), p. 3.

39 The population of Munich, and of all other Bavarian municipalities, since 1840 is reported in 'Historisches Gemeindeverzeichnis: die Einwohnerzahlen der Gemeinden Bayerns in der Zeit von 1840 bis 1952,' *Beiträge zur Statistik Bayerns,* 192 (1953), 14. For the cultural impact of cities

values were to become the cultural norms of the new lower classes whom social change was causing to appear, deforming the symmetry of traditional social structure.

Bavaria was turned topsy-turvy by the fourth of the great social changes at work upon Europe: the advance of the centralized, bureaucratic state. Between 1799, when Maximilian I became elector of Old Bavaria, until 1817, when Count Maximilian von Montgelas resigned as the king's first minister, Bavaria transmuted itself from a sleepy old regime principality into a dynamic state. Montgelas was one of a breed of enlightened administrators, devoted to French precepts for organizing and ruling a centralized country, who descended upon Germany in these years. He caused the judiciary and legal code to be reformed, the state bureaucracy to be professionalized, and government control over local fiefdoms to be asserted. Every aspect of public life underwent a wrenching reorganization in these years, something which simultaneously happened in much of the rest of Europe as well.

These governmental changes shook the old hometown elites, though not entirely displacing them. Bavarian small towns and villages had traditionally been run by an oligarchy of the wealthy and established citizens: the prosperous master craftsmen in elite trades, the merchants, peasant farmers with substantial holdings, and the local cleric, most likely Protestant in Franconia or Swabia, Catholic in Old Bavaria. In the old regime the state government in Munich, or Ansbach, or wherever, was so remote and its authority so intermittent that these local types could act pretty much as they chose in enforcing local standards of behaviour upon the citizenry, punishing miscreants, and in general arranging the moral and social environment of their communities to suit themselves.[40]

The reforms of the Montgelas era changed all this. Local citizens who felt themselves abused by the arbitrary exercise of municipal authority could appeal to echelons of the national government hovering just above the communal administrations, avid for a chance to reach into the local arena and intervene. In a period of secularization the churches were stripped of much of their property, the clerics of much of their influence and authority. There would, for example, be no more compelling people to go to church on Sundays. The controls which master craftsmen could exert upon the journeymen and apprentices who lived with them, as well as the controls which farmers could apply to the servants and agricultural labourers housed in their garrets, became circumscribed. The entire range of penalties for premarital intercourse, illegitimacy, and adultery which civil authorities had employed formerly against 'immorality' were abolished. An ordinance of 1808 stated specifically that the 'fornication penalties' were outlawed. Henceforth no criminal or civil sanction could be invoked against those who had sex outside

---

we have the testimony of the anonymous author of 'Suggestions as to how Barriers may be Placed Against the Vice Spreading to the Countryside': 'The curse of vice ... is creeping out from its previous abode – the cities – in order to inundate the countryside and its thriving fields with ravaging torrents. Young flowerlike maidens by the thousand have been seized in this wild current and thrown to the ground.' *Vorschläge wie dem auf dem Lande um sich greifenden Uebel der Unzucht könnten Schranken gesetzt werden* (n.p., 1814), p. 3.

40 On the quality of social control under the old regime, see Jos. von Destouches, *Ueber den Verfall der Städte und Märkte und die Mittel, ihnen wieder aufzuhelfen* (Ulm: Verlag Stettinischen Buchhandlung, 1803), passim; Mack Walker, 'Reform Invades the Hometown Communities' (draft paper of December 1967). See also Felix Joseph von Lipowsky, *Bayerns Kirchenund Sittenpolizei unter seinen Herzögen und Kurfürsten* (Munich, 1821), especially pp. 123-44.

of marriage, aside from seldom-used provisions which permitted the authorities to put 'chronically immoral' women in workhouses and to break up 'concubinage.' These were the means with which traditional society compelled obedience to its codes of sexual morality, and they were all swept away.[41]

Thus the Napoleonic era left the local elites, not only in Bavaria but in all of western and central Europe except England, in a very much different situation than it had found them. The traditionalists believed in a value system which stressed curbing 'egoism,' keeping chaste until marriage, and exalting the inheritance requirements of the family above all personal considerations. After the Napoleonic era they continued to believe in these things, but they had lost the power to impose their own views of moral right-eousness upon a younger generation – and upon a swelling mass of lower orders in gen-eral – which was rapidly acquiring different social values and moral standards.

The next step in the argument is to demonstrate how these major social changes – population growth, rural and perhaps industrial capitalism, urban migration and the urban way of life, and government centralization – transformed sexual morality with a consequent increase in illegitimacy. And I believe that they made themselves felt by creating new lower classes who participated in a new subculture, and that this subculture stressed individual self-development and experimentation. Here we run into major evi-dential problems. It is not difficult to demonstrate a population increase or the growth of cities since these things are quantitatively ascertainable. It is difficult to verify the emergence of a subculture among an inarticulate social class, and to specify the con-tents of this new culture. The lower classes have left few personal testimonials behind, written historical evidence being generated almost solely by members of the upper orders. So, if we wish to find out what the lower classes and the young were thinking, we must read the accounts of their activity handed down by middle- and upper-class observers, people who had every cause to be hostile to these subcultural developments. This is much like trying to study the heresies of the Middle Ages through the writings of the theologically correct, the heretical materials themselves having long been de-stroyed.

Whatever the reality of lower-class culture early in the nineteenth century, the fact is that upper-class observers certainly thought that a new subculture was emerging. They believed a decisive historical change had taken place, in which the lower classes rejected the modesty of dress, the humility of behaviour, and the propriety of morals traditionally expected of them for high-quality, fashionable apparel, an assertive de-meanour, and libertine moral standards. I have made no attempt to quantify these judgments, impressionistically asserting the existence of this strain in nineteenth-century thought. Yet such evidence may have some validity.

41 Among the few competent studies of administrative reorganization and centralization of this time, Horst Clément's may be especially recommended. *Das bayerische Gemeindeedikt vom 17. Mai 1818: Ein Beitrag zur Entstehungsgeschichte der kommunalen Selbstverwaltung in Deutschland* (Diss. Freiburg i. B., 1934). Revisions in the administrative law on social control may be followed in Georg Döllinger, *Repertorium der Staats-verwaltung des Königreichs Baiern*, 6 vols. (Munich, 1814-17); and Döllinger, *Sammlung der im Gebiete der inneren Staats-verwaltung des Königreichs Bayern bestehenden Verordnungen, aus amtlichen Quellen geschöpft und systematische geordnet*, 33 vols. (Munich, 1835-54), especially vols. 11, 12, 14, 26, and 27; the 1808 ordinance abolishing fornication penalties may be found in vol. 5, 179-80. Fornication penalties were abolished in the Franconian principalities of Ansbach and Bayreuth in 1795.

We may examine some samples from an enormous literature on the 'immorality' question. In the province of Oberbayern it was customary for 'masses' of single women to appear at dance locales, wishing to be asked to dance, and hoping to find a man to escort them home. The district poor-relief board of Landshut thought this practice repugnant to public morality, and the source of much illegitimacy. The observer who reported these facts noted that 'the daughters of respectable peasants, millers and such – in general of well-to-do landowners – are not permitted to take part in this practice.' Or there is the 'dying sister' story from the Bamberg official newspaper: 'How far the demoralisation of the lower classes of people has progressed is seen in the following incident in a nearby village. A young man sitting in a tavern was called by his mother to hurry to the bedside of his dying sister. He however replied: "You run ahead and tell her to wait until I have finished my beer." '[42]

Finally, we note the report of a provincial official in 1859 on the condition of the lower classes in the province of Oberfranken. He observed that the severe economic crises of earlier years had by now largely vanished and the land was prospering. Nonetheless the 'moral misery' of the past years had not receded. 'The damage egoism causes in public and social life through overweening ambition (*Selbstuberhebung*) and megalomania (*Grossmanssucht*) appears in private and family life through status-seeking (*Standesüberhebung*) and pleasure-seeking (*Genussucht*) ... The population of Oberfranken does not lack alertness, industriousness and perseverance. But it lacks indeed the moral power to oppose inner passions and bad examples which corrode and undermine discipline and custom.' The writer concluded that the frivolity and immorality of the population had led to great increases in illegitimate births.[43]

This middle-class perception of immorality pervades government reports, newspaper accounts, political pamphlets, social writings, parliamentary speeches, and diary observations. Whether the lower classes were acquiring a subculture of their own, with the above-mentioned qualities, remains to be definitively established. Beyond dispute is the fact that the middle classes thought a radical departure from traditional patterns was taking place.

The last part of my argument is the assertion that the new value systems which prevailed among the young meant, in fact, more sexual intercourse and a higher incidence of illegitimacy. This may be indirectly demonstrated in several ways. Contemporaries agreed that the cities were the seedbed of immorality. And independent of their outraged assertions I have suggested that urban life did promote a new subculture by aggregating people naturally open to new moral standards, by guaranteeing them anonymity, and by imbedding within the very fabric of the environment a different view of life. Consequently we would expect urban illegitimacy rates to be higher than rural ones.

And, in fact, they are. The level of illegitimacy in the larger Bavarian cities was considerably higher than that of the surrounding countryside. Between 1879 and 1888 an average of 30 per cent of all births in Munich were illegitimate; only 16 per cent were illegitimate, however, in the rural districts of the province of Oberbayern, where Munich was located. This difference is not due merely to the fact that the cities had more un-

42 For these quotations, see Munich Hauptstaatsarchiv, MI 46556, memo of 22 Feb. 1837; clipping from *Bamberger Regierungsblatt* preserved in MI 46560.
43 MI 46560, 7 April 1859.

married women available for illegitimate conceptions than the countryside. Such women actually became involved in premarital intercourse leading to illegitimate births more often in Munich than in the countryside: there were 80 illegitimate children for every thousand unmarried women in Munich, 60 in the country districts of Oberbayern. Similar results obtain for most of the other Bavarian cities as well, and not just in the 1880s but throughout the nineteenth century since 1835/36, when data on such matters first became available.[44]

In most of Europe the urban illegitimacy rate was higher than the rural. In France 15 per cent of all children born in cities were illegitimate (in Paris, 28 per cent in 1869), but only 4 per cent of those born in the countryside. Seven per cent of the Netherlands' urban births were illegitimate, 3 per cent of the rural ones. In Sweden urban illegitimacy was 27 per cent, rural 8 per cent. This was the general trend.[45] Alexander von Oettingen, the moral statistician, attributed these differentials to some cultural peculiarity of the urban environment, noting that in the cities both the marriage rate and the incidence of prostitution – factors which should drive down the illegitimacy rate, all other things being equal – are higher than in the countryside. Something about urban life was clearly producing a lot of premarital intercourse without subsequent speedy trips to the altar. I argue that that something was the cultural climate prevailing in the city.

Another type of statistical technique will permit us to relate illegitimacy not just to cities, but to 'modern' occupations and proletarian social constellations. Bavarian census data taken by district from the censuses of 1840 and 1880 permit us to spot an ecological relationship between the presence of illegitimate children and of the socio-economic characteristics of the district. The technique employed was multiple curvilinear regression. The relationship between the dependent and independent variables was derived using the backward elimination procedure. This will be gibberish to any reader not versed in statistics. The technique simply involves calculating correlations between different independent variables, such as the percentage of farmers in the district, and the dependent variable of illegitimacy. Each variable is observed in *simultaneous* conjunction with all others. The trick is to determine which combination of independent variables will explain a maximum amount of the variation in the dependent variable. At the same time, one tries to keep the number of independent variables to a minimum. The procedure lets us construct the ideal-typical profile of a district with high illegitimacy.

The census of 1840 reported for all the rural districts and the towns of the kingdom a large number of socio-economic characteristics: marital status of the population, a

44 Lindner, *Uneheliche Geburten*, pp. 81-112, 226-38.
45 Oettingen reproduces these urban–rural differentials calculated by the statistician Wappäus. *Moral-statistik*, pp. 316-19. Adna Weber believed that urban 'immorality' was not greater than rural, for data available to him on illegitimate births per 1,000 unmarried women showed no appreciable difference between town and countryside. If the rates of illegitimate births per 100 total births were higher in cities than in the countryside, Weber said it was because many young country girls came to the urban lying-in hospitals to bear their children, then returned to their home villages. *Growth of Cities*, pp. 404-6. I contend that in Bavaria, at least, illegitimacy – measured however one chooses – was higher in big cities than in the countryside. More research is needed to see if this differential holds up across Europe. But it would be a mistake at this point to assume that the 'lying-in hospital' effect operates in all cities, for the Thüringen Statistisches Bureau reported that city girls who became pregnant went out into the *countryside* to have their babies, and then returned home ('Zur Statistik der unehelichen Geburten in den Thüringenschen Staaten,' p. 342).

crude age breakdown, religion, economic structure with reference to whether agricultural, whether self-employed, and whether propertied. In addition it asked whether the children under fourteen years of age were of legitimate birth. Multiple curvilinear regression analysis was applied to these data.[46] Let me emphasize that of the fifteen or so census variables originally used in the regression analysis, I report in the following pages *only* those found to correlate closely with illegitimacy.

Interesting results were obtained for rural areas, using the number of illegitimate children per 1,000 juvenile population as the dependent variable. As Table 1 demonstrates, 54 per cent of the variation was explained on the basis of the following characteristics: (1) the absence of married couples; (2) the absence of Catholics; (3) the absence of people exclusively in agriculture (we are observing here the square of the variable);[47] (4) the presence of landless labourers (*landwirtschaftliche Taglöhner ohne Grundbesitz*); (5) the presence of farmhands (*Dienstboten*); (6) the absence of propertied craftsmen (*Gewerbetreibende mit Grundbesitz*; this observation is based on the square of the variable); (7) the presence of small-town lower-class types (*städtische Taglöhner*. I am, again, going by the square of the variable. Small towns count as rural for census purposes.).

The results obtained for rural areas when the dependent variable was the number of illegitimate children per 1,000 unmarried women were not substantially different from those just reported.

To summarize, Table 1 permits the construction of an ideal type of rural county with high illegitimacy in whose profile some kinds of social characteristics are prominent, others conspicuously absent. I emphasize that such a county must combine all of these qualities simultaneously. The district will, of course, have some obvious distinguishing characteristics: few married couples and numerous common-law unions, to take the evidence of rural rate 2. Most important, however, the district will be abundant in the landless lower classes, agricultural labourers, farmhands, and similar types. I have hypothesized that the illegitimacy explosion is partly a consequence of the growth of these orders of people, not tied in their sexual activities to the inheritance patterns of the traditional family farm. There appears to be empirical confirmation here.

The relationship between illegitimacy and these various characteristics drops way off in urban areas. Table 1 shows that when the dependent variable is the per mille of illegitimate children in the juvenile population, the most propitious combination of independent variables accounts for only 22 per cent of the variation. In urban areas some of the correlations noted in the countryside either disappear or are reversed: the presence of Catholics becomes positively, not negatively, correlated with illegitimacy; the presence of widows means a positive, not a negative correlation. (Urban widows have illegitimate children after their husbands' deaths; rural ones don't, apparently.)

The point about urban areas is that relationships which held up well in the countryside, accounting in a significant manner for illegitimacy there, almost vanish in the

---

46 The 1840 census data are from 'Stand und Bewegung der Bevölkerung, 1818-1846,' *Beiträge zur Statistik des Königreichs Bayern*, 1 (1850), 30-113.

47 Using the square of a variable in a regression model rather than the variable itself is a crude way of spotting curvilinear relationships among the independent and dependent variables. On this technique see Jerome C.R. Li, *Statistical Inference*, vol. II (Ann Arbor: Edwards Brothers, 1964), pp. 215-18, and Robert A. Gordon, 'Issues in Multiple Regression,' *American Journal of Sociology*, 73 (1968), 592-616 and especially 611.

city. This means that *some quality of urban life itself,* not just some feature of the socio-economic mix of the urban population, produces the high levels of urban illegitimacy. That is perhaps the major conclusion of this particular analysis.

I have examined a few of the figures Friedrich Lindner published from the census of 1880, using the same technique.[48] Lindner gives data on only a few variables, adding to our knowledge solely the average amount of arable land per farm by district. The dependent variables are the number of illegitimate births per thousand total births, and the number of illegitimate children in the population per thousand unmarried women, for both indices the 1879–88 average. The independent variables are the percentage of the population in agriculture, the percentage in agriculture who also practice a craft, the hectares of both land in general and arable land per landowner, and whether inheritance in the district was partible. The results are reproduced in Table 2. It is obvious that this latter variable turned out to be unimportant because the land was generally not split among inheritors anywhere in Bavaria except in the province of Unterfranken. And among the counties in that province a wide range of illegitimacy levels existed.

The key predictor variables were the percentage of the population in agriculture, the percentage simultaneously practicing a craft, and the hectares of arable land per landowner. The first two were negatively correlated with both dependent variables, the latter one positive, up to a point. These three independent variables explained 44 per cent of the variation for each dependent one.

These results confirm the findings of the 1840 census. Illegitimacy does not flourish in heavily agricultural areas because of the continuing moral grip of the single family farm. Yet when the average farm size starts to increase, illegitimacy also rises for the obvious reason that a rural proletariat, highly prone to illegitimacy, is required to run big farms.

VI

In conclusion let me summarize these results. The problem was to account for the gradual, massive liberalization of the sexual mores of much of Europe's population over the last two centuries in terms of modernization. The difficulty in bringing evidence to bear on a subject as private and intimate as sexual behaviour is overpowering, but I have claimed that, taken with a few grains of salt, we may use illegitimacy statistics as evidence of sexual activity. The phenomenon we are trying to judge, of course, is the incidence of premarital intercourse, for its acceleration was essential to the sexual revolution. A good measure of this phenomenon would be the frequency of prebridal pregnancies. Yet because arduous local digging is required to turn up such data, perhaps illegitimacy may stand as a surrogate. The data on illegitimacy seem accurate for the most part, and certainly in central Europe some significance for sexual behaviour may be attached to fluctuations in illegitimacy because official delay of lower-class marriages often made it impossible to mask an illegitimate conception with a shotgun wedding.

The major empirical finding of this paper is an explosion in illegitimate births between 1750 and 1850, taking these years as rough guideposts, not precise turning points. An upsurge in illegitimate births from the negligible levels, perhaps one or two per cent, of traditional western society to the 10 or 20 per cent of modern society constitutes a remarkable occurrence. This increase occurred sooner or later in every western country for which data are available, although the precise timing of the increase varies. We may explain this increase in illegitimacy as a consequence of a fundamental transformation of the sexual attitudes of the lower classes: they abandoned the sexual abstemiousness prescribed for them in traditional society for a more easy-going style of interpersonal relations, coming to see sexual experience as an important part of personality development. This emphasis upon social class in accounting for differentials in sexual activity is fully in keeping with empirical sociological research on sex. If recent work has taught us anything, it is that styles of sexual activity, differences in attitudes towards, and frequency of sexual relations are not distributed randomly throughout the population; they are rather a close function of social class.

I submit that four of the major social changes, which together make up much of Europe's experience with modernization, caused this shift in sexual attitudes. Population growth and the advent of capitalist farming and of cottage industry caused the ranks of the lower orders to swell rapidly: a great class of landless proletarians began to appear for whom there was no place in the family farm, the traditional social and economic unit of rural Europe. Inheritance considerations meant that the European family, concerned about the future of its little farm and about making advantageous marriages for its daughters in particular, enforced a sexual puritanism upon its offspring. With the appearance of propertyless groups, the need for such controls vanished.

At the same time, the expansion of the centralized state caused many of the traditional elites in the villages and small towns of Europe to suffer a loss in status and authority. More particularly they were deprived of the administrative devices, such as the 'fornication penalties,' with which they once commanded sexual conformity within the community as a whole. So two sets of inhibiting factors – the controls of the family and those of the village elders – become seriously weakened in the course of modernization.

The argument, however, has a further step. A sexual revolution is not produced merely by dropping mechanical controls on the opportunity for intercourse, or by abandoning civil and criminal penalties for premarital pregnancies. A positive change in the internalized values of the population must also accompany the abandonment of these social controls. Here I suggest that urbanization encouraged people to reorient their value systems. The freer, easier life of the city militated against the repressiveness and fear of one's inner emotions, evaporated the hostility to self-understanding and rational analysis one finds in traditional society. Numerous investigations have discovered the value transformation which involvement with modern situations brings about: people become more eager for ego gratification, more concerned to develop their personalities at the cost of their formerly strong identification with the community. True love, a sign of strong ego development, blossoms.

So as the cities of Europe waxed and news of their way of life spread out into the countryside, the lower-class youth of the late eighteenth century embraced a new subculture. The rational destruction of traditional institutions which the Enlightenment represented, and the development of individualism which comes with romanticism, conspired to replace the old culture with a new one. Part of this culture asserted a positive value to sexual experimentation. And its consequence was illegitimacy.

TABLE 1

The results of multiple regression analysis applied to 1840 census (260 census districts)

Variable		Partial regression coefficient (b_i)	T-test	Standard partial regression coefficient (B_i)

Rural rate 1 (illegitimate children/total population of children × 1000)

$X1$	% of married couples in the population	-1.6407	-9.88*	-0.5010
$X1^2$	% of married couples squared	0.0155	2.77*	0.1258
$X2$	% of Catholics	-0.0409	-5.81*	-0.3065
$X3$	% of population exclusively in agriculture	0.0027	0.10NS	0.0060
$X3^2$	% of population exclusively in agriculture squared	-0.0004	-2.96*	-0.1566
$X4$	% of landless labourers (*Landbau-Taglöhner ohne Grund- oder Hausbesitz*)	0.3098	3.83*	0.3022
$X4^2$	% of landless labourers squared	-0.0011	-1.74†	-0.1254
$X5$	Live-in farmhands (*Gesinde*)	0.1682	4.82*	0.2597
$X6^2$	Self-employed tradesmen with property	0.0278	0.71NS	0.0423
$X6^2$	Self-employed tradesmen squared	-0.0007	-2.60‡	-0.1422
$X7^2$	Small-town labourers (*Städtische Taglöhner*)	-0.0494	-0.36NS	-0.0264
$X7^2$	Small-town labourers squared	0.0020	2.51†	0.1683

% of variation explained ($R^2 \times 100$) = 53.68%

Equation: $Y = 121.0686 - 1.6407 \times 1$
$+ 0.0155 \times 1^2 - 0.0409 \times 2 + 0.0027 \times 3$
$- 0.0004 \times 3^2 + 0.3098 \times 4 - 0.0011 \times 4^2$
$+ 0.1682 \times 5 + 0.0278 \times 6 - 0.0007 \times 6^2$
$- 0.0494 \times 7 + 0.0020 \times 7^2$

Rural rate 2 (illegitimate children/unmarried women (widows excluded) × 1000)

$X1$	% of married couples in the population	-1.2789	-5.15*	-0.2612
$X2$	% of common-law unions	18.4657	3.25*	0.1599
$X3$	% of widows	-1.1679	-1.88†	-0.0935
$X4$	% of Catholics	-0.0864	-7.28*	-0.4240
$X5^2$	% of population exclusively in agriculture	-0.0587	-1.39NS	-0.0864
$X5^2$	% of population exclusively in agriculture squared	-0.0005	-2.30†	-0.1236
$X6$	% of landless labourers (*Landbau-Taglöhner ohne Grund- oder Hausbesitz*)	0.4016	4.91*	0.2620
$X7$	Self-employed tradesmen with property	0.0089	0.15NS	0.0090
$X7^2$	Self-employed tradesmen squared	-0.0012	-3.01*	-0.1664

X_8	% of urban labourers	-0.3062	-1.44^{NS}	-0.1095
X_8^2	% of urban labourers squared	0.0032	2.63*	0.1816

% of variation explained ($R^2 \times 100$) = 50.49%

Equation: $Y = 162.71 - 1.2789 \, X1 + 18.4657 \, X2 - 1.1679 \, X3 - 0.0846 \, X4 - 0.0587 \, X5 - 0.0005 \, X5^2 + 0.4016 \, X6 + 0.0089 \, X7 - 0.0012 \, X7^2 - 0.3062 \, X8 + 0.0032 \, X8^2$

Urban rate 1 (illegitimate children/total population of children × 1000)

$X1$	% of married couples in the population	-0.5420	$-3.04*$	-0.2945
$X2$	% of widows	0.6487	1.25^{NS}	0.1330
$X2^2$	% of widows squared	0.0629	$2.32\ddagger$	0.2561
$X3$	% of Catholics	0.0408	$2.79*$	0.2968
$X4$	% of landless labourers (*Landbau-Taglöhner ohne Grund- oder Hausbesitz*)	0.3131	$2.48\dagger$	0.2443
$X5$	% of servants	-0.2972	$-1.68\dagger$	-0.1748
$X6$	% of apprentices	0.2093	$2.65*$	0.2625

% of variation explained ($R^2 \times 100$) = 21.77%

Equation: $Y = 109.3848 - 0.5420 \, X1 + 0.6487 \, X2 + 0.0629 \, X2^2 + 0.0408 \, X3 + 0.3131 \, X4 - 0.2972 \, X5 + 0.2093 \, X6$

Urban rate 2 (illegitimate children/unmarried women (widows excluded) × 1000)

$X1$	% of married couples in the population	-0.4764	-1.53^{NS}	-0.1590
$X1^2$	% of married couples squared	0.0147	$2.71*$	0.2745
$X2$	% of widows	2.5238	$2.99*$	0.3179
$X2^2$	% of widows squared	0.1343	$3.04*$	0.3364
$X3$	% of Catholics	0.0691	$1.95\dagger$	0.3086
$X3^2$	% of Catholics squared	0.0003	$2.68*$	0.4097
$X4$	% of landless labourers (*Landbau-Taglöhner ohne Grund- oder Hausbesitz*)	0.7745	$3.97*$	0.3712
$X5$	% of servants	-0.5444	$-1.94\dagger$	-0.1967

% of variation explained ($R^2 \times 100$) = 28.62%

Equation: $Y = 78.2763 - 0.4764 \, X1 + 0.0147 \, X1^2 + 2.5238 \, X2 + 0.1343 \, X2^2 + 0.0691 \, X3 + 0.0003 \, X3^2 + 0.7745 \, X4 - 0.5444 \, X5$

NS = not significant at 10% level
† = significant at 10% level
‡ = significant at 5% level
* = significant at 1% level

TABLE 2

The results of multiple regression analysis applied to 1880 census (126 census-districts)

Variable	Partial regression coefficient (b_i)	T-test	Standard partial regression coefficient (B_i)
Rate 1 (illegitimate births/total births $\times$ 1000)			
X1 % in full time agriculture	-0.1128	-2.60‡	-0.2060
X1² % in full time agriculture squared	0.0056	2.04‡	0.1545
X2 Hectares of arable land	1.8287	7.89*	0.6255
X2² Hectares of arable land squared	-0.4733	-5.43*	-0.4438
% of variation explained ($R^2 \times 100$) = 44.2%			

Equation: $Y = 13.6601 - 0.1128 \times 1 + 0.0056 \times 1^2 + 1.8287 \times 2 - 0.4733 \times 2^2$

Variable	Partial regression coefficient (b_i)	T-test	Standard partial regression coefficient (B_i)
Rate 2 (illegitimate population/unmarried women $\times$ 1000)			
X1 % in full time agriculture	-0.0434	-2.82*	-0.2149
X2 % in part time agriculture	-0.0591	-1.95†	-0.1786
X3 Hectares of arable land	0.5134	4.71*	0.4758
X3² Hectares of arable land squared	-0.2051	-6.06*	-0.5212
% of variation explained ($R^2 \times 100$) = 43.8%			

Equation: $Y = 5.0703 - 0.0434 \times 1 - 0.0591 \times 2 + 0.5134 \times 3 - 0.2051 \times 3^2$

H. NISHIO

Political centralism and economic consequences: an analysis of early Japanese modernization

In the analysis of a productive system, Schumpeter's notion of 'Social Climate' suggests to social scientists a need for inquiry into the underlying relationships between economic and non-economic factors which provide the social basis for development of a productive system.[1] However, economic studies of Tokugawa commercialism (most of which are in Japanese) lack any systematic treatment of the interplay between economic and socio-political structures. To delineate the Japanese 'social climate' this paper focuses on selected major political institutions of Tokugawa Japan (1603–1867) so as to account for the degree and intensity of political pressure exerted by centralist political policies which, with no intention of the part of the Tokugawa policy-makers, generated some degree of entrepreneurial opportunity and encouraged economic growth during the period. We shall also assess here the degree to which the developing economic order in turn affected the basis of political authority by causing economic strain within the political system.

Before looking at Tokugawa centralism and its consequences, we must explain two things which are equally important to an understanding of the Tokugawa political system. First, the Tokugawa political system was antithetical to the preceding decentralized feudalism.[2] Second, the Tokugawa system was originally based on an ideal society

---

1 Joseph Schumpeter is quite explicit about the multi-variate causation of a productive system. In *The Theory of Economic Development* he states: 'When we inquire about the general forms of economic phenomena, about their uniformities, or about a key to understanding them, we *ipso facto* indicate that we wish at that moment to consider them as something to be investigated ... as "unknown"... *When we succeed in finding a definite causal relation between two phenomena, our problem is solved if the one which plays the "causal" role is non-economic'* (italics mine). Joseph A. Schumpeter, *The Theory of Economic Development* (Cambridge, Mass.: Harvard University Press, 1934), p. 4.

2 The words 'feudalism' or 'feudal' are used in this paper as defined by Coulborn: 'To obtain a usable concept of feudalism we must eliminate extraneous factors and aspects which are common to many types of society; feudalism is not synonymous with aristocracy; feudalism is not a necessary concomitant of the great estate worked by dependents or servile labour; feudalism is not merely the relationship between lord and man, because this existed in a non-feudal society. *It is only when*

as constructed by the twelfth-century Chinese philosopher, Chu Hsi (1130–1200) and other neo-Confucian scholars.[3]

HISTORICAL LEGACY OF TOKUGAWA CENTRALISM

The first point may be explained in a brief historical sketch. After seven centuries of imperial court administration, a highly centralized administrative and judicial system was established by the Minamoto clan in 1184.[4] During the following five centuries, until 1602, a succession of military rulers governed the nation, not as independent rulers but rather as military agents of the emperor. Throughout this period, which was marked by the rise and fall of many 'feudal' shogunates, the effectiveness of the administrative and military powers of *daimyō* (feudal lords) increased to the point where local representatives of the *shōgun* (the military ruler of Japan) saw a threat in the assumption of prerogatives by the local officials appointed directly by the Imperial Court. This situation was particularly noticeable during the early periods of military domination over military and political affairs. Consequently, an increasing number of officials and noblemen in Kyōto began to see the necessity of trimming the powers of the military regimes and of regaining for the Imperial Court more direct and complete control over the affairs of the country.

In addition, local *daimyō* were granted a substantial degree of political autonomy within their own domains. In Japan, this decentralization with its complex relationships between the Imperial Court and the central military governments had considerably weakened the political system by the end of the sixteenth century.

It became evident that a centralized political system[5] was necessary if a military ruler was to retain control. After a successful unification of the nation, the founder of the Tokugawa regime, Ieyasu, sought to reorganize the political system, particularly the

rights of government are attached to lordships and fiefs that we can speak of fully developed feudalism' (italics mine). R. Coulborn, *Feudalism in History* (Princeton, NJ: Princeton University Press, 1956), p. 16. For the distinction between a 'decentralized' and a 'centralized' feudal system, see pp. 139-45 of this chapter.

3 (a) The new metaphysical, psychological, and ethical theories of the Sung period; it borrowed much from Buddhism and Taoism in order to supplement and expand the teachings received from the classical exponents of this school, whereas, the more practical thought of the Sung school seemed to follow traditional lines, dealing with age-old Chinese institutions and with social problems. Neo-Confucian scholars include Chu Hsi, Fan Chung-yen, Ou-yang Hsiu, Cheng Hao, and Cheng I. See W.T. De Bary, 'A Reappraisal of New-Confucianism' in A.F. Wright (ed.), *Studies in Chinese Thought* (Chicago: University of Chicago Press, 1956), pp. 81-111.

(b) The Japanese neo-Confucian scholars include Fujiwara Seika, Hayashi Razan, Nakae Tōju, and later Yamazaki Anzan. Fujiwara Seika and Hayashi Razan rejected mere absorption of knowledge and a contemplation of interpretation of the Chinese classics as 'useless learnings.' Instead, they asserted a need for more pragmatic knowledge which could be put into practice for the realization of an ideal social and political order. See Yomiuri Press, *Nihon no rekishi* (Japanese History) (Tōkyō: Yomiuri Shimbunsha, 1958), pp. 161-71.

4 It was only a highly centralized system relative to the political systems which existed prior to the Kamakura period (1192-1392).

5 The distinction between 'centralized' and 'decentralized' feudalism is made as characteristic respectively of Tokugawa and pre-Tokugawa feudalism, the latter including the systems under Kamakura (1192-1392), Ashikaga (1392-1569), Oda (1569-84), and Toyotomi (1585-1603). H. Norman, *Emergence of Japan as a Modern State* (New York: Institute of Pacific Relations, 1940), p. 12.

power relations between the central government and the local *daimyō*. The antithetical nature of the decentralized and the centralized political systems needs further emphasis in view of Chu Hsi's 'ideal' society on the one hand, and of the 'power' society established by Ieyasu and his successors on the other.

Because of his concern with the weaknesses of the decentralized system of the previous periods, Tokugawa Ieyasu studied various Chinese social and political systems, particularly those of the neo-Confucian school.[6] In seeking an adequate social and political system, Ieyasu was attracted by Chu Hsi's view of an 'ideal' society. He incorporated much of Chu Hsi's thinking into his own philosophy, and made use of it in his reorganization of the political order.

CHU HSI'S IDEAL SOCIETY
AND TOKUGAWA POLITICAL STRUCTURE

Chu Hsi's 'ideal' society is a moral–legal society. 'Of All Things,' says Chu Hsi, 'each has its law. These innumerable laws all proceed from one source, and this one source of all laws is the Supreme Ultimate.'[7] 'The Supreme Ultimate is the most excellent and supremely good ethical principle.'[8] For Chu Hsi, it was identical with Moral Law; and those principles which constitute that Moral Law, Love, Righteousness, Reverence, and Wisdom are really attributes of the First Cause, the Supreme Ultimate. Chu Hsi further explains the relationship between the Supreme Ultimate and its social components, and the units of the universe: 'There is but one Supreme Ultimate, which is received by each individual of All Things; but this one Supreme Ultimate is received by each individual in its entirety and undivided, just as in the case of the moon shining in the heavens, when it is reflected on river and lake and so is visible in every place, we would not say that it is divided.'[9]

He thus conceives of society as an organic entity, an aggregate of small units, each containing the identical substance. We can extend this conception of the Supreme Ultimate to his image of social and political order. The Supreme Ultimate is, in the social context, the source of loyalty, benevolence, and recognition of self-limits, according to which each unit fulfils assigned obligations and duties, and hence contributes to the social order under the direction of the Supreme Ultimate.[10] Chu Hsi's ideal society was

6 Tokugawa Ieyasu, who acquired early an interest in learning, hoped to extend through knowledge his historical perspective and political acumen. As a political man, he was not interested in involvement with any one particular theory or school of thought. Therefore, he was not a 'neo-Confucian' politician or scholar. He was more eclectic and flexible in his attitude towards the application of knowledge. For adoption of the Chinese system by the Tokugawa, see Horie Yasuzō (ed.), *Kinsei Nihon no keizai to shakai* [Economy and Society of Contemporary Japan] (Tōkyō: Yuhikaku, 1960), pp. 10-12.

7 As quoted in J. Percy Bruce, *Chu Hsi and His Masters* (London: Probsthain and Company, 1923), p. 137.

8 *Ibid.*

9 *Ibid.*, p. 141.

10 Yomiuri Shimbunsha, *Nihon no rekishi*, pp. 164-5. Chu Hsi's system necessitates an emperor representing Heaven, as the ultimate source of loyalty on earth. In Tokugawa Japan, however, the ultimate source of loyalty was associated with the *Bakufu*, not with the Imperial Court, as will be shown.

thus one in which social and political institutions were structured and functionally co-ordinated according to a moral law. Because of the moral–legal integration of society, there could be no conflict but only eternal harmony; and no external coercion but rather voluntary adherence of individuals to the values of the Supreme Ultimate.

Tokugawa Ieyasu was a military genius and a political realist. To achieve a morally integrated, harmonious society, he did not hesitate to utilize his almost unlimited power. His implementation of Chu Hsi's ideal society was astute, and his use of power realistic, but he forced consensus, and this later had many unexpected consequences. We shall treat some of these consequences in detail later, but first we shall analyse the measures of Tokugawa Ieyasu and his successors which established a centralized political system and achieved the aim of 'permanent' ascendency for the Tokugawa family.

In analysing Tokugawa centralism, we emphasize three measures which were carefully implemented by the early *shōgun* and institutionalized by their successors throughout the period. These are: (1) a policy of isolation, (2) a system of checks and balances, and (3) a system of class and status. These measures represented a conscientious effort to overcome the weaknesses of decentralized feudalism. Each of them contributed substantially to the political and social order under the Tokugawa regime; in fact, it can be tentatively stated that these policies sustained Tokugawa centralism. After we provide evidence for this assertion, we can look at the social and economic consequences of political centralism in general, basing our analysis on the consequences of each of these three measures. First, however, we must discuss these policies in an historical context before placing them in sociological perspective.

Isolation policy (sakoku seisaku)
From the middle of the Ashikaga period (1392–1569), foreign trade with western nations such as Spain, Holland, Portugal, and England expanded greatly with export of Japanese gold coins, copper products, camphor, and lacquer wares, to China and South East Asia in European vessels.[11] Prior to the Tokugawa period, gold drainage often caused currency deficits but, in general, foreign trade was quite profitable to the pre-Tokugawa merchants and those lords engaging in the enterprise. In fact, the founder of the Tokugawa dynasty, Ieyasu himself, was in favour of leaving the door open to western merchants.[12]

However, after the death of Ieyasu in 1616, his successor, Tokugawa Hidetada, became suspicious of the activities of the European missionaries and the Japanese Christian movement.[13] Control over the movement tightened, and strain between the *Bakufu*

---

11 Nakamura Kōya, *Edo Bakufu sakoku shiron* [Treatise on the Edo Bakufu Isolation Policy and Its Historical Background] (Tōkyō: Hōkōkai, 1913), pp. 39-98.
12 *Ibid.*, pp. 171-82.
13 An estimate of the Japanese Christians at that time is not available. However, according to the one made in 1920, there existed some two hundred churches with 250,000 to 300,000 Japanese converts who were baptized by 59 European missionaries. Further fragmentary records show the figures below. Reliability of these figures is quite doubtful, however. These are cited in Nakamura Koya, *Edo Bakufu sakokushi-ron* [A Treatise on the Isolation Policy of the Tokugawa Administra-

(the central government) and the Christians was intensified. The height of the tension was marked by a series of riots in the northern part of Kyūshū, the Mecca for Japanese Christians. The battles between the central government and the local Christians cost thousands of Christian lives. These are known in Japanese history as the Shimabara Riots (1637-8).[14]

Until the riots, the Portuguese, Spaniards, Dutch, and English were all competing for trade privileges, each group being only too ready to slander the other by suggesting to the Shogunate officers that those European nations with trade interests had political designs in the Far East.[15] This situation together with the Shimabara Riots, compelled the Shogunate's office to move for the elimination of western threats to Japan's security. Christianity had become linked with foreign aggression.[16]

Thus, isolation was adopted,[17] first as an immediate internal measure to control the Japanese Christians and to check the further propagation of Christianity, and second, as an external defence measure to protect Japan from possible outside threat. Internally, isolation had indirect consequences for the implementation of the other two measures yet to be discussed.

The social significance of 'isolation' was far more extensive than the immediate consequences. For practical purposes, the isolation policy closed the society off from outside contact for over two and one-half centuries. In the meantime, the society could not vitalize its social movements and cultural activities through outside contact; dynamic social change could not come about through cultural exchange.[18] Under such condi-

tion] (Tōkyō: Hōkōkai, 1914), pp. 27, 116. Also, see C.R. Boxer, *The Christian Century in Japan* (Berkeley, Cal.: University of California Press, 1954), pp. 320-21.

Year	No. of missionaries	Year	No. baptized
1603	129	1605	793
1606	124	1606	8,000
1611	127	1613	4,350

14 It is recorded that some 37,000 men, women, and children seized any available weapons and succeeded in taking over a local castle. The *Bakufu* sent approximately 50,000 samurai to quash the uprising. Nearly every one of the half-starved defenders was massacred. For this event, the *Bakufu* expended approximately 398,000 *ryō* paid from the Ōsaka treasury. This expenditure was the beginning of the financial difficulties of the *Bakufu*. See C.R. Boxer, p. 379.

15 George Sansom, *Japan: A Short Cultural History* (London: Cresset Press, 1952), p. 447.

16 *Ibid.*, pp. 453-4. See also Delmer Brown, *Nationalism in Japan* (Berkeley, Cal.: University of California Press, 1955), p. 46, and Sawade Shō, 'Financial Difficulties of the Edo Bakufu,' translated by H. Borton, *Harvard Journal of Asiatic Studies* (November 1936), 314.

17 The Spaniards and Portuguese, whose Christianity required efforts at conversion of non-Christians, were the first to be expelled. The Spaniards left Japan in 1624, and the Portuguese in 1638. The English had voluntarily closed their agencies by 1623. Certain authorized Chinese and a handful of Dutchmen were allowed to stay in a small settlement at Nagasaki. Otherwise, no foreigners were seen after 1640, and no Japanese were permitted to leave the country during the period.

18 During the period of isolation, many European inventions and technological scientific developments became known through books. This means that the Japanese elites had this stimulus. In actuality, however, Dutch science, for instance, did not appear significantly until almost the very end of the Tokugawa period.

tions, almost any social change had to be spontaneous within the closed society. There-fore, historians tended to associate the prolonged isolation policy with what is termed the 'static' nature of the Tokugawa society.

The system of checks and balances
The second factor considered indispensable to the maintenance of Tokugawa centralism was the system of checks and balances, established to maintain the existing power rela-tions between the Imperial Court and the *Bakufu* on the one hand, and between the *Bakufu* and the *daimyō* on the other.[19] In examining this system, we find two broad categories of aims.

A/*Neutralization of power conflicts* It is commonly agreed that feudalism is character-ized by a reciprocal relationship between lords and their retainers; the former granting benevolence and rewards to the latter; the latter returning an unequivocal loyalty to the former. In a *decentralized* feudal society, the loyalty and benevolence relationships were primarily confined to personal contact between the *local* or *provincial* feudal lords and their subservients; that is, on the level of province or fief. However, in a *centralized* system, the loyalty relationships between the dominant lord (in this case, Tokugawa) and minor lords (*daimyō*) were not necessarily maintained on a local basis. On the na-tional level, mutual feudal 'ties' were in some cases non-existent: some *daimyō* were traditionally friendly and probably loyal to the dominant lord, Tokugawa, but some were potential or former enemies.[20] Thus, superordination and subordination were characterized rather by a relatively unstable balance of power within the system.

Tokugawa designed a system to neutralize power so as to resolve this rather precarious 'disloyalty' problem. To put it differently, some rational calculation to resolve the 'tra-ditional' power conflict became imminently necessary after establishing control over the feudal lords. Tokugawa Ieyasu, aware of the balance of power relations, distinguished the 'loyal' vassals, *fudai*, from the *tozama*, literally, outside lords, assigning differential status and prestige to the two groups.[21]

Naturally, the *fudai* held a higher status and enjoyed more prestige than the *tozama*. The *fudai* were given the neighbouring province of Edo and other strategically pivotal areas. The larger outlying territories which yielded more revenue were awarded to the *tozama*. The more loyal the *daimyō*, the less discontent they expressed about smaller territorial rewards. Conversely, the less loyal the *daimyō*, the greater the rewards re-quired to keep them content. Possible political conflict was expected to be neutralized by this means. The basic idea behind this allocation of territories was to 'divide and rule' (see Table 1).

We see a clearer application of the 'divide and rule' principle in Ieyasu's appointment of traditionally antagonistic *daimyō* to neighbouring districts to maximize the hostility between them. He expected this device to divert the *daimyō's* antagonism away from

19 Throughout the Tokugawa period the number of *daimyō* remained relatively the same, about 260. Increases and decreases in the number were due to suspension of *daimyō* for violating the rules and regulations applied to them or who had no male successors.
20 Mikami Sanji, *Edo jidaishi* [History of the Edo Period] (Tōkyō: Fuzanbo, 1941), pp. 254-61.
21 *Ibid.*, p. 255

TABLE 1

Relationship between political loyalty/hostility and geographical distance
as indicated by rice revenue (N = 130)* (To = tozama; Fu = fudai)

Amount of rice revenue (in units of 10,000 *koku*; *koku* = 5 bushels of rice)	Location & type of political relationship							
	Tōhoku & Kyūshū (distant)		Chūgoku & Shikoku (intermediate)		Kantō & Kinki (central)		Total	
	To	*Fu*	*To*	*Fu*	*To*	*Fu*	*To*	*Fu*
50–100+	4	0	0	0	1	2	5	2
20–50	3	2	6	0	1	5	10	7
5–20	12	8	8	5	7	23	27	36
1–5	13	2	3	2	7	16	23	20
TOTAL	32	12	17	7	16	46	65	65

* All of the small, *politically unimportant daimyō* less than 20,000 *koku* of both types are eliminated from this study, the selection being based on *Nihon no rekishi* (History of Japan), p. 134.

the central government towards their more immediate neighbours; any accumulation of political discontent was to be exhausted on the local level without becoming a serious threat to the *Bakufu*.

Ieyasu's utilitarianism was ingenious. His approach was rational in that it involved a long-range view of a political status quo wherein conflicting forces were neutralized. However, the idea was not to resolve traditional conflicts but to utilize them for the purpose of control. In this respect, Tokugawa centralism was based on a series of rational manipulations of irrational characteristics of the traditional power situation. In succeeding passages, we shall see a few other manipulative devices applied by the early Tokugawa *shōgun* to maintain the balance of power, some containing a number of irrational elements.

B/*Positive steps towards a reduction of conflict* For the system of checks and balances to operate most effectively, Tokugawa needed a guarantee of the *daimyō* 'loyalty'; he was clearly aware of the doubtful loyalty of some. His solution to this problem was the establishment of requirements for quasi-loyal relationships between the *daimyō* and the *Bakufu*.[22] The major requirement was one involving residency, which was inaugurated in August 1635. To minimize hostility, it was necessary for the Tokugawa regime to keep the *daimyō* close, thereby holding them in check, and precluding any mutual understanding between traditionally hostile *daimyō*.[23]

22 The alternate residency requirement was enacted for all *daimyō*. Prior to this, Tokugawa Ieyasu requested Maeda Toshinaga, the Lord of Kanazawa, to pay homage in Edo in 1602. Maeda was indignant at the request, but unwillingly obeyed for the sake of his family. From that time on his feelings toward Tokugawa were never friendly. Maeda's obedience was strictly to secure his family's continuation. *Ibid.*, p. 124.

23 Various devices were utilized for this purpose. One of the most common was to establish blood-relationships through intermarriage with powerful *tozama daimyō* (the outside lords). For example,

The *sankin kōtai* (alternate residency requirement) was devised to prevent any build-up of hostility through dissociation; it was also intended to implement a quasi-loyalty relationship in which the *daimyō* were requested to pay loyal homage to the *Bakufu* periodically. Each *daimyō,* whether *fudai* or *tozama,* was required to remain in the Tokugawa castle town, Edo, for one year every other year. During alternate years, they administered their home affairs. The Tokugawa regime further requested that they leave their wives and children in Edo upon their return home. Thus a hostage system supplemented the *sankin kōtai* system as a check on subversion.

These devices for reduction of possible conflict were only for the *daimyō.* In addition, however, some manner of dealing with the Imperial Court was required. The court was at that time the highest locus of political office; it was the court which appointed the shōgun. While all of the Tokugawa *shōgun* were awarded this official title during their administration, they were required to submit their credentials upon assuming their position in the *Bakufu.* The Imperial Court did not at that time have any real power over the appointed, the Military Ruler (*Taishōgun*) but it did represent for the *Bakufu* and *daimyō* the final source of legitimization for the exercise of political and military power. This relatively differentiated authority–power structure existed even before the Tokugawa period, as the Imperial Court had existed above the level of conflict among the lords since the Kamakura period (1192–1392).

Thus an early problem for Tokugawa was the determination of what could be done to secure compliance of this legitimizing authority which provided an essential basis for political stability and social order. The Imperial Court was a necessary institution, but it could possibly become detrimental to Tokugawa's domination by co-operating with the *daimyō* to eliminate Tokugawa control. Tokugawa Ieyasu and his successors knew that any attempt to deliberately curtail the court would have undesirable repercussions. Instead, they moved to bring about positive results by disassociating the court from the *daimyō.* It was felt that close relationships between the *Bakufu* and the *daimyō* would be reinforced by decreasing the contacts between the *daimyō* and the Imperial Court.[24]

These measures for the control of power relations were institutionalized during the Tokugawa administrations. The following major points are apparent: (1) Tokugawa political centralism was established in an isolated and exclusive society which included local *daimyō* legitimately governing their home provinces (*han*); (2) the exercise of political power by the *Bakufu* was aimed at diminishing any source of conflict within the

most influential *daimyō* such as Katō, Asana, Fukushima, and Ikeda married Tokugawa's daughters or close relatives of the Tokugawa family (e.g. the Matsudaira family). For detail, see *ibid.,* pp. 137-41.

24 (a) For the implementation of this policy, the *Bakufu* adopted an inspection system to seek out co-ordinated political moves by the Imperial Court and the *daimyō*; the Kyoto Magistrate, disguised as a liaison officer between the Court and the *Bakufu,* functioned to detect any subversion on the part of the *daimyō* and the Court. The *Bakufu* further required submission of a petition when the *daimyō* wished to stay in Kyoto on the way to Edo upon the *sankin kōtai.*

(b) In 1613, the Imperial Court Members' Regulations (*kugeshū hotto*), and also in 1625, the Imperial Court and the Imperial Court Attendants' Regulations were issued by the *Bakufu.* The main intention of these regulations was to make learning the primary concern of the Emperor and the court nobles, thereby keeping them away from involvement in politics. See Yomiuri Shimbunsha, *Nihon no rekishi,* p. 33.

system by institution of an arrangement of checks and balances; and (3) to ensure un-challenged political domination, a peripheral seat of authority was disassociated from any possibility of insurgency. These measures, firmly institutionalized in the system, were intended to maintain a static political order. However, the order was not one based upon any fundamental or spontaneous consensus on the legitimacy of the central government, but was maintained by political manipulation which resulted in the creation of a quasi-feudal relationship between the *daimyō* and the *Bakufu*. The *sankin kōtai*, alternate residency requirement, was a particularly heavy burden; the *daimyō* had to show his loyalty by maintaining dual residency and periodically commuting to and from Edo.

Thus, Chu Hsi's model society, based on 'the Supreme Ultimate which is received by each individual of the All Things' was realized by the Tokugawa's replacement of the previously decentralized feudal system by a centralized government; extending the loyalty relationships on the local level to those on the national level; and further, es-tablishing statutory relationships between the *daimyō* and the *Bakufu*, characterized by the alternate residency requirement, the hostage system, and many other obligations. While these requirements were designed to secure an ideal static political order, the maintenance of that order had many non-political repercussions, particularly on the economy. This will be taken up in detail later. There were yet other measures devised for maintenance of the static social equilibrium.

Class and status systems
The third aspect of the Tokugawa's political centralism differs from the other two in that it was not a program directed specifically at power relations, but was essentially a social rearrangement towards better maintenance of a static social order. Isolation and checks and balances were designed to neutralize power conflict within Tokugawa soci-ety. Within the political framework, however, a system of social stratification based on Chu Hsi's model was firmly established. The purpose of the stratification system was the establishment of a social hierarchy based on the ideas of 'loyalty, benevolence and recognition of self-limits' throughout the social strata of the Tokugawa society.[25]

While this model was consistent with the prior cultural orientation of Japan, its appli-cability to the current Japanese society wherein occupational differentiation was already considerably advanced was questionable. The problem was a matter of the effec-tive application of such a medieval social model.[26] In spite of the problems, this func-tionally co-ordinated and organically structured societal model was extremely appealing to Tokugawa Ieyasu and his successors; it satisfied their goal of political domination within a static social arrangement.

25 These ideas are explicitly stated in much of the widely read literature of the Tokugawa period. To cite a few: 'What ought to be the principal duties of a ruler? First of all, he should have a parental feeling of benevolence toward the people in order to practice benevolent administrations.' (Kuma-zawa Banzan, *Daigaku Imon*, vol. I.) 'Even the rich exercise self-control to confine themselves to a limit; even the poor should know the value of what they are.' (Yamage Sokō, *Yamaga gorui*, vol. 21.) Both cited in Nomura Kanetarō, *Tokugawa jidai no shakai keizai shiso gairon* [Introduction to the Social and Economic Thoughts of the Tokugawa Period] (Tōkyō; Nihon Hyōronsha, 1933), pp. 91-2.
26 For detailed information, see *ibid.*, pp. 36-61.

Tokugawa class and status system was in accord with the idea basic to the maintenance of political centralism,[27] i.e., 'to divide the society into different segments, freeze the social dynamics in each of the groups, and then control all of them separately.' To apply this, changes were required, since the ranking system prior to the Tokugawa period was flexible in that it allowed a certain degree of status and occupational mobility. Particularly during the War Period (1467-1569) the military class emphasized values of superiority according to criteria by which able individuals were accepted into the elite samurai class. This achievement–orientation had to end when the Tokugawa finally established their military supremacy over the other *daimyō*; instead, the 'adjustment' of individuals to their given status and occupation was required.[28]

The transition from an achievement–orientation to an adjustment–orientation was made in accordance with the Chinese system; the Tokugawa system placed the samurai class at the top, the peasants next, the artisans below them, and the merchants at the bottom. Finer classification was made within each of these categories. Priests, monks, scholars, and medical doctors were considered 'alternate' members of the samurai class, holding a social position distinct from other non-samurai classes. It should be emphasized that a strict social distance was maintained between the samurai and non-samurai classes by the application of laws and regulations regarding living standards, rights, and prestige of the various classes. Contacts among the different classes were minimized to protect the prestige of the higher-status groups.

This was an explicitly moral functional order; the samurai placed the highest social value on the peasant class because of their productive capacity, upon which the samurai were dependent for existence. Since the samurai also needed artisans for armaments, castle-building, and aesthetic pursuits, they were regarded as next in importance to the farmers.[29] As the merchants contributed nothing substantial to the samurai's basic needs, but were, rather, looked on as 'scheming profit-seekers' or 'parasites' upon the wealth of the samurai class, they were relegated to the bottom of the hierarchy.[30]

The behaviour of the members of each order was regulated according to the need of the samurai for the respective orders. This does not mean that the farmers, occupying the formal status next to the samurai, enjoyed more social privileges than the artisans and merchants. On the contrary, as the farmers' services were so indispensable to the samurai, their behaviour was most restricted.[31] The attitude towards the farmers held

27 See Takahashi Kamekichi, *Tokugawa jidai hōken keizai no kenkyu* [Study on the Tokugawa Feudal Economy] (Tokyo: Teito Mainichisha, 1932), pp. 3-16.
28 More empirical studies should be made to clarify various historical explanations, as very few reliable studies are available so far.
29 Many Tokugawa economic and social writings are concerned with the importance of the farmers; 'Saints divide a society into four (classes): they are warriors, farmers, artisans, and merchants. Only the warriors concern themselves with learning' (Kaibo Sekiryō); 'Agriculture is a fundamental of society, on which a peace or war may be dependent' (Muro Kyūso); 'It should be emphasized that the farmers are the foundation of a nation; they are the head of the people. The latter's survival hinges upon the first' (Yamagata Bantō). All cited in Nomura Kanetarō, *Tokugawa jidai no shakai shisō gairon*, pp. 45-56.
30 Miyamoto Mataji, Kinsei shōnin ishiki no kenkyū [Study on the Social Conscience of the Contemporary Merchants] (Tōkyō: Yuhikaku, 1940), p. 22.
31 Ogyu Sorai, *Seidan* (Political Dialogue) in *Nihon Keizai sōsho* [A Collection of Japanese Economic Works], vol. III, 435.

that they should be kept just about at subsistence level. The idea was that insufficiency of food would provide more incentive for labour as the farmers would work better if slightly hungry, but would be lazy if their stomachs were full. This logic was extended to all aspects of the farmers' lives; they could not wear silk *kimono,* could not live under a tiled roof (only straw), could eat no polished rice, to cite a few examples.[32] These and many other restrictions were imposed upon the farmers so that a maximum amount of rice revenue could be obtained. Merchants, however, though at the bottom of the social scale, were less restricted, more prosperous, and geographically more mobile.

Status positions within each class were also narrowly specified so as to reduce the possibilities for social mobility. For instance, in the administration, Ieyasu classified the *daimyō* into two categories, *fudai* and *tozami.* Only the *fudai* were allowed to participate in *Bakufu* policy-making, and even among the *fudai,* pivotal positions were reserved for those with certain ascribed status. For example, the position of *tairō* (Elder Statesmen) was attained by only a few prominent *daimyō*: only those *fudai* who had previously served as Guard of the Osaka Castle (Osaka *Jōdai*) and/or Kyoto Magistrate (Kyoto *Shoshidai*) could occupy the position of *rōchu* (Ministers).[33] At that time no examination system existed, as it did in China, for the recruitment of government officials. By this arrangement the Tokugawa could appoint to pivotal administrative positions those who were carefully selected from the highly qualified status groups, without jeopardizing the static status system.

The restriction of status, exemplified by the administration occurred also in the administration of *han* (fief) affairs. In the whole Tokugawa political and administrative system there were well-defined and functionally co-ordinated ranking systems in each of some two hundred and fifty local subpolitical units (*han*). The effects of this 'traditional' status system were quite pronounced; political affairs passed from one generation to another with a minimum of conflict and confusion, as only a highly selected group of qualified people at each status level were involved. The traditional authority of the Tokugawa family was maintained and perpetuated by the performance of explicitly designated roles within each status group.

CONSEQUENCES OF THE TOKUGAWA POLITICAL CENTRALISM
We have been concerned with the centralized political system which, as will be brought out, had implications for the provincial economic structure, and we have focused on three fundamental features, the isolation policy, the system of checks and balances, and the class and status structure. We have seen the social and political implications of Tokugawa centralism: socially, it was an isolated, closed, and exclusive society based on rigidly stratified status and class systems; politically, the society was administered by a *centralized power* through maintenance of a balance of power among the *daimyō,* partly utilizing and partly forcing the *daimyō* loyalty.

These intentional political measures of the Tokugawa administration were being exercised in a small, closed society. Various political institutions, including the three fundamental ones, remained relatively unchanged throughout the period: their consequences

---

32 Takahashi Kamekichi, *Tokugawa hōken keizai no kenkyū* [A Study on the Tokugawa Feudal Economy] (Tōkyō: Teito Mainichisha, 1933), p. 32. Also see Ogiu Sorai, p. 394.
33 Takahashi, *ibid.,* pp. 6-7.

were, therefore, seen mostly in non-political spheres, particularly in the economic structure. Tokugawa Ieyasu and his successors were extremely careful in setting up their ideal form of government, but they failed, as we shall see, to plan in advance an effective economic policy, particularly in regard to centralization of the age-old taxation system. As Professor Takekoshi Yosaburō has pointed out, Tokugawa domination might have lasted much longer, had the administration initiated a centralized taxation system, collecting revenues directly from the local *daimyō*. [34] Tokugawa Ieyasu was a master politician in the utilization of his power, but as Gamau Kumpei once commented, '... he (Ieyasu) was a man who undertook only what he could accomplish but avoided what was beyond his power.' [35]

Our next concern then is to examine the various consequences that arose from the Tokugawa political domination, and to account for the unintentional encouragement of a certain type of commercialism through political pressure. With this in mind, we return to our original discussion of the three indispensable and enduring institutions of Tokugawa.

Economic implication of the isolation policy
In assessing the impact of the isolation policy upon the Japanese economy, we should bear in mind the fact that the period from 1603 to 1640 was one of rapid transition in the Tokugawa view of foreign trade; it changed from a relatively favourable to an extremely unfavourable view during the reign of the first three *shōgun* (i.e., Ieyasu, Hidetada, and Iemitsu).

The founder of the Tokugawa regime, Ieyasu, for example, took a liberal attitude towards trade with the western nations, leaving all ports and harbours open, and levying no duties on goods. Further, he granted extraterritorial rights to the European traders while they resided in Japan. [36]

The second *shōgun*, Hidetada, began the transition by adopting a negative policy towards foreign trade in response to the alleged political activities of the European missionaries; in 1616, he issued an order to close all ports of trade except Nagasaki and Hirato, both in Kyushu. (This law did not apply to Chinese traders and their vessels.) Within two weeks after the issuance of this order, in August, Hidetada ordered enforcement of another law prohibiting even the use of Nagasaki, leaving only Hirato for English traders. [37] These restrictive moves reached their culmination shortly after the Shimabara Riots of 1637-8, when the *shōgun*'s office decided upon complete closure of the nation from the outside world, leaving only one port, Nagasaki, open for certain authorized Chinese and a handful of Dutch who were confined, almost imprisoned, in a small settlement there. [38]

Closure and the consequent isolation of Japan from that time undoubtedly stultified the rich cultural life of pre-Tokugawa Japan, destroying the spirit of progress, curiosity,

34 Takekoshi Yosaburō, *Nihon Keizaishi kenkyū* [Study of the Japanese Economic History], vol. III, 355.
35 Sawada Shō, p. 310.
36 Nakamura, pp. 39-46, 85-98.
37 *Ibid.*, pp. 248-63.
38 *Ibid.*, pp. 309-58; also, Sansom, pp. 445-52.

and adventure-seeking, and narrowing the scope of world view. For example, during the isolation period, the Japanese came to regard their country as a world in itself, and to view the feudal fiefs and provinces as national boundaries. Japan became the earth, subdivided into some two hundred and fifty small nations. The Japanese word *tenka* meaning 'all under the heaven' referred to Japan itself, and similarly, *kokka*, literally 'nations,' connoted the feudal provinces.[39] As we shall see, a general lack of initiative, attitudes of reserve, and narrow economic views typically found among the Tokugawa merchants seem to have resulted directly from the low morale engendered by the Tokugawa policies.

These ethnocentric, microcosmological national concepts moulded a pervasive economic passivity which was undoubtedly a major negative consequence of prolonged isolation. Nevertheless, the isolation policy had some positive consequences as well. We should note that the policy contributed significantly not only to the maintenance of the Tokugawa regime but also to the preservation of Japan's national independence from encroaching western imperialism, which was expanding in all of Asia from the seventeenth century onward. This factor contributed to the national security in which peace and order were sustained – a condition favourable for the development of commerce and industry.

Furthermore, there were more direct and immediate consequences of isolation. We might automatically assume that exclusion of foreign traders from Japan meant the loss of any profit accruing from trade with these countries. While this was true, there has been a good deal of debate among Japanese historians over the amount of 'gain' from the policy.[40] Those who favour the policy argue that trade with the European nations had made no sizable contribution to the Japanese economy before that time; it consisted mainly of the importation of silk, weapons, medicine, and some other items, with the export, in turn, of large quantities of gold and silver coins to these countries.

This argument has some merit, for during the early periods of the Tokugawa administration, the western mercantile nations were eager to acquire gold for improvement of their monetary positions in world trade. At that time, the gold coins minted by the early Tokugawans were considered of good quality, containing twenty karats of gold in each piece. In addition, Ieyasu's free-trade policy during the early years of his administration made dealing with Japan even more attractive (to the western traders). It is certain that a considerable quantity of gold flowed out of Japan during the hundred years from 1528 to 1628.[41]

In this sense, it may well be true that the isolation policy saved the Japanese economy from gradual deterioration from excessive gold drainage over a long period of time. Aside from this direct gain from the isolation policy, what other economic implications can we see in this closed and isolated Japanese economy? Sir George Sansom makes the

39 Miyamoto Mataji, *Ōsaka chonon-ron* [A Study on Osaka Merchants] (Kyōtō: Mineruva Shobo, 1959), pp. 45-8.

40 Cf. Mikami Sanji, *Edo jidai-shi kōgi* [Lectures on the History of the Tokugawa Period] (Tōkyō: Fuzanbō, 1944), chap. 6.

41 According to a rough estimate made by the administration, 6,192,800 gold coins, 1,122,687 silver coins, and 228,997,500 copper coins were used in exchange for western commodities. Nakamura, p. 266.

following remark about a long-range consequence of it: 'Her problem now was not how to obtain and utilize wealth and wisdom from abroad, but *how to conserve and increase her own resources*' (italics mine).[42] There must have been profound psychological anxiety as well as a determination among the rulers to cope with various economic adversities which might occur in the closed, economically self-reliant nation. Such anxiety would be quite understandable, with anticipation of such economically important conditions as population increase leading to unbalanced relationships between productive capacity and demand, or as crop failure owing to floods, typhoons, fires, and other disasters.

These anxieties were overcome by their determination to increase agricultural productivity within their own domains, this being the only available alternative after closure of the ports by the *Bakufu*. In this sense, the isolation policy may be seen as indirectly giving impetus to the conservation of Japan's resources and the increase of agricultural production.

The attempts by the *Bakufu* and the *daimyō* to increase agricultural production through the adoption of the so-called Agricultural Encouragement Policy (*Kannō seisaku*) substantiate these assumptions. This policy had both negative and positive aspects.

The negative aspect involved such restrictive rules for farmers as making it illegal for them to change residence or occupation, to transfer inherited lands to residents of other fiefs, or to produce agricultural items other than those officially allowed. These negative aspects were intended to secure sufficient agricultural production for assurance of the needed rice revenue for the *daimyō* and samurai.

On the other hand, the positive aspects of this policy encouraged improvement of productive conditions. In fact, in many fiefs, the *daimyō* provided funds for betterment of irrigation systems, or for improvement of the quality of fertilizers and seeds. Towards the middle of the Tokugawa period, the *daimyō* abandoned determination of the kinds of agricultural items to be produced, so as to bring in additional revenues. These measures added to agricultural production and thereby, as we shall see in the following discussion, unintentionally stimulated commercial activity in the urban castle towns.

Economic consequences of the system of checks and balances
In treating the economic consequences of the system, we now take up the following two subjects: first, the *Bakufu*'s occasional requests to the *daimyō* for funds and labour; second, the *sankin kōtai* or alternate residency requirement which compelled heavy expenditures by the *daimyō* for the annual journeys and for maintenance of two residences.

As was noted, these two devices were part of Tokugawa's program for establishment of a system of quasi feudal relationships, which, as was intended, weakened the financial position of the *daimyō*. The two measures effectively contributed throughout the period to Tokugawa's checks and balance system. With institutionalization, these devices began to provide essential pre-conditions for the rise of commerce and, furthermore, generated some degree of entrepreneurial opportunity. The *goyōkin* (*Bakufu* requests for donation) involved two types of projects; construction of shrines and temples, and public works projects such as flood prevention and road construction.[43]

42 Sansom, p. 455.
43 Nakamura, pp. 267-9.

In regard to the first type of *goyōkin*, requests for donations were frequent during the first sixty years of the Tokugawa administration; the *daimyō* contributed money and labour for construction of the Nikkō Shrine, Sentō Palace, Nijō Castle (partial reconstruction), Katsura Palace, and others. All of these were luxuriously designed and lavishly decorated at enormous cost, far beyond the financial capacity of the *Bakufu*.[44] The contributions were to be regarded as evidence of loyalty to the *Bakufu*, but the *daimyō* could hardly refuse. In time, successive requests for *goyōkin* led to financial difficulties for the *daimyō*.[45]

In comparison with the first *goyōkin* category, the *daimyō* contribution to public works projects had a far more extensive impact upon the economy. The intention of the *Bakufu* was to improve transportation and communication systems in such a way that they would strengthen the military position of the *Bakufu* in relation to that of the *daimyō*, and at the same time to keep the economic strength of the *daimyō* in check through successive donations for public works. The idea was, then, an integral part of the system of checks and balances. To this end, the *Bakufu* itself made some financial contributions. By use of *Bakufu-daimyō* resources, major rivers such as Ōi and Tenryū were equipped with effective flood prevention systems. This guaranteed safe travel from Edo to other parts of Japan. Furthermore, considerable improvements and extensions of major roads were made: completed during the early Tokugawa period were Tōkaidō (Edo-Ōsaka), Ōshūdōchū (Edo – the Ōshū region), Nikkō Dōchū (Edo-Nikkō), and Kōshū Kaidō (Edo – the Kōshū region). These major highways, constructed as part of the *Bakufu* program to keep the *daimyō* financially weak, consequently paved the way for the expansion of commercial activity by their contribution to a better communication and transportation system for commercial use.

We now turn to the economic consequence of the *sankin kōtai*, or alternate residency requirement. As noted above, this system required the *daimyō* to remain in their home territory for one year, and then in Edo for the following year. The journey to and from Edo placed a financial burden on the *daimyō* which varied with distance and geographical conditions. The *tozama*, of course, had more distance to travel than the *fudai*, whose fiefs were usually within five hundred miles of Edo. These journeys accounted for approximately five to ten per cent of the total expenditures of each *daimyō*.[46] In addition, each one maintained two or three mansions in Edo, depending upon his status. During the Tokugawa period, a large portion of the entire Edo city area consisted of *daimyō* mansions.[47]

Some features of the *daimyō* procession to and from Edo are worthy of description: the processions were colourful and extravagant, the *daimyō* often competing with one

---

44 For example, on the Nikko Shrine, completed in 1641, the administration spent 568,000 gold, one hundred *kan* (one *kan* equals 3.75 kilograms) of silver, and 1,000 *koku* (one *koku* equals approximately 5 bushels) of rice. To alleviate the deficit, the *daimyō* supplied considerable amounts of gold and labour. Mikami, p. 314.

45 *Ibid.*, p. 317.

46 Yomiuri Shimbunsha, *Nihon no rekishi*, p. 83.

47 According to a survey made by the Ministry of the Interior in 1869, the total area of Edo consisted of: Area occupied by the samurai residences 11,692,000 *tsubo* (one *tsubo* equals six *shaku* [one shaku = 33 cm] square); area occupied by the shrines and temples 2,661,000 *tsubo*; area occupied by the commoners (non-samurai) 2,696,000 *tsubo*. Cited in Kōda Naritomo, *Edo to Ōsaka* (Edo and Ōsaka) (Tōkyō: Fuzanbō, 1933), p. 17.

another in order to enhance their family reputation and demonstrate their *kakushiki* protocol. Powerful *daimyō* such as Maeda of Kanazawa, Date of Sendai, and Shimazu of Satsuma (all *tozama*) were accompanied by no less than four thousand retainers, and smaller *daimyō* normally by two to three thousand. Financing such flamboyance was by no means easy under the *daimyō*'s weakening fiscal circumstances, and the more elaborate the procession, the larger the concomitant treasury shrinkage.[48]

Thus, the *sankin kōtai* system continued, serving its function of draining off the *daimyō*'s military and financial power. Certain unintended consequences of the system are more significant to our analysis, however. As a result of the increased traffic, many small commercial towns appeared along the highways. These were known in Japanese as *shukubamachi* or post towns.[49] In these towns, supplying of post horses, keeping of inns, and maintenance of ferries were important economic pursuits. These towns were connecting points for long-distance trade, and they became especially important as routes employed by the lords for transport of their land tax proceeds. Some fifty such post towns flourished along the Tōkaidō road which connected Edo and Ōsaka, the two Tokugawa commercial centres. These towns along the five major highways were essential to the development of commercial activity as it increased from local to national dimension.[50]

We should make a final remark about the contribution of the alternate residency system to the Tokugawa economy. Professor Endō Masao makes this characterization: 'the Tokugawa economy may be summarized in one word. It is a money-lending economy.'[51] Though this statement needs careful explanation, the implications are clear: Tokugawa feudalism was in transition from a rice to a money economy. During the transition the samurai elite were caught in two different economic systems. They attempted to resolve the problem not by revising the fundamental economic structure, but by borrowing from money-lenders. A money economy had existed since the eighth century, but it attained a new stage of development during the seventeenth and eighteenth centuries. It was not yet an independent institution, but it was of major importance to the economy within the feudal political framework.

The *sankin kōtai* system undoubtedly accelerated the transitional process by forcing the *daimyō* to use cash for their journeys and for other associated expenses. Also, while they stayed in Edo, out of their own political jurisdiction, they could not spend their own *han* currency but were forced to use gold and silver coins.[52] Thus, the *daimyō* were annually obliged to allocate sizable amounts of money for fulfilment of utterly unproductive feudal obligations. The more they spent, the more impetus they provided for the expansion of commercialism, and the wider the expansion of commercial activity, the worse the results for the *daimyō*'s financial conditions.[53]

48 Yomiuri Shimbunsha, *Nihon no rekishi*, p. 83.
49 Toyoda Takeshi, *Nihon no hoken toshi* [Feudal Cities in Japan] (Tōkyō: Iwanami Shoten, 1952), pp. 148-50.
50 It should be added that there arose another type of *machi: Minato-machi* or port-towns connecting sea communication and transportation between ports and cities, for example, Nagasaki.
51 Endō Masao, *Kinsei Nihon shōgyō shihon hattatsushiron* [History of the Development of Commercial Capital in Modern Japan] (Tōkyō: Nihon Hyōronsha, 1936), pp. 50-1.
52 Sakumichi Yotarō, *Kinsei Nihon kaheishi* [A History of Japanese Currency] (Tōkyō: Kobundō, 1956), p. 139.
53 Takahashi, pp. 2-5.

Thus, the consequences of the *sankin kōtai* were ironic; Tokugawa adapted the system to achieve a static political order with a balance of power, but though a static equilibrium was maintained, it stimulated a dynamic commercialism which in turn weakened the political equilibrium. This assumption might lead to the conclusion that the Tokugawa political system committed economic suicide. As this has no historical validity, we must seek the factors that functioned to counter those elements. We shall treat some of them later, but first we shall analyse the economic consequences of the Tokugawa stratification system.

Economic consequences of the stratification system
Before further analysing the Tokugawa status system, we should note that the stratification system itself had few economic consequences. It is true that some of the wealthy merchants, at the bottom of the class system, raised their prestige considerably with the expansion of commercial activity and their consequent accumulation of wealth, but this only indicates that wealth led to a more general social acceptance of the merchants so that some of the wealthier merchants were placed almost on a par with the samurai.[54] It does not imply any direct economic consequences of the stratification system. Class and status factors were thus not causal but rather dependent factors in the course of economic development. Therefore, we shall deal only with the economic consequences of professional differentiation, urban settlement of the samurai, and the widened functions of the merchants in the changed pattern of rural–urban relationships.

Prior to the Tokugawa period, the professional roles of samurai and peasants were somewhat diffuse. The samurai, particularly those of the lower class, engaged in combat during the wars but many settled down during peaceful periods as resident landowners or, if of the lower class, as farm labourers. This diffusion lasted until the late sixteenth century, just a few decades before the establishment of the Tokugawa family. Their predecessor, Toyotomi Hideyoshi, for instance, confiscated swords from the peasants so as to differentiate the samurai from the farmers.[55] To cite another example, both *daimyō* and samurai retainers collected rice revenue directly from their respective fiefs; this not only decentralized the locus of the local political authority but also attached the *daimyō* and the samurai to the land, wherein both thereby continued to be involved in agricultural production.

Professional differentiation became clear with the establishment of the Tokugawa social system of four classes (warriors, farmers, artisans, and merchants). Moreover, there was a rapidly growing trend towards a revision of the rice revenue system so as to enable the *daimyō* to control all of it within their respective jurisdictions. This meant that the samurai could no longer exercise political power in their fief, but became administrators receiving fixed rice revenue from the *daimyō*. The *daimyō* was thus the sole political authority in a fief which had previously been subdivided into parts, each controlled by a samurai subordinate to the *daimyō*.

54 Shirayagi Shūko, *Chonin no tenka* [The Merchant World] (Tōkyō: Ryūbunkan, 1910), p. 70. The wealthier merchants with prestige were those who were privileged to function as *Bakufu* or *daimyō* protégé merchants or as *kuramoto* (warehouse custodians) or *kakeya* (purveyors). For detailed information, see chap. III.

55 Toyotomi Hideyoshi was the founder of the short-lived Toyotomi Administration (1585–1602); this event was known as Hideyoshi's 'sword-hunting.'

Under the new system, the samurai retainers had no need to remain on the land;[56] they moved into the urban castle towns where the lords resided. This urbanization of the samurai was widespread throughout Japan during early Tokugawa times, and continued until the end of the period.[57] The traditional attachment of the samurai to the land thus came to an end, though there was frequent expression of desire to return to the land, where the samurai spirit was born.

Thus, most of the samurai became urban, salaried retainers, breaking from their rural traditions and joining other non-productive groups in the castle towns. With this rapid samurai urbanization, the number of *jōkamachi* (castle towns) increased.[58] Edo was undoubtedly the largest *jōkamachi* in Japan during the period, the rest ranging from those of more than 50,000 population to small towns with one thousand population or less. Some representative castle cities were:[59]

Jōkamachi	Daimyō	Population	Year
Kanazawa	Maeda	68,636	1697
Kagoshima	Shimazu	59,728	1772
Nagoya	Tokugawa	54,932	1654
Sendai	Date	23,098	1772
Hiroshima	Asano	31,203	1677
Okayama	Ikeda	28,659	1667
Kōfu	Tokugawa	14,334	1689
Morioka	Nambu	13,370	1788
Kagi	Mori	5,300	1677
Ueda	Matsuda	2,424	1710

There was much variation, but the model castle city in the seventeenth century probably had a population of between fifteen and twenty thousand. The proportion of samurai residents in a castle city was high, frequently more than fifty per cent.[60]

The impact of samurai urbanization was felt throughout the Tokugawa period: a better transportation system was required for movement of goods from the rural areas to the non-productive urban areas. In addition, it was essential that the functions of merchants expand in the interest of more effective commerce. A description, extremely

56 This is the basic difference between Japanese and western feudalism. The European feudal retainers long held the right to collect revenue from their own fiefs as landed aristocrats. In Japan, however, the administrative authority was monopolized by the *daimyō*. Norman, p. 12.

57 As of 1690, the overwhelming majority of the *daimyō* had adopted this new wage system. Only 17 per cent of the total number of the *daimyō* still allowed their retainers to collect revenue from their own fiefs. Yomiuri Shimbunsha, *Nihon no rekishi*, p. 81.

58 *Jōkamachi* can be traced back at least to the twelfth century. But as late as the second half of the sixteenth century, when overseas trade flourished, there were no more than two or three population centres that justly deserved the name 'city.' T. Smith, *The Agrarian Origin of Modern Japan* (Stanford, Cal.: Stanford University Press, 1959), p. 67.

59 Cited in Henry Rosovsky, *Capital Formation in Japan, 1868-1940* (Glencoe: Free Press, 1960), p. 69.

60 *Ibid.*, p. 70.

simplified, of the economic structure of a *han* (fief) will point up the rural–urban relationships, the role of merchants in these two communities, and the circulation of rice and money.

There were four key economic institutions in a *han* political boundary: The productive households in the agrarian community, those of farmers and those of artisans; the *daimyō*'s households located in the castle-town; the retainers' households which were functionally dependent upon the *daimyō*; and the merchants' households which connected the production and the consumption functions of the rural and urban communities.

During the Tokugawa period, almost half of the annual product of the farmers and artisans was collected by the *daimyō* as rice revenue, the household consuming half of the remainder.[61] The surplus, one-quarter of the total, was marketed by the merchants.[62] The amount of rice for market could only be increased by elevating productivity or by cutting down on home consumption. The latter method, being easier, was more common.

Roughly seventy to eighty per cent of the *daimyō*'s total revenue was paid to retainers; only twenty to thirty per cent remained as net revenue.[63] This had to be used for various purposes, military and political administration, agricultural improvements (irrigation, water control, etc.), living expenses and various miscellaneous services. Some was retained in the treasury to meet the occasional requests of the *Bakufu* for road construction, waterway maintenance, and other public works projects. As was noted, the expenditure for the *sankin kōtai* (alternate residency) requirements consisted of five to ten per cent of the total income of the *daimyō*.[64]

The retainers subordinate to the *daimyō* followed a relatively similar pattern of expenditure. However, they were not responsible either for agricultural improvements or for contributions to *Bakufu* projects. Towards the middle of the Tokugawa period, because of fluctuations of rice prices in the city[65] and requirements for increased expenditures, the *daimyō* came upon harder times. Frequently, it was necessary for them to reduce the retainers' wages or to postpone payment indefinitely so as to maintain their financial position.[66]

In contrast, the merchants realized a relatively high rate of profit from the exchange of *daimyō* rice for money, and resale of the rice to other households. At that time, rice exchange was at least a part of the enterprise of most merchants.[67] The Tokugawa economy was a rice economy since rice was the measure of wealth; however, with the rise of the city and increased diversification of goods, a more convenient exchange unit, money, became necessary.[68]

61 Etō Tsuneji, 'Tokugawa jidai no keizai kōzō' [The Economic Structure during the Tokugawa Period], *Hikone ronso* (September 1958), no. 15, 8.
62 Uemura Genkaku, *Gyōshōken to ryōiki keizai* [The Commercial Boundaries of the Itinerant Merchants and the Provincial Economy] (Kyōto: Mineruva Shobo, 1959), p. 67.
63 Yomiuri Shimbunsha, *Nihon no rekishi*, p. 80.
64 Takahashi, p. 12.
65 Honjō Eijirō, *Tokugawa Bakufu no beika chōsetsu* [The Regulation of Rice Prices during the Tokugawa Period] (Kyōto: Hōgakkai, 1916), pp. 408-10.
66 Yomiuri Shimbunsha, *Nihon no rekishi*, p. 115.
67 Endō Masaō, pp. 22-4.
68 Sakumichi Yotarō, p. 115.

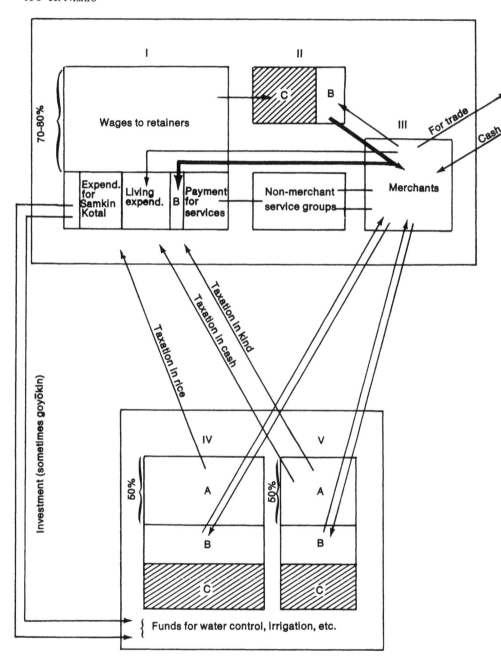

FIGURE 1 *Flows of rice and money between major economic sectors of a local han (fief)*
I: *Daimyo* household; II: retainer's household; III: merchant's household; IV: agrarian's
household; V: artisan's household. A: Taxation in rice or in kind; B: surplus crops or
funds; C: household consumption

Figure 1 shows the flow of payment in the *han* rice economy. Wealth originates in the agrarian household, moves from there to the *daimyō*'s treasury, and thence, to his retainers. In this flow, the need arises to change rice to money; this is where money economy becomes the economic medium of the society. It should be kept in mind that the merchants determined the prices, not the *daimyō*: while *daimyō* attempted to fix prices in their favour, they were unsuccessful, as the merchants' position was fully established in the economy.[69]

Thus, the economic functions of the merchants were indispensable for both rural and urban elements as they supplied necessary goods and services, and exchanged money for the surplus crops of the *daimyō*, the samurai, and the farmers. However, their social position was not felt to be comparable to that of the samurai, or even that of the artisans. Only a few merchants in the commercial cities gained in status as a result of their newly won affluence.

So far, our concern has been with economic consequences resulting from Tokugawa's three fundamental institutions. The consequences discussed point to the fact that Tokugawa centralism, which was designed to maintain a static social and political equilibrium, had the effect of stimulating a dynamic, expanding economy which, in turn, had consequences for Tokugawa political structure. To evaluate the impact of the new economy on this structure, we must look at some of the forces that arose within the political framework to counteract the economic threat to the system. We shall examine the interplay between these economic dynamics and the economic structure which counterbalanced the new pressures by limiting the possibilities of the expansion of commercialism.

In an analysis of the whole Tokugawa economic structure, we shall make use of a concept developed by Professor Miyamoto Mataji. In assessing the Tokugawa economy, he refers to it as having a 'provincial' economic system, noting the fact that it consisted of some two hundred and fifty independent economic units (*han*), each maintaining its geographical and political integrity. These units varied considerably in size, population, stage of agricultural technology, quality of land, and kinds of crops. The essential characteristic of the system was that each unit functioned as an economically self-sufficient entity in a manner generally analogous to the nation in the international economic structure.[70]

In adopting today's international economy as the model for analysis of the Tokugawa economic system, Professor Miyamoto treats inter-*han* trade as analogous to international trade. It is interesting to view the Tokugawa economy with this conception in mind. As noted above, the *daimyō* and *Bakufu* encouraged increased agricultural production after the sudden suspension of foreign trade. Each local *daimyō* was anxious to trade his surplus with other *han* to gain extra revenue. However, inter-*han* trade was complicated by the fact that each *daimyō* wanted to export but was extremely reluctant to import goods from other *han*. The *daimyō* often enacted laws to limit or curtail imports; examples are regulations limiting the stay of outside merchants, and requirements for reporting to local offices the purposes of their visit and details about

69 Honjō Eijirō, p. 408.
70 Uemura Gennosuke, pp. 18-21. See also Miyamoto Mataji, *Osaka chronin-ron*, p. 47.

the trading they hoped to do. Another device to discourage imports from other *han* was the issuance of *han* currency which could only be used in the *han*. In addition, local *daimyō* often adopted a policy of control (*tsuru*) over certain trade commodities.[71] Such items as crops, wax, lacquer ware, and oil were prohibited from export in many *han*; textiles and dyestuffs were mainly prohibited from import.[72] Like tariffs or barter systems in today's international trade, *tsuru* was essentially a measure to protect *han* economic autonomy.

The new dynamics had to contend with the restrictions of *ryōiki keizai*. The restrictive nature of the provincial economic structure undoubtedly allowed the progress of the new commercialism which required the allowance of widespread economic activity with minimum political intervention. Application of the utilitarian rationale of commercialism was thus hindered by political particularism. However, as long as the *daimyō* needed revenue from their surplus crops, they had to seek markets. By definition, the most logical situation for a flourishing commercialism is one with the least political restriction, one wherein freedom for the rational pursuit of economic gain is guaranteed.

We have associated political intervention with limitation of the scope of the economy, and hindrance of the free development of commercial activity. With this in mind, it seems that commercialism could only develop by accident within a tight net of *ryōiki keizai* under Tokugawa centralism.

However, several areas were directly administered by the *Bakufu*. All of these areas including Ōsaka, Sakai, and Nagasaki were located from several hundred to a thousand miles from Edo. Hence, we find relatively loose political restrictions in these areas in comparison with those of the castle towns. For instance, Ōsaka, the second largest city during the Tokugawa period, had only two municipal courts, one in the north, the other in the south. *Bugyō*, head of the judicial court officers appointed by the *Bakufu*, were in charge; they supervised fifty junior officers, twenty-five each in the north and the south. In addition, there were twenty-five *Bakufu*-appointed castle guards to protect the city. More of the actual city administration was thus left to the representative councils (Sō) which consisted mainly of merchants.[73] Indeed, Ōsaka enjoyed more commercial freedom than any other castle town; *tsuru* and other political controls were non-existent there; trade commodities could be freely shipped in and out of the city, to and from other *han*.[74] This commercial freedom may have been accidental in that the Tokugawa administration was simply afraid of undesirable repercussions from the residents of these areas since most of them were traditionally anti-Tokugawa family.

We have seen that Tokugawa economic provincialism was unable to cope, through inter-*han* trade, with the problems presented by diversification of commercial goods. However, the effects of this weakness were compensated for by the activities of the *Bakufu*-directed territories, where restrictions on economic activity were almost non-existent. Commercial development in these cities in a sense rescued the provincial economic system which, owing to the *daimyō* financial deficits and the incapacity for

71 Uemura, *ibid.*, p. 26.
72 Uemura, *ibid.*, p. 27.
73 Miyamoto Mataji, pp. 257-93. See also Kōda, *Edo to Osaka*, pp. 34-75.
74 Miyamoto, *ibid.*, pp. 48-50.

economic expansion, was not able to function fully. The extremely inflexible provincial system only managed to escape economic stagnation because of these points of release for the pressures generated by increasing local trade needs in conjunction with local economic restrictions.

However, we have seen no proof that the trend towards a national economy critically threatened the existence of the provincial system. The growing commercialism may have been the most important factor contributing to the degeneration of the Tokugawa feudalism, but we have not so far seen evidence to indicate this. At this point, we can only make the following conclusion: Tokugawa centralization which was initially established for political and military reasons, unintentionally resulted in economic conditions which were conducive to an increase in commercial activity, as it utilized power for the maintenance of a 'static' political system. The consequences were dynamic in the sense that they challenged the existing political and economic structures, and forced modification of these structures.

The dynamic qualities within Tokugawa centralism were to a large extent absorbed by the trade activities in the unrestricted *Bakufu*-controlled cities. This in turn prevented a breakdown of the provincial political and economic system. Tokugawa feudalism thus embraced two economically contradictory systems within a politically closed system; the possibility of politically dysfunctional consequences of this arrangement was minimized by an effective safety valve, the existence of national trade centres by means of which provincial economic strains and pressures could be released. Such a situation could not have perpetuated itself had there been rapid technological advancement on the local *han* level, as this would have made it impossible for the limited number of trade centres to handle the increased volume of goods; the inflexible local trade barriers would have been destroyed; the provincial economic structure would have been rapidly pushed toward establishment of a national economy. However, no technological innovations which would have effected this were evident during the Tokugawa period.

STANLEY R. BARRETT

Crisis and change
in a West African utopia

Aiyetoro is a small utopia located in the depths of the Niger delta in Nigeria.[1] It was founded in 1947 by a group of uneducated fishermen who were being persecuted because of their religious beliefs. The significance of the community stems from its special social organization. It is a theocracy: according to the ideal belief system, religious values have primacy. It is communistic: there is no exchange of money among members for goods or services. Food, clothing, and housing are provided free. In turn, no member receives payment for working; all profits are retained by the community, to be administered by the *oba* (king). Finally, the community is very wealthy: in spite of its isolated location and brief existence it has achieved a remarkable degree of industrialization. It now has several factories, as well as a half-dozen mechanized fishing trawlers.

The potential causal relation of the system of religious beliefs and the communal social organization to the rapid development constitutes a logical focus of research. This relation has been considered elsewhere.[2] There it was argued that the industrialization of Aiyetoro is mainly a consequence of its communal organization. Following the normal procedure of the social sciences the dynamic role of communalism was not demonstrated; rather an attempt was made to disconfirm the alternative hypothesis. Since the evidence overwhelmingly refuted any causal relation between religion and the economy, the communal social organization was accepted tentatively as the major determining variable.[3]

I shall not be concerned here to explain why Aiyetoro has industrialized. The causal status of communalism will be assumed. My purpose is to describe a recent and radical

I am indebted to the Wenner-Gren Foundation for Anthropological Research whose grant made this research possible.

1 For a general description of the community, see E. McClelland, 'The Experiment in Communal Living at Aiyetoro,' *Comparative Studies in Society and History*, vol. 9 (1966-7), 14-32.
2 S.R. Barrett, 'The Protestant Ethic and the Holy Apostles,' unpublished paper, School of African and Asian Studies, University of Sussex.
3 An extensive comparative study was undertaken in a village located near Aiyetoro which shared almost the same religious beliefs, but had not developed and was not organized along communal lines. It is this comparative material that rules out most strongly the causal role of religion in Aiyetoro.

structural change in the economy itself. Since approximately 1968 a form of private enterprise has been introduced into the community. The modification has been effected covertly, and the village continues to describe itself as a communal society. As will be shown, such denial is necessary to reduce tension resulting from the change.

The structural change in the economy has extensive theoretical significance. However, with the exception of modest interpretations of why capitalism was introduced and why this did not result in the dissolution of the community, as well as a brief consideration of some implications of the communal system for modernization theory, this paper will be mainly ethnographical. Its purpose is to describe the economy as it was in the past and as it is now. The restriction to data does not imply any antagonism towards theory. It is a necessary consequence of the range and subtlety of the changes themselves.

CONCEPTS AND METHODS
A potential source of ambiguity concerns the concepts of communalism and capitalism. What precisely is meant when it is said that the latter has been introduced into Aiyetoro? An adequate definition of the two entities would encompass several pages, or more. Durkheim, for example, devoted an entire book to his brilliant exposition of the distinction between communism and socialism.[4]

I do not intend to present a thorough definition, but instead to isolate only those elements in both communalism and capitalism that are essential for the comprehension of the Aiyetoro case. This means that the aetiology of the two entities in historical terms, reflecting different philosophies of life, will be excluded from discussion.[5]

The minimal definition offered for the communal system in Aiyetoro is as follows: there is no private ownership; labour is a collective affair; and all profits are claimed by the central committee, to be administered as it sees fit. The minimal definition of capitalism is the converse: there is private ownership; labour is an individual affair in the sense that the actor sells himself on the market to the highest bidder, and in the sense that, while operating within a structure of social relations (or an organization), he is oriented primarily to his own direct gratification rather than to that of the collectivity; and profits are retained by the individual himself. By the introduction of capitalism, then, will be meant the transition from the elements in the first entity to those in the second.

It is relevant to add that some of the more educated members use the term 'communism' to describe their village. The term has no international political connotation in Aiyetoro. Members often exchange it with communalism and community, with a preference for the latter. In order to avoid confusion I have decided not to follow these

4 Emile Durkheim, *Socialism* (Collier Books, 1967).
5 Even if the problem is limited to the explanation of capitalism alone, the task is overwhelming. The entire bulk of literature concerning Weber's *Protestant Ethic* thesis is relevant. Moreover, the different explanations provided by Weber and Marx are of central importance. As Parsons remarks, Weber is of the opinion that the Marxist framework is adequate to explain the fully developed capitalist system, but not to explain its genesis. See Talcott Parsons, *The Structure of Social Action* (Free Press Paperback, 1968), vol. II, 510.

For quite a different interpretation of Marxism and its relation to industrialization, see Ernest Gellner, *Thought and Change* (London: Weidenfeld and Nicolson, 1969). See also N. Birnbaum, 'Conflicting Interpretations of the Rise of Capitalism: Marx and Weber,' *The British Journal of Sociology*, vol. IV (June 1953).

definitions exactly. First, communism will not be used at all. Second, community will not be employed as a synonym for communalism or communism. Instead it will be used to mean a village or a town.[6]

The material presented is based on three months of fieldwork. It was revised after almost a year in the field, thus enabling me to take into account subsequent discoveries. Quantitative material has been collected by the techniques of the questionnaire, the structured interview, and the card-sorting method,[7] but this material has not been used here. The main sources of data are informal interviews, participant observation, and informants. The interviews were limited to selected specialists, such as the managers of the factories and the *oba*. In the capacity of participant observer I usually worked alongside the members, especially during communal labour. Almost never did I become a complete participant, which has many limitations for the fieldworker; instead my role fluctuated from an observer who participates to a participant who observes.[8]

With respect to informants, efforts were made to draw them from different strata in order to provide a representative cross-section. It has been difficult to develop suitable candidates from both the female sector and from the elderly males. To some extent this flaw in methodology has been corrected by the use of the structured interview to tap the inaccessible sectors. However, the data are primarily drawn from several male informants, both members and non-members, who are under 30 years of age and educated beyond the average of the community.

Finally, the indigenous language is Ilaje, a Yoruba dialect. With the exception of the few expressions I have learned since the beginning of fieldwork I can speak no Ilaje or Yoruba. This has not proved to be an obstacle. Almost everyone in the community speaks English. For this reason an interpreter rarely has been required for any interview or casual conversation.

EARLY ECONOMY

Prior to depicting the structural changes in the economy, it is necessary to describe the community's setting, origin, and subsequent growth along communal lines. Aiyetoro is located along the coast of the Atlantic Ocean in the Western State of Nigeria. Its population according to the 1963 Federal Census is 1,240.[9] The community is inaccessible by road, but numerous rivers connect it to the mainland. The nearest large town is Okitipupa. It is fifty miles to the interior. The entire expanse between Aiyetoro and Okitipupa is dense mangrove swamp, broken only by the rivers that cut through it. The banks of the rivers and the coast of the Atlantic are populated by two major ethnic

6 Communism also has a religious connotation in Aiyetoro, but it will not be considered here. Members of ten say that nearby villages have no religion because they are not a 'community.'
7 For an explanation of this technique, see S.S. Silverman, 'An Ethnographic Approach to Social Stratification: Prestige in a Central Italian Community,' *American Anthropologist,* vol. 68 (1966).
8 For a clarification of these and other roles of observation, see Raymond L. Gold, 'Roles in Sociological Field Observations,' *Social Forces,* 36 (March 1958), 217-23; and Buford H. Junker, 'Social Roles for Observation,' chap. III, *Field Work* (Chicago & London: University of Chicago Press, 1962); see also Howard S. Becker, 'Problems of Inference and Proof in Participant Observation,' *ASR,* vol. 23, no. 6 (December 1958), for an excellent discussion on how to improve the quality of data derived from participant observation.
9 This estimate remains valid, for according to my own census in 1969 there are now 1,239 residents.

groups, the Ilaje and the Ijaw. The Ilaje, who trace their origin to Ile-Ife and thus are Yoruba, live along the coast. Almost all the original members of Aiyetoro are drawn from this group.[10]

The majority of the Aiyetoro people originate from nearby villages. Before 1947 they belonged to the Cherubim and Seraphim Mission. This is an indigenous Yoruba prophetic movement connected with the Aladura churches.[11] Around 1942 several members of Cherubim and Seraphim began to preach against the killing of twins, which was practiced in Ilaje-land.[12] This roused the anger of the Ilaje people. The responsibility of killing twins was held by a male secret society (oro). In order to eradicate the practice the dissident members of Cherubim and Seraphim began to reveal the secrets of the oro to the women. This elicited greater persecution, and consequently the rebel members decided to establish their own community, which became known as Aiyetoro.

Aiyetoro was not founded with the anticipation that it would be organized along communal lines. Indeed, almost a year went by before a decision to this effect was taken. According to the members two factors inspired them to adopt communalism. The first is related to biblical teaching: they wanted to live by the example of early Christians. The second is related to conflict: the members felt they would be in a stronger position to withstand the persecution of their neighbours if they were united.

Once the decision to live communally was taken, all personal possessions were turned over to the community. This included watches, rings, and cash. It also included clothing and women; some wealthy members, for example, had brought along all their garments and all their wives. They were allowed to keep one suit of clothes and one wife; the remainder was claimed by the community, to be distributed among those who had none. The profits from the salable items were used to purchase food, fishing gear, and carpentry tools. The profits also paid legal fees that resulted from the defence of members who were put in jail.

The ideology of communalism extended to the kinship system. Husband and wife did not form a household. Instead the village was divided into male and female sectors. Four or five men lived together in one house in the male sector; their mates were dispersed in similar accommodations in the female section. Children were not brought up by their own parents. Each child was given to an adult, who became his master or guardian. According to the members, this is done partly for purposes of discipline; one can correct another's child with much less hesitation than one's own child. A further reason is suggested: the distribution of the children contributes to the sense of community. It is the community, not the kinship unit, that is paramount.

10 The Ilaje in turn are composed of two peoples: the Ugbo and the Mahin. A good account of their rivalry for control of Ilaje-land is given in a secret British Intelligence Report that I was fortunate to discover. The report is dated 1937, but the author's name is not revealed.

11 See J.D.Y. Peel, *Aladura: A Religious Movement among the Yoruba* (London: Oxford University Press, 1968).

12 It is generally assumed that the Ilaje practice of killing twins is not representative of Yoruba society, where twins enjoy special privileges. However, in a recent publication Bascom states that even outside Ilaje-land twins are feared, and can cause the death of their parents. See William Bascom, *The Yoruba of Southwestern Nigeria* (New York: Holt, Rinehart and Winston, Inc., 1969), p. 74. Johnson also indicates that twin-killing was prevalent in former times among the Yoruba. See S. Johnson, *The History of the Yorubas* (London: Routledge & Kegan Paul, Ltd., 1966), p. 25.

These examples reflect the extent to which communalism pervaded Aiyetoro almost from its founding. It emerged as the central feature of the value system. I now want to focus upon communalism as it relates to the economy. Of initial importance is the manner in which labour was organized. Work was a collective rather than an individual activity; members laboured in large gangs. This pattern of work made possible some outstanding achievements. Consider, for example, the construction of the town itself. At first, all houses were made with poles and thatch cut from the swamp. It was then decided to replace this material with wood. The members were fishermen, not carpenters, and they lacked the tools required for large-scale construction. Nevertheless, working in gangs they felled timber in the swamp, floated it to the site of the town, and split it into planks by the use of machetes. Within three years enough buildings had been constructed to accommodate all members. The result was a standard of housing remarkably high, relative to the nearby villages.

A second difficult task was made necessary because of the environment. In the wet season the ground is flooded. For this reason all the houses had to be built on stilts. This was not a novelty, for all houses in the traditional villages were elevated in a similar manner. However, the members of Aiyetoro decided to connect every dwelling in the community with a walk, which itself had to be built four or five feet above the swamp. As a result of communal labour a central boardwalk almost a quarter of a mile long was constructed, as well as numerous shorter walks connecting rows of houses to the main walk. When compared with the situation in neighbouring villages this achievement is outstanding. In spite of the fact that dwellings in the traditional villages are only a few yards from each other, it is necessary to use a canoe to move from one house to another.

Another major job at the beginning was the construction of a seven-mile canal to a lagoon in the interior. Such a canal already existed, but the neighbouring villages would not allow the members of Aiyetoro to use it. Access to the lagoon was imperative since from it a natural water route led to Okitipupa and to Lagos, as well as to other points on the mainland. Without an outlet to these places Aiyetoro could not market her fish. Working in gangs of hundreds of men, the community completed the canal in 1949.

These large projects were the work of communal labour, for which no payment was received. Instead, the community assumed responsibility for all necessities. As already indicated, members did not pay for food, clothing, or housing. Furthermore, several young men were sent to schools outside Aiyetoro with the community paying their fees. In addition, if a person wanted to travel, he approached the *oba* and explained the purpose of the trip. If the journey was reasonable, the community supplied the necessary funds.

At first fishing was the only industry. Gradually several other enterprises were established, including boatbuilding, shoe making, weaving, tailoring, and bread factories. As the several new industries were introduced, the organization of the work was modified. Three distinct patterns emerged. The most important pattern involved the adoption of the department as the main unit of administration. Each factory and other major industry such as fishing, carpentry, and boatbuilding became a separate department. All adult members of both sexes were assigned to a particular department. Even children of primary school age were included under this organizational unit. After school closes at 2 PM each child must report to the department where the guardian of the same sex is employed. This not only permits an early start as an apprentice, but it also enhances socialization into those norms having to do with attitude towards work.

The department emerged as the most important formal organization in Aiyetoro. Its functions are instrumental: every economic enterprise of significance was taken into its structure. Its functions are also expressive: it is a locus of identification for members, with departments sometimes holding their own parties. As well, any type of collective activity in Aiyetoro has a moral connotation. The implication is that each department constitutes a distinct moral community within the larger community. Finally, the creation of departments marked the beginning of internal competition in Aiyetoro. Departments began to compete with each other for reward – a moral, not a material reward.

The second pattern of work was communal labour. As stressed, this was the dominant type at the beginning. With the emergence of the department its importance declined, but did not disappear. Communal labour continued to occur whenever there was a job to do that was either too big for a particular department, or not the direct responsibility of any department. As an example of the initial case, members often were summoned to help draw the fishing trawlers onto land for repair. As an example of the second case, the entire community periodically gathered to cut grass and weeds that grew around the town. Such labour occurs now on an average of twice a week.

A third pattern of work was not formally organized at all. It involved individual labour. For example, before the factories opened in the morning an individual might go to the seashore to catch crayfish to be dried or smoked. What was not consumed was sold to strangers in the community market, or in nearby villages. Some members also kept chickens and ducks or attempted to grow oranges, bananas, and paw paw. This was the only type of work in Aiyetoro that was not a collective enterprise.

In spite of the changes in the organization of work, there was no modification of the system of rewards. In the case of the departments all profits were regularly turned over to the community. This occurred at the end of each month, when a bell was rung. Then a representative of each department took the money to the treasurer of the community. As well, those members who had earned a pound or two from individual effort, such as fishing at the seashore, gave their earnings to the treasurer. Since communal labour never resulted in any profit, it posed no problem when the new patterns of work emerged.

To conclude, within a few years Aiyetoro had become industrialized. Its achievements are outstanding when compared to its environment. The neighbouring villages have no electricity; their housing, relative to that in Aiyetoro, is primitive; their income is miniscule; and migration from these villages to the larger towns in the interior has been extensive. Those who remain are increasingly dependent upon Aiyetoro for employment. As a result there has been a complete shift in power relations. The nearby villagers no longer can afford to be overtly hostile to Aiyetoro; it is Aiyetoro that wields the power – in this case economic power.

The achievements of the village are significant even when compared with those of the nation as a whole. For example, as far back as 1951, only four years after its founding, Aiyetoro was described as the most successful community development project in Nigeria.[13]

13 E.H. Duckworth, 'A Visit to the Apostles and the Town of Aiyetoro,' *Nigeria Magazine*, no. 36 (1951).

And in 1957 it was said to have the highest standard of living of any town in the country.[14] It has been discovered in the course of fieldwork that communalism is a necessary but not a sufficient cause of the rapid development. A number of supporting variables exist, the absence of which would have precluded such development. Nevertheless, the communal system remains the major causal variable.[15]

PRESENT ECONOMY

It will now be demonstrated that the communal economic structure has been modified extensively. It has been replaced partly by a form of capitalism. Two factors must be stressed. First, as already indicated, the change has been effected covertly. The community has attempted to conceal the incipient capitalism, and its success in doing so is reflected in the ignorance of the surrounding villagers. The villagers are aware that something unusual has occurred, for they notice that members now wear a wide range of clothing styles, where previously a uniform was worn. They also observe that several members have recently purchased expensive items such as radios. But they are unaware of the capitalist intrusion. Second, the change has been salutary. Given the central position of communalism in the value system of Aiyetoro, it may be assumed that any deviation from it would be dysfunctional. This assumption is not tenable. Aiyetoro has encountered the capitalist modifications, absorbed them, and become rejuvenated in the process.

The major index of the transformation in the economy is that members are now allowed to have a personal income. This has been achieved partly by an incentive system that rewards individual initiative. Members now compete with each other in the marketplace. However, there is no direct correlation between individual industry and the size of one's private purse. This is because the system of rewards is more complex: in addition to individual competition, there is also collective competition. These two levels of competition have been introduced through the existing organizational structure of the economy. As described previously, there are three patterns of work. These include work in departments, communal labour, and individual labour. What has happened is that the system of rewards corresponding to two of these organizational types has been modified. First, all profits from individual labour are now retained by the members. Second, *some* profits from departmental work are presently shared by the workers of each department. This has meant a shift in the relative importance of the three types of labour, although this statement must be qualified according to whether it is judged by the individual member or by the community as a whole. From the perspective of a particular member, individual labour has replaced communal labour as the second most important type, because it is now a source of personal income. From the

14 'Aiyetoro,' *Nigeria Magazine*, no. 55 (1957).
15 An interesting problem, but one I am unable to consider here, is how Aiyetoro came upon the idea of a communal society. Suffice it to say that no model of similar communal proportions to my knowledge exists in West Africa. However, communalism of a less extensive range can be found. See, for example, David W. Ames, 'Wolof Cooperative Work Groups,' in W.R. Bascom and M.J. Herskovits (eds.), *Continuity and Change in African Cultures* (University of Chicago Press, 1963); and J.R. Goody, 'The Fission of Domestic Groups among the Lo Dagaba,' in J.R. Goody (ed.), *The Developmental Cycle in Domestic Groups* (Cambridge University Press, 1958).

perspective of the community, it is difficult to determine which contributes more – individual or communal labour. As will be seen, the first has reduced some of the conflict in the community, and to a certain extent increased productivity. However, communal labour epitomizes the central values of the community, and for this reason remains significant.

I now propose to examine in some detail both levels of competition in Aiyetoro, and the corresponding system of rewards. With respect to individual competition, there are two types. One is legitimate, the other is semi-legitimate. Legitimate competition is conducted both on a part-time and a full-time basis. Two examples of individual competition that is part-time and legitimate will be given. One of the cases has been referred to previously; until recently, however, it was not a source of personal income. It involves those members who go to the seashore early in the morning before one's regular job in the department begins. The men wade into the water with their nets and catch different kinds of fish. The women usually assume the responsibility of processing and marketing. When the fish is dried or smoked it is sold in the Aiyetoro market or in markets farther away. Previously the profits of this work were turned over to the community. Now all profits are kept by the individual.

The second example also is connected with the fishing industry. In the past three years a few members have begun to build fish-ponds. This is done by digging a rectangular hole approximately twenty feet square. The hole must be boarded off to keep the fish from escaping during the floods of the wet season. It must also be deep enough so that it will not evaporate in the dry season. After the pond is constructed, small tarpon about two inches long are caught in the fresh-water rivers. If left in the rivers they make their way to the sea after reaching a certain stage of maturity. The tarpon are fed small fish caught by net and spear. Eventually they grow to about two or three feet in length, are delicious to eat, and can be sold for 15 shillings or one pound each. Most are marketed during the Christmas celebrations.

These types of individual labour are not new to the community. However, in the past they were not a focus of individual competition, nor were they pursued with the same intensity as at present. This is especially the case with the fish-ponds. A few years ago a similar pond was built, which supposedly was the property of the community, but in reality belonged to the first *oba*. The members did not attempt to build other ponds at that time, and the *oba*'s pond was soon discarded. In contrast, the fish-ponds now are almost epidemic, around 30 of them having been constructed recently.

These are examples of legitimate competition at the individual level, carried out on a part-time basis. Two examples of such work which is carried on full-time will now be given. It must, however, be stressed that most individual labour is on a part-time basis. The cases to follow, then, are not normal, but they are indicative of the transformed structure of the economy.

The first case involves the community photographer. He has performed this function for Aiyetoro since 1962. When he first began, the community gave him the funds required to purchase equipment, but it no longer provides such service. For example, in 1968 the photographer decided he needed equipment for enlarging, as well as new cameras. The cost of the equipment was approximately 180 pounds. Instead of supplying the photographer with this amount, the community decided to lend him 100 pounds.

Now the photographer has charged members for photographs for the past three years. From the profits of this work he saved 60 pounds. He waited until he had earned the remaining 20 pounds and then purchased the new equipment. His work is good, and the members constantly require his services. He expects to repay the 100 pounds loaned by the community by the end of 1970.

A second case has to do with conflict. The community has many disputes with other villages and groups of people. The quarrels usually concern women who have joined the village without the consent of their relatives, or competitors in the economic arena. One member has gradually emerged as the community's lawyer. He has no formal training in law, but he continued to study law in his spare time, and now represents Aiyetoro whenever a conflict arises with non-members. The member does not receive a regular wage from this work. Instead, whenever there is a conflict he is immediately summoned by the department in trouble. If it is, for example, the Fishing Department, they will give him 40–50 pounds to represent them. Out of this he may spend half, and thus have a profit of 20–30 pounds. It is important to stress that it is not the community in general who pays him, but instead a particular department. This suggests once more the degree to which the departments are autonomous structures.

I now want to describe a form of competition among individuals that is only semi-legitimate. This is what the community calls 'business.' For example, if one wants to purchase a desk from the carpentry department he may be asked to pay ten pounds. Instead of agreeing to do so, he may approach one of the carpenters and ask him to do the work privately at a reduced cost. In one such case a member agreed to build a desk for a resident of a neighbouring village. He did the work in an empty building at night. When the desk was completed it was sent by canoe to the outsider under cover of darkness and sold for five pounds.

A further example involves the Tailoring Department. Perhaps one wants to buy a shirt. It is easy to persuade one of the tailors to do the work after hours. The buyer is happy because the price is less than that asked by the department. The tailor is pleased because the profits are his own.

'Business' is also called 'dodging,' and is only semi-legitimate. However, the new *oba* is reported to be in favour of it. He interprets it as another source of healthy competition for the community. It should be stressed that business is not new in Aiyetoro. However, in the past it was called corruption. With the introduction of private enterprise it has achieved some degree of legitimacy.

Both legitimate and semi-legitimate individual competition result in direct monetary reward. In each case all profits are retained by the individual, and the size of the reward corresponds to the individual's output. I shall now describe the second major type of competition. This type occurs at the level of groups, is carried out entirely on a full-time basis, and takes place within the structure of the department. It was stressed that the department is much more than an impersonal place of labour. Each department is a locus of identification for the member, at times even rivalling the kinship unit. It was for this reason that the departments were described as moral communities within the larger community.

Now the emergence of departments as distinct moral communities within the structure of the economy probably contributed to production. It created competition, which otherwise was alien to the communal system. Furthermore, the departments competed for moral reward, which was measured in terms of productivity. The effect of the changes in the reward system has been to augment, not replace, the system of moral reward. Departments are still praised for high production. But in addition to immaterial reward there are now material benefits. These take two forms. First, members of departments still are not allowed to retain their profits, but when the money is handed over to the community treasurer at the end of each month, the manager will keep out a few pounds and distribute it among the workers. The amount received varies according to the post of the worker. The manager, for example, receives two or three pounds more than the others. This monthly source of income may be termed a 'dash.'

Second, while the members of each department do not receive a salary, a form of payment called a 'bonus' has been introduced. Each member receives a bonus three times a year. The members are concerned to explain that the bonus is not a salary, in order to maintain the appearance of communalism in Aiyetoro.

A further example of group competition is also related to the various departments. Before 1966 there was only one store in the community where small items could be obtained. This was called the Aiyetoro Community Shop. In the last three years six other shops have been opened. Each shop is owned by one of the departments, and all carry an identical range of stock. Given a communal society in which competition is supposedly foreign, such overlap is not rational. In effect, the several new shops are indices of the transformation of the economy of Aiyetoro. They are extensions of departmental competition. For example, both the Bread Department and the Tailoring Department own a shop. When a member goes to collect bread he is enticed into making a further purchase at their shop. The same thing occurs in the tailoring shop. Before 1967 no money was charged in the original shop, but now in all the shops, including the original one, members must pay for what they buy.

A final example of group competition concerns the fishing industry. The catch from the trawlers is carried in carts to a specific building where it is dumped on the floor. The task of separating the fish according to type belongs to the women. As a reward for working, each woman is allowed to keep a pile of the culled fish. The size of the pile varies according to the age of the women. The older one is, the larger the pile.

After the fish are separated they are weighed and sold to customers. These customers are mainly female members of Aiyetoro. Since 1968 they have not been allowed to collect the fish free, but must pay for it. The women take the fish away, dry it, and in turn sell it in the market.

In spite of the fact that the women pay for the fish, their profits are still immense. A pile that they purchase for one pound may bring in a return of one pound ten, or one pound fifteen, after it has been dried. It is unreasonable to suppose they keep all the profits. Indeed, they do not. Each month the accumulated profits are turned over to the community. It may be suspected that the female members will attempt to 'dodge.' However, their work is organized in such a way as to reduce 'business' to a minimum. No woman works alone. Instead, all work in groups of four or five. Each group has a leader who is a trusted member. It is her responsibility to make certain all profits from her group go to the community at the end of each month.

Now the system of reward here is identical with that in other departments. First, at the end of the month the group leader retains a few pounds cash and distributes it among her mates. Second, the community provides each group of women with a bonus.

The size of the bonus varies according to the output of the group. As in the case of the other departments, the basic system of reward is indirect; it is not the individual who is rewarded, but the group as a whole.

In summary, group competition is more dominant than individual competition. It is carried out entirely on a full-time basis. Its rewards are primarily indirect, and the size of the reward varies according to the output of the entire group, rather than in terms of individual productivity within the group.

A final source of reward warrants attention. This is related to a year-end ceremony in Aiyetoro. As part of the community's ideology of modernity all indigenous ceremonies and rituals are rejected as time-wasting and evil. However, they do celebrate the end of each year with countless parties and one major ceremony. Work comes to a stop, and members conducting community business at points throughout Nigeria are summoned home. It may be speculated that the year-end ceremony fills a necessary social gap in the community, given the absence of traditional rituals. However, this interpretation suffers a little too much from functional indispensability. Irrespective of its ritual significance the ceremony has a specific important function. It is then that rewards are distributed for outstanding performance.

Coincident with previous descriptions, such rewards are both immaterial and material, both individually and collectively determined. The epitome of immaterial reward is an appointment to the Supreme Council of Elders or the Faith and Work Council, two elite organizations in the community. Material rewards include clothing, bicycles, and motorcycles. These are donated to both individual actors and corporate groups. In the first case, a particularly industrious member may be given a bicycle. In the second case, a department that has greatly exceeded its estimated productivity may benefit from a department that has not done so well. For example, if the carpenters have worked hard, and the tailors not so hard, the latter department may be ordered by the *oba* to give a shirt to every member of the carpentry department.

In summary, there are now several sources of personal income in the community (see Table 1). First, money can be gained by individual initiative outside one's regular occupation. This includes both legitimate and semi-legitimate work. Second, one can gain money from one's regular occupation in a department. This includes both the monthly 'dash' and the thrice annual bonus. Finally, one can be rewarded at the year-end ceremony.

The preceding cases reflect the extensive transformation of the economic structure of Aiyetoro. Members are now allowed to have a private purse. Given this basic change in the structure of the economy, it may be suspected that the range of amenities provided by the community has diminished. This is true. For example, bread previously was collected without payment by any member. Now free bread is provided only on a limited basis. On each line connecting rows of houses to the central boardwalk there is a specific house where all people in that line eat. Every morning and evening bread is distributed to the eating house. If at other times of the day a member wishes to have bread to eat in his own house, he must pay for it.

A further example relates to housing. It was stated that all houses were provided without charge. Now, however, the community does only part of the construction. Community carpenters will drive the stilts into the mud and erect the framework, but

TABLE 1
Summary of types of competition and reward

Type of Competition	Basis of Work		Degree of Legitimacy		Type of Reward	
	Full-time	Part-time	Legitimate	Semi-legitimate	Direct	Indirect
Individual	x	x	x	x	x	
Collective	x		x			x

the individual occupants must complete the construction. Wood is provided without charge, but such items as light bulbs now must be paid for by the occupant.

Finally, as suggested previously, school fees were paid by the community. Aiyetoro now has its own primary and secondary schools. Fees are still free, but the guardians and kin relations of students are responsible for buying many of the required books. In addition, the community has decided that next year it will not provide the school uniforms. Instead, each student must purchase his own.

THE MIXED ECONOMY

Although a form of capitalism has been introduced into Aiyetoro, it must be stressed that the changes in the economy have been limited. By retaining the structure of the departments, and the consequent system of rewards in terms of collective rather than individual achievement, the development of capitalism has been inhibited. As a result, the present economy represents a mixture of both capitalist and communal systems. It is the purpose of this section to emphasize the continued communal nature of much of the economy in spite of the introduction of the private purse.

The initial factor of importance is that, while individuals are now allowed to keep a private purse, the size of this purse relative to the collective profits of the community is miniscule. Indeed, community policy allows members to retain only 7 per cent of all profits. The remaining 93 per cent is claimed by the community treasurer.[16] Given such a disproportionate percentage claimed by the community, it might be thought that the incentive of the private purse would be nullified. It might further be assumed that many, perhaps the majority, of the members would attempt to 'dodge.' With respect to incentive, it must be realized that in the past *no* private income could be retained. Thus even a small personal income now is valued. It may also be suggested that, in comparison with the average income of neighbouring villagers, 7 per cent of the collective profits in Aiyetoro represents a significant amount.

Insofar as dodging is concerned, it must be remembered that most work occurs in the departments. This labour is well organized. It is not difficult to assure that the stipulated 93 per cent of the profits are delivered to the community. In cases where super-

16 This figure was provided by the *oba*. From other sources I have been told that members are allowed to retain 1/6 on every pound, which works out to approximately 7 per cent.

vision is more difficult, steps have been taken to ensure delivery. The system of control with respect to the women who sell fish has already been described: all women work in small groups. Further, the income derived from individual part-time work, such as catching fish at the seashore in the early morning, or conducting 'business,' is, in fact, quite small. The community treasury does not suffer by allowing members to keep it. Indirectly, then, the private purse benefits the community as much as the individual. By permitting it, the incentive of individual reward is fostered. By restricting its size, the community treasury is not jeopardized.

The second policy reflecting the mix in the economy has to do with what the community calls 'the circulation of profits.' This is an ingenious method in which the recent novelty of the private purse again ultimately enriches the communal purse. The system works as follows: a restriction is placed on how one's private money is spent. No goods should be purchased outside the community. Since basic necessities such as bread, clothing, and shoes, as well as minor items from combs to brassieres, are available in the village, the objective is to a great extent realized.

The advantage of this system to the community can readily be explained. First, radios, rubber boots, yams, etc. are all bought in bulk from outside the community. This constitutes a significant reduction in price. Those in charge of purchasing such goods know the exact price; in an economy where bargaining is a normal procedure the advantage held by the expert again reduces the cost of the item. This factor, it may be added, is especially relevant in Aiyetoro. Because until recently members did not pay money for goods received, they often did not know their value. For this reason they were easily cheated outside the community. This was particularly true in the case of the younger members who were born in Aiyetoro and knew no other system than their own brand of communalism.

These are not the most important advantages. Consider the following process: when a member decides to buy a lamp or a flashlight, he makes the purchase in one of the community shops, or departments. Now this means that the profit of the sale remains in the community. It is not lost to the outside world. Furthermore, most of these profits gradually find their way to the community treasury, because departments retain only a portion of what they earn.

It is not only individual members who are encouraged to make their purchases in Aiyetoro. When possible the various departments buy goods from each other. For example, if the Shoe Department requires nails, it will buy them from the Carpentry Department at a slightly increased price.

In order to encourage members and departments to spend their money in Aiyetoro, some departments are allowed to supplement their stock with goods obtained from Lagos or elsewhere. For example, in addition to the shoes made by the community, one can purchase Bata models at the showroom. A stock of shirts and trousers purchased from Lagos is also carried by the Tailoring Department. The Shoe Department increases the price of the Bata shoes by three or four shillings. The Tailoring Department makes a similar profit on its imported stock. The size of the profit on such sales is not unlimited. If each department were permitted to charge what it wished, the members would be reluctant to make their purchases in the community. In order to avert this danger the *oba* has decreed that profits from the sale of expensive goods must not exceed 10 per cent, and from petty items must not be greater than 15 per cent. According to the members this decree is frequently ignored.

In effect, central to the system of 'the circulation of profits' is the perpetual flow of capital. Members are not encouraged to hoard their money. It should be spent, but only in Aiyetoro. There is some exchange of cash among individuals. This occurs, for example, when one buys a chicken or a fish from one of the members. Most purchases, however, are made from the various departments, or from the several shops belonging to them. The major flow of capital, then, is from individuals to departments and among the departments themselves. In both cases the bulk of the capital is claimed eventually by the community treasurer. Thus each time a transaction is made, whether between an individual and a department, or between departments themselves, the community purse is replenished.

A final example of the retention of some degree of communal social organization will be described. This involves communal labour. The introduction of private enterprise has not led to the cessation of communal work. It still occurs on an average of twice a week. When the towncrier rings his bell and announces a specific project to be done, all members are expected to respond. Usually about two or three hundred men appear at the designated spot, and perhaps 15 or 25 women. This work does not bring in any direct material reward. However, its importance, both for the work achieved and for the individuals contributing, is significant. Large-scale projects requiring hundreds of men still can be done quickly in Aiyetoro. Communal work is symbolic of the values that have always defined Aiyetoro and this means that an individual's contribution is a moral contribution. It is for this reason that no ambitious member can afford to miss communal labour. Thus whenever the bell is rung to summon the members to cut grass or clear logs from the canal, there is an over-representation of both established and aspiring members of the elite.

DISCUSSION

The original economy of Aiyetoro was communal. It has been modified by the introduction of capitalism. No attempt has been made to explain two outstanding problems: Why did the change occur? Why did it not result in the dissolution of the community?

To provide satisfactory solutions to these problems would entail an extensive theoretical discussion, which is beyond the scope of this presentation. Nevertheless, I do propose to take steps toward their solution. First, I shall relate how the members themselves account for the modification of the economy; this retains the emphasis upon data rather than theory. Second, I shall suggest, but not develop, the type of theoretical explanation that may account for both the change in the economy and the subsequent state of health of the community.

With respect to the initial problem, the *oba* suggests two reasons. He describes the state of affairs that existed in Aiyetoro prior to the change. The members had grown lazy. Many of the most industrious of them at the time of the founding of the community were now old men. They no longer provided inspiration. In addition, the community had become corrupt. Members stole from each other and sold the goods in neighbouring villages. In order to rectify the laziness and corruption a change of some kind was required. The *oba*'s second explanation is that people simply need a change every few years regardless of how the existing system is functioning. His argument is that people grow weary of the status quo. With this in mind, he predicts that in another twenty years a further modification of the village may be necessary.

In virtually all interviews with other members of Aiyetoro the *oba*'s initial explanation is supported. For example, people did not show up for work in the departments, let alone go to the seashore before their regular job began. There was also increased difficulty in social control. Prior to the present *oba*'s assumption of the throne all primary and secondary students were withdrawn from classes because of corruption. Corruption refers mainly to the breaking of sexual codes, but also includes laziness, theft, and general disobedience.

Relative to the *oba*'s second explanation, no other informant has offered a similar statement. Nevertheless, it is an imaginative interpretation of the changed economy. It is relevant to add that the attitude towards work has shifted dramatically since the insertion of some degree of private enterprise. Now the seaside is crowded in the early morning by both male and female members. Even many of the old men have started to work again. It must be stressed that their willingness to work may have little to do with the acceptance of the new system. Instead, it is a question of necessity. The community no longer provides them with all they need.

This is how the members interpret the introduction of capitalism. Relative to theory, four related models may be drawn. The first has to do with the process of rationalization.[17] In the beginning the community stressed its uniqueness. For example, members shaved their heads and did not wear shoes. In recent years many of the esoteric practices have been terminated: members no longer shave their heads; they now wear shoes. As well, a regular Sunday church service has been established. All of this has reduced social distance between Aiyetoro and the outside world. Insofar as capitalism is part of the external world, this has enhanced its influence in the community.

The second and third models both focus upon conflict. In order to stress their differences they will be described separately. One has to do with the state of crisis that confronts the community. It is characteristic of utopias that they are short-lived. The first major period of trial is not determined randomly. It probably sets in a generation or so after the utopia has been in existence. This is long enough for the message of the prophet to lose its momentum, resulting in a dissipation of the collective spirit of the chosen people. It also is adequate time for a new generation to mature. For them, the founding principles are abstract phenomena. Aiyetoro was settled a little over twenty years ago. It has entered the period of crisis. The structural modification of the economy is a response to the crisis.

While the crisis model indicates that some kind of change was inevitable, it does not explain the particular response of capitalism. This is the task of the third explanation, which for purposes of clarity may be termed the conflict model. It consists of two elements. The first is the communal system of Aiyetoro. The second is the capitalist system of Nigeria as a whole. In the beginning strain was neutralized by isolating the antagonistic organizations from each other. This was achieved by fostering social dis-

17 See Max Weber, *Theory of Social and Economic Organization,* edited by Talcott Parsons (London: William Hodge and Co., 1947).

tance from the outside world. At present the potential conflict has been reduced temporarily by permitting capitalism to claim part of communalism. Given the imbalance between the two systems, it is assumed that the intrusion of capitalism into Aiyetoro was inevitable.

The fourth and last model has to do with succession. It would be wrong to assume that the pressures that brought about the change in the economy have only emerged recently. Problems of theft and laziness are as old as the community itself. Further, a great number of members left Aiyetoro at the beginning, and to a lesser extent over the succeeding years, because of a dislike of communalism. While strains generated by the esoteric system accumulated over the years, the probability of a major change was minimal until the death of the first *oba* in 1963. This is because of the tendency for changes to take place during periods of succession. The new *oba* attempted to solve the problems that loomed most obviously by redefining Aiyetoro as a community of worshippers. Given a taste of development, this was not acceptable to the populace. When the third and present *oba* came to the throne in 1966, the community was still in turmoil. He swung value priority back to the economy, and then supervised the structural modification of the economy itself. The implication is that there always have been strains in Aiyetoro that threatened the communal system. But it is during periods of succession that they finally find outlet.[18]

The formal interpretations (as well as those offered by the members) are complementary. All are addressed to the problem of why the structure of the economy was modified. But differences exist among the models in terms of their power to explain more specific aspects of the problem. For example, why did the change take the direction it did, and why did it occur when it did? With respect to direction, the crisis model is devoid of content; it simply forecasts disintegration (or alternatively the maintenance of the status quo, given a successful confrontation). The rationalization model suggests a logical transition from the sacred to the secular, from the unique to the ordinary. The conflict model is the most specific of all. It *defines* the secular and the ordinary. Given the capitalist environment, these elements are by necessity capitalist elements. Similar to the crisis interpretation, the model of succession has nothing to say about direction. But in another respect it is the most specific of all: it predicts the time when changes occur.

Several explanations of why capitalism was introduced have been suggested. The second and third are said to focus upon conflict. Yet in varying degrees all underline the strain that was widespread in the community. The laziness and corruption referred to by the *oba* and his subjects are signs that the crisis was imminent. The process by which esoteric beliefs and practices are replaced by more rational (i.e. normal) elements, however slow and unflamboyant, is also a subtle form of strain. The succession model exposes the degree of tension that had built up over the years. The implication is clear: in a thorough analysis the various explanations should be subsumed within a more general model of conflict.

18 It would be wrong to assume that the correlation of structural and value changes during periods of succession is restricted to cases of royal succession. Gouldner provides an interesting test of the correlation in an industrial plant. See A. Gouldner, *Patterns of Industrial Bureaucracy* (Glencoe, Ill.: Free Press, 1954).

I now want to consider the second problem. Why did the intrusion of capitalism not result in the dissolution of Aiyetoro? It is the capacity of the community to roll with the change – not the modification itself – that is the surprising feature. Unlike the first problem, no systems of explanation have obvious relevance. The following factors, however, may have contributed to the adaptability of the community. First, it must be remembered that the transformation of the economy was not absolute. Capitalism did not replace communalism. Instead a mixed system emerged. As a result Aiyetoro can continue to describe itself as a communal society, thus maintaining continuity with the original ultimate values. Second, the change was kept covert. This again has the purpose of protecting the central value system. The nearby villagers have always scorned communalism in Aiyetoro. By concealing the change, the community has not been forced to face the inevitable accusations that they have failed. In addition, the hidden nature of the capitalist modification has contributed to the maintenance of social distance from the outside world. Social distance performs two main functions. It keeps the surrounding villagers at bay; if they were permitted to compete freely in the Aiyetoro market, it is likely that the sensitive balance of the mixed economy would collapse. Its second purpose is to create conflict. Such conflict has an integrative function in the community, in that it fosters a sense of in-group values which facilitates the pursuit of common goals.

Further, it was previously noted that the members in the departments receive a bonus, not a salary. Given the fact that outsiders know nothing of the transformed economy, the term bonus can not be intended for their consumption. This implies that it is not only strangers that must be kept in doubt about what has happened. To some extent members must deceive themselves.

A non-sociological variable also may be relevant. It concerns the environment of Aiyetoro. Its significance can be made clearer by introducing a comparative element. The Hutterites also are organized along communal lines.[19] This enables them to accumulate large sums of money. However, wealth is not likely a major incentive for membership, because it is possible to make a good living outside their community as well. The case of Aiyetoro is very different. The rest of Ilaje is very poor. Even on the mainland unemployment is high. Thus there is a real economic advantage for the members of Aiyetoro to maintain the community, no matter how grave the obstacles.

Finally, the successful adaptation of the community may be attributed to the role of the *oba*. Without a strong leader it is not likely that the present mix in the economy could be maintained. Its success requires able administration at the top, complete obedience at all levels of stratification, and an information system that alerts the leader to tension in the community. The role of the *oba* fulfils these requirements.[20] In Aiyetoro the *oba*'s rule is absolute. He is the economic, political, and religious leader of the community. The population is small enough for the *oba* to have complete information on

19 See John W. Bennett, *Hutterian Brethren* (Stanford, Cal.: Stanford University Press, 1967).
20 See P.C. Lloyd, 'The Traditional Political System of the Yoruba,' *Southwestern Journal of Anthropology*, 10 (Winter 1954), 366-84; 'Traditional Rulers,' in J.S. Coleman and C.G. Rosberg, Jr. (eds.), *Political Parties and National Integration in Tropical Africa* (Berkeley and Los Angeles: University of California Press, 1966); and 'Sacred Kingship and Government among the Yoruba,' *Africa, 30,* 221-37.

every member's movement. Regardless of the specific person fulfilling it, the role of the *oba* is appropriate for the task of maintaining the delicate balance between communalism and capitalism.

The emphasis placed on the *oba*'s role rather than his personality is intentional. For the same reasons given by Durkheim[21] long ago and by Radcliffe-Brown[22] and Gluckman[23] more recently, I am reluctant to reduce the explanation to a level lower than the role. If the lines between sociology and psychology are blurred, the probability of either developing a consistent body of theory is diminished. At the same time there is a point where the sociological explanation can go no further. Its range is likely to vary with different problems. The introduction of capitalism, for example, is readily accounted for in structural terms. Indeed, the purpose of the entire preceding analysis has been to demonstrate the sociological conditions that made change inevitable. The structural framework is less successful in explaining the ability of the community to absorb the radical transformation of its economy. It is here where the personal qualities of the *oba* may have exerted their greatest influence. For example, the policy of the circulation of profits, which is perhaps the major concrete manifestation of the mixed economy, was the brainchild of the *oba*. To argue thus does not detract from the sociological theme, as long as it is made clear that the level of analysis has shifted.

CONCLUSIONS

The structural change in the economy has extensive theoretical significance. The preceding discussion has the limited objective of suggesting a framework for dealing with the problem. An adequate analysis would require a rigorous development of the several ideas. Other systems of explanation not referred to would need to be introduced. For example, the method of requisite analysis may be fruitful.[24] Given the central position of communalism in the system of ultimate values, it may be entertained as a structural requisite. At the same time social distance may be considered to be a functional requisite. As has been seen, social distance contributed to the reduction of conflict between Aiyetoro and its environment during the early years. In addition, a major purpose of hiding the change in the economy from the outside world is to maintain social distance. It must be stressed that the conditions to test the requisite status of communalism are not favourable. This is because the transformation of the economy was only partial. It is emphasized, too, that social distance is not the sole functional requisite that supports communalism. A well-developed system of social control is probably one among other necessary conditions.

While our focus has been on the structural modification of the economy – not the communal system itself – in concluding I should like to entertain some of the implications of communalism for modernization theory. Does Aiyetoro with its centralized, collective system approximate to the model of development that currently prevails?

21 See Emile Durkheim, *The Rules of Sociological Method* (Glencoe, Ill.: Free Press, 1950).
22 See A.R. Radcliffe-Brown, *A Natural Science of Society* (Glencoe, Ill.: Free Press, 1964).
23 See, for example, the long introduction in Max Gluckman, *Order and Rebellion in Tribal Society* (London: Cohen and West, 1963).
24 Levy has provided probably the most extensive and lucid statement on requisite analysis. See Marion J. Levy, Jr., *The Structure of Society* (Princeton, NJ: Princeton University Press, 1952).

It is argued that it does. However, a great deal of confusion surrounds the question of development, and some attention must be given to it. The main difficulty concerns the relation between the political and economic systems. The disciplines of sociology and social anthropology rely heavily upon the concepts of 'system' and 'structural interdependence.' The assumption is that the various parts of a society (subsystems or substructures) are related to each other. Thus a change in one will have consequences for the rest.

These concepts appear to be unambiguous and useful. However, the problems begin when one tries to attach weights and content to the various parts. Consider the economic and political systems. Which (if either) has the greater causal weight? At the time that Weber was writing, the economy enjoyed priority. However, many analysts would argue that this is no longer the case. Instead, development is now primarily a political act. Parsons,[25] Eisenstadt,[26] Black,[27] and Anderson, von der Mehden and Young[28] are only a few of those who have argued in this vein.

The ambiguity is similarly great with respect to content. What type of political structure is most conducive to development – democratic or authoritarian? The arguments that have surrounded this problem amply reveal the degree to which our discipline is value-prone. Two early influential works that supported the hypothesis that there is a direct correlation between political competitiveness (democracy) and development are those by Lipset and Coleman. Lipset accepts the hypothesis as confirmed in a comparison of Western European and Latin American democracies.[29] Coleman confirms it in a comparison of Asia, the Middle East, and Africa, with special reference to the latter.[30]

Other authors have taken exception to the conclusions arrived at by Lipset and Coleman. They contend that the relation between the political system and development is exactly the converse: a direct correlation exists between an authoritarian political system and development. Horowitz is one of those to argue in this vein. As he states: 'The end of traditional society, the rise of modernization, has been accompanied by a decline in competitive party politics.'[31] Horowitz makes this statement in explicit reference to Coleman.

Janowitz shares the position taken by Horowitz.[32] He considers the arguments of Coleman and Lipset and concludes that they are not justified in confirming their hypothesis. It is correct that Janowitz arrives at this conclusion in the context of an investi-

25 Talcott Parsons, 'Some Reflections on the Industrial Framework of Economic Development,' in *The Challenge of Development: A Symposium* (Jerusalem: Hebrew University, 1958), pp. 107-36.
26 S.N. Eisenstadt, 'Political Modernization: Some Comparative Notes,' *International Journal of Comparative Sociology*, vol. V (1964), 3-24.
27 C.E. Black, *The Dynamics of Modernization* (New York: Harper and Row, 1966).
28 Charles W. Anderson, *et al., Issues of Political Development* (Englewood Cliffs, NJ: Prentice-Hall, Inc., 1967).
29 S.M. Lipset, 'Some Social Requisites of Democracy: Economic Development and Political Legitimacy,' *American Political Science Review,* 53 (March 1959).
30 James S. Coleman, 'The Political Systems of the Developing Areas,' in Gabriel A. Almond and James S. Coleman (eds.), *The Politics of the Developing Areas* (Princeton University Press, 1960).
31 I.L. Horowitz, *Three Worlds of Development* (New York: Oxford University Press, 1966), p. 229.
32 Morris Janowitz, *The Military in the Political Development of New Nations – an Essay in Comparative Analysis* (Chicago and London: University of Chicago Press, 1964), pp. 22-3.

gation of the role of the military in development, rather than more conventional concrete political organizations. This, however, would not seem to invalidate his remarks. His criticism of the arbitrary nature of Coleman's three basic categories - competitive, semi-competitive, and authoritarian - is especially well grounded.

In summary, it seems to me that the bulk of evidence supports those who argue that not only is development at the present time more of a political than an economic fact, but that an authoritarian and centralized political system is more conducive to development than a democratic one. What this means is that the Aiyetoro case can be presented as a model of modernization that has wide applicability. It follows then that those investigators that continue to operate within the Weberian framework - or within variations on it such as McClelland's[33] thesis of n Achievement - are in error.[34]

This argument must be qualified. As has been shown, the communal system has given way partly to private enterprise. It is inviting to explain this in evolutionary terms. In other words communalism is the first stage in a developmental process that necessarily leads to capitalism. I am hesitant to accept this explanation. It would seem that the crucial variable is not the type of economic organization - communal or capitalist - but the nature of the relation between the unit and its setting. Thus (other factors being constant), given a capitalist village within a communist environment, it would be expected that there would be a comparable transition towards communalism.

It is relevant to add that Levy suggests that a highly authoritarian political structure is dysfunctional in a complex society.[35] This remark shades off into a value statement in the same way as do those of Lipset and Coleman. And in the case of Aiyetoro it is only marginally relevant, insofar as the change in the structure of the economy has not resulted in a reduction of the legitimate authority of the king. However, it is a fact that among the populace in general there is now much greater scope for individual expression, manifested in such small ways as using one's private income to purchase food not provided by the community. Thus, Levy's assumption may contain a grain of truth.

A further theoretical implication will be considered. Again it is tangential to the focus of the paper. It concerns the concepts of modernization and industrialization. Considerable ambiguity surrounds these concepts. Are they synonymous? And if so, do they also mean Westernization as Lerner would argue?[36] An admirable attempt to weed out the confusion has been made by Nettl and Robertson.[37] They stress that the empirical referent for modernization should be the international stratification system.

33 David C. McClelland, *The Achieving Society* (Princeton, NJ: Princeton University Press, 1961).

34 It is relevant to point out that Dr Weinberg was moving towards the position taken by Horowitz and others. See Ian Weinberg, 'The Concept of Modernization: An Unfinished Chapter in Sociological Theory,' unpublished paper, University of Toronto, 1968.

35 Levy, *The Structure of Society,* p. 502.

36 As Lerner remarks: 'The ethnocentric predicament is confounded by failure to realize that modernization appears as Westernization by historical coincidence.' He adds: 'The "Western Model" is only historically Western; sociologically it is global.' Lerner published these remarks in an ambitious study that first appeared in 1958. This suggests how quickly a set of ideas can become dated. See D. Lerner, *The Passing of Traditional Society* (Glencoe, Ill.: Free Press, 1958), p. viii.

37 J.P. Nettl and Roland Robertson, 'Industrialization, Development or Modernization,' *British Journal of Sociology,* vol. 27, no. 3 (Sept. 1966), 274-91; see also their more extensive treatment, *International Systems and the Modernization of Societies* (London: Faber, 1968).

An earlier effort to clarify the concepts was made by Apter. He argues that moderni-zation and industrialization are not the same: 'Although most of the new nations will not industrialize, they will continue to modernize. Internal markets and resources are too poor and limited in size for rapid industrialization.'[38]

If by modernization it is meant that roads and airports will replace donkey and canoe, libraries and hospitals will be built, and traditional value systems modified, Apter's argu-ment appears to be sound. The significance of the Aiyetoro case is that it is a reversal of Apter's thesis: it has industrialized but not modernized. With the exception of a handful of members who have been abroad or have received a higher education on the mainland, and with the exception of the attitude towards work, most members con-tinue to embrace the values and attitudes that are central to traditional Ilaje society. Thus witchcraft still conditions their behaviour. This is particularly the case with the women. Most of them, for example, prefer to take their meals while resting comforta-bly on the floor rather than sitting on a chair at the table. I realize the value-proneness of this statement. I should not have made it except for the fact that numerous men in Aiyetoro have referred to the women as backward for this very reason. In other words, they have accepted implicitly an ideal type of modernity that is arbitrary in the sense of intrinsic value, but meaningful in the sense of the manner in which Nettl and Robert-son advocate that the concept be used; that is, a product of power on an international scale.

This argument too must be qualified. As Parsons remarks, the concept of interdepend-ence of substructures of a social system does not mean that all change in the same way simultaneously.[39] Instead the economy, for example, may be modified and at a later date the family may change as a result. Similarly, van den Berghe stresses with respect to South Africa that one structure may change slowly or not at all (the political struc-ture in his case) and another structure change quickly (the economy).[40]

Thus there is no theoretical problem about disproportionate change in the substruc-tures of a social system. What is interesting in the Aiyetoro case is that it diverges from the thesis of Apter inasmuch as it has industrialized before it has modernized. And what would be surprising is if those aspects that have been referred to as evidence that the village has developed but not modernized do not change within a few years.

This leads to a final question. What does the future hold for Aiyetoro? Almost cer-tainly significant changes in the entire social system will emerge, because the conse-quences of the introduction of capitalism extend beyond the economy. Evidence of its effect already can be seen in the system of stratification. Since the founding of the com-munity the ideal of equality has been central to the value system. Equality in the past was interpreted to refer primarily to material objects, rather than to power and prestige. For this reason most members enjoyed a similar standard of living, but a small elite ruled the community and received differential respect.

38 David E. Apter, 'Political Religion in the New Nations,' in Clifford Geertz (ed.), *Old Societies and New States* (Glencoe, Ill.: Free Press, 1963), p. 61.

39 Talcott Parsons, 'The Problem of Controlled Institutional Change,' in *Essays in Sociological Theory* (Glencoe, Ill.: Free Press, 1964), p. 244.

40 Pierre L. van den Berghe, *South Africa, A Study in Conflict* (Middleton, Ct.: Wesleyan University Press, 1965), p. 3.

Since the introduction of capitalism there has been a tendency for material reward to correspond with an actor's power and prestige.[41] For example, the *oba* recently decided that large, two-storey houses will be built for the managers of the various departments. The change in the economy has resulted in a redefinition of power in the community. Power is increasingly determined by the individual's ability to adapt to the mixed economy. The sector of society most able to cope is the young, energetic, and well-educated, many of whom have been trained in technical or secondary school. This has resulted in a generation drop in the locus of power, and consequent hostility from the elders who have lost their influence. Since the *oba* is one of the younger and well-trained generation, the hostility is unlikely to develop into a problem.

The stratification system has thus become much more sensitive to the economic order. It is the *oba*'s intention to increase private enterprise as time goes on. To do so will place more strain on the delicate balance between capitalism and communalism. However, the capacity of the community to survive its recent crisis makes prediction about its future confident: it will absorb its strain; it will persist for years to come.

41 In a project drawing from simple random samples of three different status categories a direct correlation was found in terms of an actor's status and the probability of recently acquiring a radio, record player, and motorcycle. The same trend held with respect to polygyny. Prior to the change in the economy the men in the three status categories had roughly an average of one wife each. Since the change those in the lowest category still only have one wife, while those in the highest group now have an average of over four wives each. While it is impossible to develop the assumption here, I should strongly argue that women in this case are to be considered material rewards in the same way as are radios and record players.

L.R. MARSDEN, E.B. HARVEY, AND J. BULCOCK

Language barriers to modernization: African examples

In the sociological literature on modernization, education is often central to the issue. Whether it be in the political, cultural, or social spheres, one of the agreed-upon changes is the necessity for various groups in the modernizing society to communicate with each other in new ways.[1] Whether one is talking about mobilizing the work force to the necessary occupational changes, spreading information about public health techniques, or taking a census, the fact is that education relates to modernization in ways that are more or less understood.[2]

In the African countries the role of education in economic development has been thoroughly substantiated.[3] Eisenstadt, among others, has demonstrated the importance of education in the process of change and the ways in which the structure and organization of education in a society crucially affects the whole process of modernization.[4]

The specific effects of formal education are diffuse and difficult to separate and calculate accurately. Values, attitudes, opportunities, actions – all may be changed when education is institutionalized into a formal system.

The cultural transition between what is called modernization and non-modernization in a society occurs in formal education through the medium of language. It is in some

1 S.N. Eisenstadt, *Education and Political Development,* Duke University Commonwealth Seminar Series (Durham, N.C.: Duke University Press, 1962/3); also his *Modernization: Protest and Change* (Englewood Cliffs, NJ: Prentice-Hall, 1963); Daniel Lerner, *The Passing of Traditional Society* (New York: The Free Press, 1958); L. Gray Cowan, James O'Connell, and David G. Scanlon, *Education and Nation-Building in Africa* (New York: Praeger, 1965).

2 See, for example, references in n. 1 and Ian Weinberg 'The Concept of Modernization: An Unfinished Chapter in Sociological Theory,' paper presented at 1968 USA meeting, unpublished; and Marion J. Levy, Jr., *Modernization and the Structure of Societies* (Princeton, NJ: Princeton University Press, 1966).

3 See, for example, Adam Curle, *Educational Strategy for Developing Societies* (London: Tavistock, 1963); Helen Kitchen (ed.), *The Educated African* (New York: Praeger, 1963); D.G. Scanlon (ed.), *Church, State, and Education in Africa* (New York: Teachers College, Columbia University, 1966); Nuffield Foundation and Colonial Office, *African Education: A Study of Educational Policy and Practice in Tropical Africa* (Oxford: The University Press, 1953).

4 Eisenstadt, *Education and Political Development.*

aspects of the relationship between language factors and socio-economic development that we are principally interested. Written language is of major importance within the context of formal education, and the common index of the effects of written language on other variables is literacy. The usual measure of literacy is the ability to read and write one's own name. Golden,[5] exploring the relationship of literacy and industrialization in 1950, has found a coefficient of correlation of 0.87. However literacy affects a society (and Golden concludes that it is tied to the growth and diffusion of an urban-industrial civilization), it provides an excellent general indicator of economic development.

But some[6] have gone beyond this general correlation to see which other factors affect the relationship. In the nations of Africa which are pushing towards modernization, the spread of literacy can be affected by many factors including available funding, skilled manpower, traditional values and attitudes towards education, the diversity of native languages used, the necessity of choosing an official, political language, and the attitudes of colonial administrations (both present and previous) towards literacy and language. It is our intention here to look at two of the complicating factors in the relationship – homogeneity of language and the language in which education takes place.

Considerable research has been devoted to the various language problems of the developing nations.[7] Thus, Fishman[8] reports the findings on linguistically homogeneous and heterogeneous polities and finds them very different on almost every score, the homogeneous side 'winning' in the sense of being more developed economically, educationally, politically, and in many other ways. Although, when per capita GNP differences are partialled out some of the differences between linguistically homogeneous and linguistically heterogeneous polities are attenuated, the differences are weakened but by no means obliterated. Linguistic homogeneity is an important correlate of the economic position of a polity.

A second factor in the spread of literacy is the language of instruction in elementary grades of school. There is widespread agreement among the new African nations that an 'official' Western (political) language is a necessity if the nation is to participate in the wider culture and economy of the world.[9] For many former colonies, the decision as to which Western language should be the official one is fairly straightforward. They use the language of the colonists of their country. In many African countries, this is either French or English. However, the question remains as to when the official language should be introduced into the formal educational system.[10] Some say early, some say late, but we ask what is the relationship between using the vernacular or the official

5 Hilda H. Golden, 'Literacy and Social Change in Underdeveloped Countries,' in J.J. Spengler and O.D. Duncan (eds.), *Demographic Analysis: Selected Readings* (Free Press, 1963), pp. 532-8.

6 *Ibid.*; see also, Joshua A. Fishman, Charles A. Ferguson, and Jyotirinda Das Gupta (eds.), *Language Problems of Developing Nations* (Toronto: John Wiley and Sons, 1968).

7 *Ibid.*; J.A. Fishman, C.A. Ferguson, and J. Das Gupta; also, John Spencer (ed.), *Language in Africa* (Cambridge: The University Press, 1963).

8 Joshua A. Fishman, 'Some Contrasts between Linguistically Homogeneous and Linguistically Heterogeneous Polities,' in Fishman, Ferguson, and Das Gupta, *Language Problems.*

9 See, for example, Robert G. Armstrong, 'Language Policies and Language Practices in West Africa,' in Fishman, Ferguson, and Das Gupta, *ibid.*

10 See, for a discussion, John Bowers, 'Language Problems and Literacy,' in Fishman, Ferguson, and Das Gupta, *ibid.*

language in the elementary grades and socio-economic development, given various levels of literacy? Is it literacy *per se* that relates to development or is the language in which literacy develops of importance? If literacy is very low anyway, what difference does the use of one language over another make in the elementary grades? If, as Golden argues, investing in education is desirable for countries wishing to develop economically, should such countries invest in teaching of the vernacular (presumably faster and cheaper since teachers would be more readily available) or would teaching in the official language be sufficient to affect economic development?

Finally, among those countries where either French or English is the official political language, at given levels of literacy is one superior to the other in terms of socio-economic development? Is English the language of business and French the language of diplomacy, as some would have us believe?

Since, during the colonial era in Africa, the two major colonial powers implemented different general policies concerning the development of their colonies, this question with its overtones of language superiority is an intriguing one. More theoretically, however, we are pursuing the indicators of a common factor in development at the level of language. We suggest that being able to communicate with as many people within the country as possible and to communicate with other modernized countries may affect the rate of economic development.

First, we expect that at any level of literacy, homogeneity of language will be associated with higher levels of socio-economic development than will language heterogeneity. Second, we expect that the higher the level of literacy in a country, the more highly correlated will be the official, political language in the elementary schools with socio-economic development. Finally, on the question of whether French or English is associated with higher socio-economic development, we have no reason to assume that either language is superior to the other and so put forward the hypothesis of no difference.

In an attempt to control extraneous variation in the relationships among the independent and criterion variables, we have chosen to limit the sample to politically independent countries of Africa which use English or French as the official language. The countries included in the sample are given in Table 1.

METHOD

An appropriate manner of examining these problems is a general regression model, and accordingly a design has been formulated on the basis of current literature in the area of multiple regression techniques.[11] In particular, a design is required which is sufficiently flexible as to permit the examination of three possible relationships between the control variable 'level of literacy,' and the dependent or criterion variable 'a measure of socio-economic development,' for each of the selected problems. One possible relationship would be a curvilinear one in which, for example, the influence of official

11 See, for example, R.A. Bottenberg and J.H. Ward, Jr., *Applied Multiple Linear Regression,* Technical Documentary Report PRL-TDR-63-6, Lackland Air Force Base, Texas: 6570th Personnel Research Laboratory, Aerospace Medical Division, March 1963; and Francis J. Kelly, D.L. Beggs, and K.A. McNeil, with T. Eichelberger and J. Lyon, *Research Design in the Behavioral Sciences: Multiple Regression Approach* (Carbondale: Southern Illinois University Press, 1969).

TABLE 1
Politically independent African countries with
French or English as the official political language

Political language

English	French
Botswana	Algeria
Ethiopia	Cameroun
Gambia	Central African Republic
Ghana	Chad
Kenya	Congo Republic
Liberia	Dahomey
Malawi	Dem. Rep. Congo
Nigeria	Gabon
Rhodesia	Guinea
Sierra Leone	Ivory Coast
Somalia	Libya
South Africa	Malagasy
Sudan	Mali
Tanzania	Mauritania
Uganda	Morocco
Zambia	Niger
	Rwanda
	Senegal
	Togo
	Tunisia
	Upper Volta

political language used in elementary school on socio-economic development across the levels of literacy was non-linear (Fig. 1, Situation 1). A second relationship might be one in which the amount of change in the dependent variable per unit change in the control variable was different under different levels of the categorical predictors (Fig. 1, Situation 2). A third relationship might be a situation in which a change in the dependent variable value per unit of change in the control variable is parallel under two (or more) categorical predictors (Fig. 1, Situation 3). The fourth possible relationship is represented by the situation in which the two (or more) categorical predictors are equally effective and, hence, best represented by a simple curved or rectilinear X-Y relationship (Fig. 1, Situation 4).

VARIABLES

Data of relevance to the problems selected for examination have been compiled by the Agency for International Development (1968).[12] Where several variables seemed relevant as a measure of the same construct, it was customary to select as an independent variable the one that had a high correlation with the dependent variable and the lowest correlations with other independent variables. Following this procedure, the variables in Table 2 were the ones available from AID which seemed to be associated with measures of modernization for developing nations.

12 *Agency for International Development Economic Data Book - Africa* (Washington: AID, 1968).

Situation 1: Curvilinear Interaction

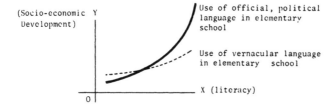

Situation 2: Linear Interaction

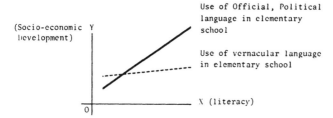

Situation 3: Parallel Lines

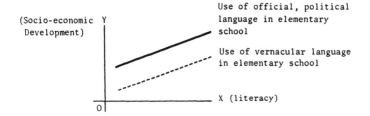

Situation 4: Superimposed Lines

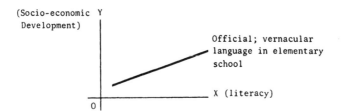

FIGURE 1 *Diagrams illustrating four possible relationships between control and dependent variables (hypothetical relationships only)*

TABLE 2
Correlation matrix of factors affecting modernization of
39 politically independent African nations (product–
moment correlations, no missing data)*

Variable	SED	GNP	LR	PPP
SED		-0.74	-0.48	-0.56
GNP	-0.69		0.27	0.47
LR	-0.48	0.40		0.59
PPP	-0.51	0.51	0.70	

* Correlations above the diagonal are based on AID (1968) data. Correlations below the diagonal have
been based on the factors SED, GNP, and LR after a logarithmic transformation of these variables
had been conducted. It will be noted that, after the transformation, half, or three, of the six possible relationships were strengthened, but of these changes only two were significant. Thus, it was
decided not to use transformed data in the analysis despite the fact that the variables SED, GNP,
and LR were skewed or leptokurtic in distribution. To check for possible distortion in the findings
due to the skewed distribution of three variables, tests were made in three of the four problems
using transformed as well as untransformed variables. Although in one problem area – the language
of instruction in the early grades of elementary school – the significance levels of the findings were
affected, in the remaining instances, the transformation had no statistically significant effect on the
reported outcomes using the untransformed data.

SED: socio-economic development as measured by the percentage of the adult male labour force in
agriculture. (As agricultural labour decreases, literacy should increase.)
GNP: gross national product per capita measured by 1965 U.S. dollars. (As GNP increases, so should
literacy.)
LR: literacy rate.
PPP: pupils as a percentage of the population.

(a) Dependent variables
On the basis of previous research literature, two variables were selected as acceptable
indexes of socio-economic development; namely, (1) the percentage of the adult male
labour force in agriculture, and (2) gross national product per capita as measured in
terms of 1965 U.S. dollars. In the case of variable (1), the lower the percentage, the
higher the development, and in the case of variable (2), the higher the GNP, the higher
the development.

(b) Independent variables
In each problem, the level of literacy was selected as the control variable for reasons
given in the first section of the paper. That is, literacy has been shown to be a good indicator of the level of socio-economic development. The objective of a covariance control design is to get a smaller denominator for the F-ratio, thus increasing the chances
of rejecting a false hypothesis.[13] Data on the literacy rates for the different countries
constituting the sample were obtained from the Agency for International Development
(1968).

The categorical independent variables in the first problem are high, medium, and low
levels of language homogeneity in the sample countries. Those countries in which from

13 William C. Guenther, *Analysis of Variance* (Englewood Cliffs, NJ: Prentice-Hall, 1964), p. 143.

71 to 100 per cent of the population speak the dominant language were classified as high on the criterion of language homogeneity. Those countries in which 41 to 70 per cent of the population speak the dominant language were classified as medium on the language homogeneity criterion, and low homogeneity indicated the category where fewer than 40 per cent of the population spoke the dominant language. The range in the low category was from 17 (Congo-Kinshasa) to 40 per cent (South Africa). The source for this data was Rustow.[14]

The variable in problem two – language of instruction in the early grades of school – is problematic because of shifting and overlapping policies in this regard in a number of the African countries included in the sample. On the basis of the most up-to-date information available in one source,[15] whenever possible the countries in the sample were classified into (i) those in which the official government policy is to provide instruction in the first two years of school in the vernacular language, and (ii) those in which the official government policy is to provide instruction in the earliest school grades in the official, political language (either French or English) of the country. It was possible to classify 37 countries using this criterion though some government policies will now differ from those listed in Table 5 below; and in some instances, where government policies were non-existent or permissive, what seemed to be the current practice was the basis for the classification. Finally, with regard to the effect of Western language on socio-economic development, the two Western languages, French and English, were chosen respectively as the categorical predictors. Sasnet and Sepmeyer (1966) provided the source for the classification.[16]

THE SAMPLE

Three criteria were used in selecting the sample: (i) the countries had to be politically independent; thus, countries which were still of colonial status were excluded; (ii) the countries concerned had to have either English or French as political languages; and (iii) the countries concerned had to be African countries. Forty countries could have been included in the sample, but Swaziland was excluded because of a lack of available data on the dependent and independent variables. Missing data from Lesotho and Burundi were estimated from prediction formulas based on multiple regression techniques in which the data from 37 African countries provided the basis for the estimates. Thus, some 39 countries qualified, and were included in the 'problem one' sample. By estimating the missing data in the two cases mentioned, it was possible to ensure that there were no missing data for any observation in the sample.

FINDINGS

Corresponding to the hypotheses presented earlier, the findings are presented in three sections.

14 D.A. Rustow, 'Language, Modernization and Nationhood: An Attempt at a Typology,' in Fishman, Ferguson, and Das Gupta, *Language Problems,* pp. 87-106.
15 Martena T. Sasnet and Inez Sepmeyer, *Educational Systems of Africa: Interpretations for Use in the Evaluation of Academic Credentials* (Berkeley: University of California Press, 1966).
16 *Ibid.*

TABLE 3
Classes of linguistic homogeneity (high, medium, and low)
for 39 African countries (based on the percentage of the
population in each country speaking the dominant language

Linguistic homogeneity

High (71–100%)	Medium (41–70%)	Low (11–40%)
Lesotho	Botswana	Malawi
Malagasy	Rhodesia	Guinea
Tunisia	Morocco	South Africa
Somalia	Dahomey	Mali
Algeria	Sierra Leone	Zambia
Libya	Upper Volta	Chad
Rwanda	Ethiopia	Gabon
Mauritania	Sudan	Kenya
	Gambia	Uganda
	Central African Republic	Burundi
	Congo Republic	Liberia
	Ghana	Nigeria
	Niger	Ivory Coast
	Senegal	Tanzania
	Togo	Congo (Kinshasa)
		Cameroun

Problem one: homogeneity of language

In Table 3, the 39 countries in the sample are classified on the basis of language homogeneity (1, 2, 3) – high, medium, and low. The results of the regression analysis for this problem are presented in Table 4. Figure 2 illustrates the results of the regression analysis.

The first problem was formulated as follows: what is the relative effectiveness of the homogeneity of language on a measure of gross national income per capita when controlling for the effects of the level of literacy? The results of the multiple regression analysis were that the relationship was one best represented by curvilinear interaction (cf. Fig. 1, Situation 1). The results are presented in Table 4.

Figure 2 illustrates a curvilinear interaction situation in which the amount of change in the dependent variable (GNP per capita) per unit change in the control variable (level of literacy) is different under the three selected categories of language homogeneity (high, medium, and low). The significance of language homogeneity is evident, which points to the conclusion that the effects of high language homogeneity are superior to those of medium and low language homogeneity.

While the findings demonstrate that countries in which 41–70 per cent of the population speak the dominant language can expect continued increases in their gross national products per capita to accompany increases in the literacy rates, this rate is considerably less than would likely be the case if language homogeneity increased. An unanticipated finding was the reversal of the trend of the regression curve for those 16 countries in the sample in which 40 per cent or fewer of the population speak the dominant language.

TABLE 4
Results of regression analysis predicting Gross National Product per capita
from homogeneity of language (1, 2, 3) and level of literacy ($N = 39$)

Row set	Question	Predictors	RSQ	Source of variance	% criterion variance accounted for	Df	F-ratio	P
1		Model 1. 9 variables: high, medium, and low language homogeneity, plus literacy levels for each, plus three 2nd degree polynomial transformation vectors	0.390					
2	1	Model 2. 6 variables: high, medium, and low language homogeneity, plus literacy levels for each	0.096	Model 1–Model 2	29.4	2/33	7.9891	<0.01
3	2	Model 3. 4 variables: high, medium, and low language homogeneity, plus a common vector for level of literacy	0.079	Model 2–Model 3	1.7	1/35	0.6589	ns
4	3	Model 4. 1 variable: level of literacy	0.074	Model 3–Model 4	0.5	1/36	0.1960	ns
5	4	Model 5. 5 variables: high, medium, and low language homogeneity, plus a common weight for literacy rate and a common weight for the polynomial transformations	0.223	Model 1–Model 5	16.7	2/33	4.538*	<0.05
6	5	Model 6. 2 variables: common weights for three categories of independence plus a common weight for the polynomial transformations	0.216	Model 5–Model 6	0.7	1/35	0.3153	ns

* Model 5, therefore, is the best fit.

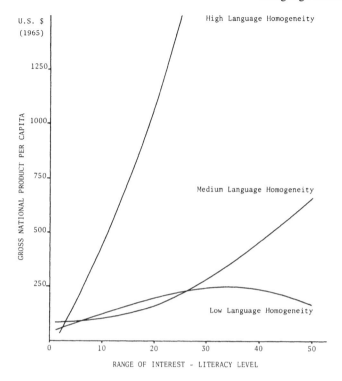

FIGURE 2 *Regression analysis of association between Gross National Product per capita (1965 U.S. dollars) and level of language homogeneity (high, medium, and low categories) across literacy level (N = 39)*

It would appear then, *mutatis mutandis,*[17] that the language factor is an important one in terms of economic growth and development.

When socio-economic development as measured by the percentage of the adult male labour force in agriculture was used as the criterion value, the findings were analogous to those reported, but the *F*-ratios in row sets 2 and 5 respectively were significant only at the alpha = 0.1 level.

17 Although we have used terms such as *mutatis mutandis* and 'other things being equal ...' it must be realized that in non-experimental research it is seldom possible to control all 'extraneous' variables or to avoid 'experimental' error. In *ex post facto* holistic studies of societies using global or 'basic' variables as opposed to unidimensional variables, it is obviously impossible to study single dimensions of social phenomena while assuming that the other dimensions are equal and unrelated. While it is possible to assume that 'other things are equal ...' in carefully controlled laboratory studies, the kinds of research reported in this paper does not lend itself to such exactitude. Many of the exploratory factors (i.e. concomitant variables) cannot be controlled statistically simply because the data are not available – either the theoretically important factors have not been measured, or if they have the data do not cover all the sample observations on the scale desired.

TABLE 5

African countries with official languages either French or
English classified according to the language of instruction
in the early grades of elementary school (N = 37)

Official language	Language of instruction in the early grades	
	Vernacular language	Official language
English	Kenya	Ethiopia
	Tanzania	Somalia
	Uganda	Sudan
	Sierra Leone	Gambia
	Malawi	Ghana
	Rhodesia	Liberia
	Zambia	Nigeria
	Botswana	South Africa
French	Algeria	Cameroun
	Libya	Dahomey
	Morocco	Ivory Coast
	Tunisia	Mali
	Guinea	Mauritania
	Dem. Rep. Congo	Niger
	Rwanda	Senegal
		Togo
		Upper Volta
		Cen. Africa Republic
		Chad
		Congo Republic
		Gabon
		Malagasy

Problem two: language of instruction in the early grades of elementary school
In Table 5, 37 countries included in the sample with either French or English as official,
political languages are classified on the basis of whether the language of instruction in
the early grades of elementary school is in the vernacular (tribal tongue) or in the official (non-vernacular) language. The results of the regression analysis for problem two
are presented in Table 6. Figure 3 illustrates diagrammatically the findings presented
in Table 6.

The statement of problem two was as follows: what is the relative effectiveness of the
language of instruction in the early grades of elementary school when controlling for
the effects of the level of literacy? The question attempts to examine the problem as to
which is the most effective approach to instruction in the early grades of schools in
multi-lingual countries. Note that model 2 (Fig. 1, Situation 2) represents the best fit.

Figure 3 illustrates a situation in which linear interaction of the two categorical predictors takes place. The rates of change in the effectiveness of the two categories associated with the literacy rates are different for the two types of language instruction.
Within the range of interest, there is a literacy level at which the two languages are
equally effective in terms of socio-economic development. This literacy rate is the 15-
17 per cent level; that is, the value of the control variable (literacy) at which the two
lines representing language instruction effects intersect. For literacy levels greater than

TABLE 6
Results of regression analysis predicting socio-economic development from categories
of language instruction (vernacular vs. official language) and level of literacy (N = 37)

Row set	Question	Predictors	RSQ	Source of variance	% criterion variance accounted for	Df	F-ratio	P
1		Model 1. 6 variables: instruction in the vernacular and official language, plus literacy levels for each, plus two 2nd degree polynomial transformation vectors	0.293					
2	1	Model 2. 4 variables: instruction in the vernacular and official language, plus literacy levels for each	0.284	Model 1–Model 2	0.9	2/31	0.199	ns
3	2	Model 3. 3 variables: instruction in the vernacular and official language, plus a common weight for level of literacy	0.098	Model 2–Model 3	18.6	1/33	8.570*	<0.01
4	3	Model 4. 1 variable: level of literacy	0.097	Model 3–Model 4	0.1	1/34	0.029	ns
5	4	Model 5. 4 variables: instruction in the vernacular and official language, plus common weights for both literacy and the polynomial transformation	0.155	Model 1–Model 5	13.8	2/31	3.009	ns
6	5	Model 6. 2 variables: common weights for (i) the level of literacy, plus (ii) common weights for polynomial transformations	0.155	Model 5–Model 6	0.0	1/33	0.006	ns

* Model 2, therefore, is the best fit.

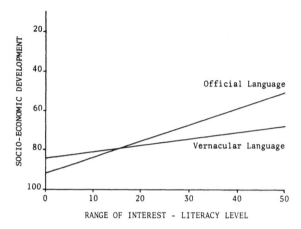

FIGURE 3 *Regression analysis of association between socio-economic development and language of instruction (vernacular vs. official language) in early grades of elementary school across level of literacy (N = 37)*

this point of intersection, it seems that the use of the official language as the medium of instruction in the early grades of elementary school is associated with higher levels of socio-economic development. For literacy rates below the point of intersection, the vernacular language is more effective in terms of socio-economic development.

Problem three: official, political language
The division of the sample of 37 African countries into those with French as the political language and those with English as the Western language has been made in Tables 1 and 5. Table 7 presents the results of the regression analysis for problem three. The best fit is represented by model 6 (Fig. 1, Situation 4). The answer, then, to the question: what is the relative effectiveness of the official language on a measure of socio-economic development when controlling for the effects of literacy? is clear-cut – there is no distinction. Figure 4 illustrates the findings in Table 7.

CONCLUSIONS
The findings above point to some general policy implications in the relationships between literacy and socio-economic development. The chief concern of the independent African countries with regard to education is educational development to aid in the solution of other national goals, for example, nationalism or socio-economic development.

From the above findings, one can see that an independent African nation can probably afford to ignore the issue of whether French or English is an advantage in the educational system from the point of view of economic development. If the choice even exists for a country, it must be made on grounds other than economic ones.

Second, a country with a low current level of literacy might place priority on developing language homogeneity, or prepare to compensate for the effects of medium or low language homogeneity in socio-economic development by other means. For ex-

TABLE 7

Results of regression analysis predicting socio-economic development from categories of official language (French and English) and level of literacy ($N = 37$)

Row set	Question	Predictors	RSQ	Source of variance	% criterion variance accounted for	Df	F-ratio	P
1		Model 1. 6 variables: official language French or English, plus literacy levels for each, plus two 2nd degree polynomial transformation vectors	0.287					
2	1	Model 2. 4 variables: official language French or English, plus the literacy levels for each	0.120	Model 1–Model 2	16.7	2/31	3.634	<0.05
3	2	Model 3. 3 variables: official language French or English, plus a common weight for the level of literacy	0.103	Model 2–Model 3	1.7	1/33	1.000	ns
4	3	Model 4. 1 variable: level of literacy	0.097	Model 3–Model 4	0.3	1/34	0.217	ns
5	4	Model 5. 4 variables: official language French or English, plus common weights for both literacy and the polynomial transformation	0.285	Model 1–Model 5	0.2	2/31	0.043	ns
6	5	Model 6. 2 variables: common weights for (i) the level of literacy, plus (ii) the polynomial transformations	0.266	Model 5–Model 6	1.9	1/33	0.850*	ns

* Model 6, therefore, is the best fit.

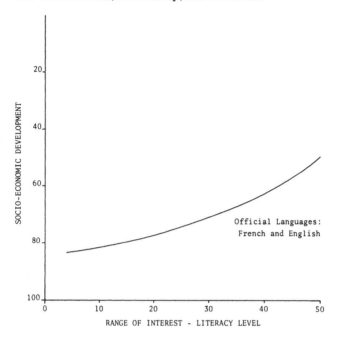

FIGURE 4 *Regression analysis of association between socio-economic development and categories of official language (French and English) and level of literacy (N = 37).*

ample, if there is no common language spoken by the majority of the people, the use of an official or Western political language might be expected to be beneficial from the point of view of economic development. This expectation follows from the findings in problem one above, all else being equal.

Finally, such a country might use teachers prepared to teach the vernacular now and plan to train skilled manpower to teach the official language in the future. This follows from the findings in problem two above.

All this assumes that the general findings from 39 different African countries can be brought to bear upon the future of a single country. Such an assumption must not be taken lightly. Special conditions in any given country will bear examination to see whether the findings reported above can be generalized to individual countries. Nonetheless, some policy implications can be deduced from our findings.

For example, in a country like Ethiopia where the rate of literacy is about 5 per cent[18] the Amharic language is official although the widespread use of other languages places Ethiopia in the 'medium homogeneity of language' category for the purposes of our analysis. Amharic is the language of the ruling family and the elite groups. As in other similar multi-lingual situations, the subordinate-language groups may try to preserve their language and culture by attempting to have their vernacular taught at least in their

18 AID, *Data Book*, 'Ethiopia.'

elementary schools.[19] Whatever the arguments in favour of such a procedure, from the point of view of economic development, the general point can be made that high homogeneity of language is associated with (not necessarily the cause of) high socio-economic development. Regardless of policy, as the level of literacy increases, if the experience of other countries predicts the future of a country like Ethiopia, the advantages of having medium rather than low language homogeneity will be reflected in increased socio-economic development (after 25 per cent literacy is reached, the line curves sharply upwards in Fig. 2). Also, while the vernacular language of elementary school curricula is an advantage in socio-economic terms at the 5 per cent level of literacy, as literacy increases, usage beyond 15 per cent of the official, political language in elementary schools will represent an advantage. This argument assumes that the experience of other countries has application to Ethiopia. Of course, this may not be the case, but such findings have direct implications for consideration by policy-makers.

In short, we are arguing that the empirical support for the propositions under consideration provides impetus for further probing of the causal connections between literacy and socio-economic development within a given set of cultural conditions. At the same time, we in no way suggest that the manipulation of language systems on the dimension of homogeneity or introduction of the official language in elementary schools will lead directly to further economic progress. The latter argument, implicit in Golden's article referred to earlier, needs considerable further specification and empirical exploration before such assertions can be made.

---

19 However, as Donald Levine has pointed out in a recent article, Amharic is a national language and a source of unity within Ethiopia. 'The Roots of Ethiopia's Nationhood,' *Africa Report*, May 1971.

9 781487 591496